PRAISE FOR
MINDSET OF SUCCESS

'Makes a compelling case that a leader's mindset can count far more than their skills in achieving breakthrough success. It has profound implications for how we think about developing leadership potential within ourselves and our organizations.'
Sharath Jeevan, CEO, STIR Education

'Down to earth and very readable, this book is full of stories to inspire and remind us what leadership is all about.'
Steve Munby, CEO, Education Development Trust

'Jo Owen provides practical advice on how to ensure a leadership mindset pervades your work in this well-written, original book which was a truly enjoyable read. I would highly recommend it.'
Brett Wigdortz, CEO, Teach First

SECOND EDITION

The Mindset
of Success

Accelerate your career from
good manager to great leader

Jo Owen

KoganPage

First published in Great Britain and the United States in 2015 by Kogan Page Limited
Second edition 2018

Apart from any fair dealing for the purposes of research or private study, or criticism or review, as permitted under the Copyright, Designs and Patents Act 1988, this publication may only be reproduced, stored or transmitted, in any form or by any means, with the prior permission in writing of the publishers, or in the case of reprographic reproduction in accordance with the terms and licences issued by the CLA. Enquiries concerning reproduction outside these terms should be sent to the publishers at the undermentioned addresses:

2nd Floor, 45 Gee Street	c/o Martin P Hill Consulting	4737/23 Ansari Road
London	122 W 27th Street	Daryaganj
EC1V 3RS	New York, NY 10001	New Delhi 110002
United Kingdom	USA	India

© Jo Owen, 2015, 2018

The right of Jo Owen to be identified as the author of this work has been asserted by him in accordance with the Copyright, Designs and Patents Act 1988.

ISBN   978 0 7494 8035 6
E-ISBN   978 0 7494 8036 3

British Library Cataloguing-in-Publication Data

A CIP record for this book is available from the British Library.

Library of Congress Cataloging-in-Publication Data

Names: Owen, Jo, author.
Title: The mindset of success : accelerate your career from good manager to great leader / Jo Owen.
Description: Second Edition. | New York, NY : Kogan Page Ltd, [2017] | Revised edition of the author's The mindset of success, 2015. | Includes bibliographical references and index.
Identifiers: LCCN 2017032049 (print) | LCCN 2017043337 (ebook) | ISBN 9780749480363 (ebook) | ISBN 9780749480356 (pbk.) | ISBN 9780749480363 (eISBN)
Subjects: LCSH: Management. | Leadership.
Classification: LCC HD31 (ebook) | LCC HD31 .O946 2017 (print) | DDC 658.4/092–dc23
LC record available at https://lccn.loc.gov/2017032049

Typeset by Integra Software Services, Pondicherry
Print production managed by Jellyfish
Printed and bound by CPI Group (UK) Ltd, Croydon, CR0 4YY

CONTENTS

Conclusion   239

LIST OF FIGURES AND TABLES

Introduction

Everyday heroes and the seven mindsets of success

This book is about how you can fulfil your true potential.

Look around the places where you work, or volunteer or support. You will always find a few people who stand out from the crowd. These are the people who make things happen. They attract followers; they create energy and transform crises into opportunities. They are nature's leaders, even if they do not have the formal title and position of a leader. They may not be the great leaders of history, but they lead anyway. They are the everyday heroes who make a difference to where we live and work.

This book goes in search of such everyday heroes, to find out what makes them special. After 17 years of researching leaders around the world, I suspected that leaders need more than formal skills to succeed. Of course, a skilled leader is normally better than an unskilled leader. But the best leaders all had something more than skills. They had an X-factor that set them apart from everyone else: you can spot such people at any level. These everyday heroes don't just improve things: they transform and disrupt. They take people further and faster than anyone expects. So how do they do it?

It soon became clear that they act differently because they think differently. This is the mindset difference. It is the invisible key to success: once you have it, you have an advantage that lasts a lifetime and works for you time and again. Mindset is the X-factor that all the everyday heroes have – and that anyone else can learn.

The mindset X-factor is good news for five reasons:

- The success mindset was consistent across all the everyday heroes who took part in research for this book. There is a clear success formula. There is no mystery or magic to it.

- Mindset is something anyone can learn. Some simple routines will help you to build the habits of mind that will let you achieve more and do more. Like learning a musical instrument or a sport, it takes time to become world class. But even a little practice will set you apart from most of your peers.

- Mindset lets you make the most of your existing talent. In a world where there is an increasing glut of skills, you need more than skills and hard work to set yourself apart from colleagues who work just as hard as you and have as many skills. Skills can be copied easily; mindset is much harder to observe or copy.

- Mindset works at any level. With the right mindset you can lead and take control of your destiny, even if you do not have a formal leadership role. The right mindset gives you the power to accelerate your career.

- Mindset is the essence of 21st-century leadership. Increasingly, leaders have to make things happen through people they do not control. Leaders can no longer rely on formal authority to succeed. Today's leaders require a new way of thinking and behaving.

At first, mindset sounds dangerous. It sounds like we have to wire our brains into machines, change our personality or mess with our heads. Fortunately, the reality is not so dramatic. Mindset is not about changing who you are. It is about becoming the best of who you are. The right mindset lets you focus on your natural strengths. On good days, we can all be positive, bold, resilient and collaborative. That is the essence of the X-factor, and you already have it. The difference is that the everyday heroes are like that every day, and they take these qualities to an extreme. With some simple tools and techniques, you can acquire your own version of the X-factor.

This book is a journey of discovery. It lets you discover what works for you, rather than forcing you to apply a rigid formula. Mindset is not about what works in theory: it is about what works in practice. Each chapter lays out one different aspect of mindset, with real-life examples from the everyday heroes who took part in the research for the book. Each chapter also gives you practical and simple ideas on how you can build your own version of the mindset.

As with any journey of discovery, it pays to do some preparation. So before you set out, this chapter lays the groundwork for your journey. We will briefly look at why mindset matters more than ever, and how it differs from skills and education. The seven steps to prepare for our journey are set out below:

1 The mindset revolution.

2 Mindset and the nature of leadership.

3 Mindset versus skill set.

4 Mindset versus education.

5 The research behind the book.

6 Why this book is different.

7 The seven mindsets summarized.

The mindset revolution

Mindset is at the heart of a revolution in management. Forget about the technology revolution and the internet. The technology revolution has been with us for 200 years, since the steam engine and railways started the Industrial Revolution. There always has been, and always will be, a technology revolution for us to deal with.

The real revolution is in how managers manage. The old paradigm of the heroic leader commanding his (and it was nearly always his) troops is over. The world is too complex for one person to master. Leadership is now a team sport. The best leaders build the best teams. Leaders no longer rely on command and control. They have to use influence and persuasion to make things happen through people they may not control and may not even like. Work is becoming more specialized and more focused. Firms are no longer like medieval walled cities that sustain themselves. The walls of the organization have come down and now our success depends on suppliers, customers and partners: we may not like them all but we have to work with them. This is the new world of influence and collaboration that leaders have to master. It is not simply a new set of skills. It is a new way of thinking. Some legacy organizations and leaders have not yet made the leap. To succeed in the future, all leaders and all organizations will eventually have to make that leap. The new world of management requires a new way of thinking.

This book does not predict a revolution. It simply maps the hidden revolution that is already happening. It shows how mindset is the factor that sorts the best from the rest. You can still have a good and worthy career by honing your skills and working hard. But you will not achieve your full potential unless you have the invisible advantage that our everyday heroes have developed: the right mindset. This book maps that mindset for you, and shows how building your mindset will help you build your career.

The nature of leadership

True leadership is about taking people where they would not have got by themselves. Nowadays, that means leading people whom you do not control. In the past, leadership was about authority, power and position. Now it is not about your title: it is about what you do. There are plenty of people with big titles such as CEO but who are no more than stewards of their organization. There is no shame in that. But the real leaders may be found lower in the organization, where they rise to the challenge of taking people where they would not have got by themselves. With the right mindset you do not have to wait for promotion to start leading. You can start leading now. If you don't lead, you don't control your destiny.

The great leader is transformative. Some may transform history, others may transform the way their service team works with customers. Transformative leaders do not simply improve the situation: they *change* the situation. These transformative leaders may be heroes of history, or they may be everyday heroes who you know and work with.

The focus of this book is on the everyday hero: if you are a wannabe Genghis Khan there are plenty of other books that claim to show you the way. But if you want to be an everyday hero, this book will show you how. The research deliberately focused on ordinary people achieving extraordinary things.

What we found is that leadership is not the exclusive preserve of business people. Instead, we looked into the worlds of education and entrepreneurship, spies and sports, public and private sectors, politics, and to business and beyond. We found truly transformative leaders who do not attempt to have their pictures on magazine covers. They are people like you or me, but who always seem to achieve more.

Mindset versus skill set

Over the past 17 years, the research for this book has shown that how we think is the new frontier of performance. The difference between the good and the great is the difference between your mindset and your skill set. In a world where skills are bountiful, and increasingly outsourced to cheaper parts of the world, we need more than skills to survive, let alone thrive. Mindset separates the best from the rest: the right mindset drives the right habits, which drive the right performance.

Skills focus has four traps for the unwary manager:

- Skills are in plentiful supply and becoming a commodity. Even the once-prized master's degree in business administration (MBA) is becoming devalued. The United States is producing over 125,000 MBAs annually,[1] up 74 per cent in 10 years; worldwide there are over 1 million MBAs granted each year.

- Skills are not a good indicator of performance, as one CEO put it: 'I hire most people for their skills and fire most for their values (mindset).'[2] The right skills are normally abundant; the right mindset is a rare commodity that is greatly valued.

- Skills requirements change when you are promoted. This is deadly for managers: the success formula that got you promoted from your last job is not the same as the success formula you need in your next job. You have to learn new rules and new skills. All the best leaders are still learning; even though they appear to be at the top of their trade, they never stop learning new skills.

- Today's skills may be redundant tomorrow. The University of Oxford estimates that 47 per cent of US jobs are at risk from technology in the next 20 years.[3] Even jockeys have been replaced by robots in camel racing.[4] South Korea has created chanting, waving robot sports fans: hopefully they will not create the swearing, drinking and fighting football hooligan robot.[5] New technology may well create new opportunities and new jobs,[6] but we have to be agile and adapt throughout our career. We may even find a robot interviews us for our next job.[7] We cannot rely on one skill set for life.

The joy of mindset is that it is hidden. You may have the same skill set as others, but with the right mindset you can do more with those skills and learn new skills as well. Your improved performance will be visible, but the causes of your improved performance will remain invisible. And that is probably what you already see in your organization. Many of your colleagues will have similar skill levels, but some outperform others by a large margin. They simply act differently and better. There is no point in trying to ape their actions: copying symptoms is as pointless as trying to deal with your child's measles by using spot remover. You have to deal with the root causes. You have to understand why they act differently: you have to find their mindset. That is very hard to do. If you asked them about their mindset, you would be met with a look of blank disbelief. And that is the purpose of this book. It makes visible the invisible advantage that the right mindset gives.

Mindset versus education

The research for this book showed that in the search for the X-factor of the best leaders, it made sense to see if they were academically outstanding. In the leadership panel we put together, several leaders were complete failures at school: dyslexia, harsh home backgrounds or simple lack of interest meant they never flourished. Yet academic failure is not a barrier to success: many of the world's top billionaires do not have a degree.

Who needs education?

If you want to prosper, education helps. The Federal Reserve Bank of San Francisco found that 'the average college graduate earns over $800,000 more than the average high-school graduate by retirement age'.[8] But the world's top billionaire's do not play by normal rules. Here are the college degrees of the world's top 10 self-made billionaires:[9]

- Bill Gates: dropped out of Harvard.
- Carlos Slim: graduated from National Autonomous University of Mexico.
- Warren Buffett: graduated from University of Nebraska and Columbia Business School.
- Amancio Ortega: did not graduate.
- Larry Ellison: dropped out of University of Illinois.
- Sheldon Adelson: dropped out of City College of New York.
- Bernard Arnault: graduated from École Polytechnique.
- Li Ka-shing: left school at 15.
- Michael Bloomberg: graduated from Johns Hopkins and Harvard Business School.
- Stefan Persson: graduated from University of Stockholm.

Five out of the ten did not graduate from college; only two out of ten took the conventional route of an MBA. They are clearly all smart, but they have something more than a formal education that propelled them to extreme wealth.

Their success was not just about skills, intelligence or having good parents. Skills and intelligence help, but are not enough. They all had something else: they had a way of thinking that set them apart from anyone else.

The brightest people are not necessarily great managers. Einstein is admired for his genius, but not for his leadership talent. If you have ever had the pleasure of observing the governing body of a university meet, you will find brilliant people who are complete strangers to the ideas of management or leadership. You do not have to be born a genius to be a great leader.

As a leader, you do not need to be the smartest person in the room. You do not need to be the best person in the room. You need to get the smartest and best people into the room and lead them.

The research behind the book

The origins of this book go back 17 years, when I first started researching leadership for Teach First.[10] Since then I have interviewed hundreds and surveyed thousands of leaders across industries and geographies. Most of the work has been focused on the skills of the leader, but it slowly became clear that there was a huge gap between the best leaders and the merely very good. To reach the status of being one of the best leaders, you need more than skills. The best leaders not only react differently from the merely very good in the same situation: the very best seek out situations that challenge them – and grow them fast.

Based on this wide experience of outstanding leaders, I decided to focus on leaders who appeared to have the X-factor. This is a non-scientific selection. But most scientific selections are bogus anyway. Jim Collins's book *Good to Great* (2001) claimed to have found genuinely great companies with the secret of success.[11] His 11 great companies include Circuit City (bankrupt 2009); the Federal National Mortgage Association, known as Fannie Mae (home loans scandal, bailed out); Wells Fargo ($25 billion bail-out) and Gillette (taken over). *Good to Great* is part of a long and ignoble tradition started by *In Search of Excellence* (1982),[12] which focused on such excellent companies as Atari, Amdahl, Digital Equipment, Eastman Kodak and Western Electric: all have been split up, acquired or filed for bankruptcy. Given these examples, it is perhaps better to use judgement than blindly accept the results of a mechanical selection process, however rigorous it appears to be.

The selection of leaders for our leadership panel deliberately went beyond CEOs of large companies, who are reliable role models in terms of career advancement, but not necessarily in terms of leadership. To the extent there was method in the selection process, I deliberately went beyond the world of business; business does not have a monopoly on leadership. I interviewed widely across sectors: Royal Marine Commandos, spies, entrepreneurs, people in sports, government, politics and education, as well as business at all levels. Each has different leadership challenges and offers different perspectives, but they all rested on the same mindset. The X-factor seems to be a constant in the best leaders, wherever they are.

When I first approached selected leaders to interview them about their mindset, I feared they would be very sceptical. I need not have worried. They all immediately agreed to talk, because they knew that this was what set them apart.

But how do you discover someone's mindset? Wiring up people to machines can be quite fun, but there is a limit to how much you can find out by scanning people's brains and watching what happens as they react under laboratory conditions to controlled stimuli. Wiring up leaders in the office would be entertaining, but impractical. Nevertheless, where appropriate, this book draws on neuroscience to support the evidence gained from interviews and observation.

The simplest way to get at mindset is through interviews. All our leaders went through a structured interview. These were revealing, but inevitably carried a propaganda risk in that during interviews we all like to present our best face to the world.

To validate the interviews, I observed the leaders at work. Watching people work is invariably more enjoyable than doing the work. Many of the interviewees I have known for years, which provided a reality check on what they said. For others, I was able to gain access to 360-degree reviews of them, and in some cases I had to resort to views of colleagues, observers and even the media.

The research started with three hypotheses:

1 Mindset differentiates great leaders from the merely very good.

2 Mindset differences are consistent and can be documented.

3 The mindset of success can be learned, to some degree, by anyone.

If we were being truly scientific about this, we would look to disprove the hypotheses rather than validate them – the good news is that the research was unable to disprove the hypotheses. So at this stage it looks like they stand.

Why this book is different

Over 11,000 business books are published each year.[13] Amazon lists over 22,000 books on leadership alone. So you have plenty of choice. Amid this tidal wave of publishing this book attempts to offer you something original, in three ways:

- *Original subject matter.* Most leadership books focus on the skills, actions or habits of effective leaders. This is useful for any prac- tising leader but it is clearly not enough. Two people with equal skills can have very unequal levels of achievement. And looking at actions and habits is to look at the symptoms of success: we can see the actions and habits work, but we cannot see what causes the leaders to act that way. This book goes behind the symptoms of success to look at the root causes of success, which lie in the way that we choose to think: our mindset.

- *Original research.* Writing this book has been a journey of discov- ery, with plenty of surprises along the way. At the outset it was not clear what mindset meant. The everyday heroes who formed the leadership panel not only defined mindset, they provided compelling and original stories to illustrate their points.

- *Original types of leader.* Many leadership books look at CEOs of large firms, or at the heroes of history. But these are flawed role models. Most of us cannot become some implausible combina- tion of Nelson Mandela and Lord Nelson, even if they are the right role models for us. And CEOs of large firms are also flawed: many successful firms today fail tomorrow. And, perhaps, focus on people such as these can lead to the conclusion that you have to be a middle-aged white male in order to succeed. This book takes a different perspective. It looks at everyday heroes in business, government, sports, not for profits and beyond. These are people who you can relate to and learn from.

This second edition adds one more, vital and original, topic. It looks at how the mindset of success changes as your career progresses. When your context changes, it is no surprise to find that the rules of success change. This edition shows how the meaning of each of the seven mindsets develops at each stage of your leadership journey.

Inevitably, no book can be 100 per cent original. It would be arrogant to ignore the valuable lessons learned from previous research by many other people over decades. So this book duly draws on a wide range of research from business, psychology and beyond, and provides sources to help you explore further any areas of interest.

The seven mindsets of success

Cutting through all the noise of the research, seven mindsets consistently came out as the ones that the great leaders, our everyday heroes, displayed to an exceptional degree. They are:

1 high aspirations;
2 courage;
3 resilience;
4 positive;
5 accountable;
6 collaborative;
7 growth.

As you look at that list, your reaction may be, 'Well, I have all of that, so why am I not a hero yet?' There are two reasons.

First, there is the problem of inflation: language inflation. We now live in a world where anyone who has had a song in the Top 20 is immediately billed as a global megastar. And hype is not just the preserve of pop music. Business also loves its hype. The old Personnel Department has become the Strategic Human Capital Division. Even the most stable businesses such as utilities and government departments are transforming their paradigms, re-engineering their value chain, implementing global customer relationship management systems and becoming best-in-class next practice operators that create meaningful core competences in pursuit of their strategic intent. It is gobbledegook and hype. But it means that powerful words such as high aspirations or resilience have lost all their power. It is only when you hear our everyday heroes speak about what they have done that you discover just how powerful these words can be. It is the same difference as being able to hit all the notes on a piano versus playing a Rachmaninov piano concerto at Carnegie Hall: both are playing the piano, but in completely different leagues.

The second problem is in our heads. We like to think we are better than we are. Most of us suffer from a sense of illusory superiority,[14] for example:

- 88 per cent of US drivers put themselves in the top 50 per cent in terms of skills;[15]
- 85 per cent of SAT students put themselves above median in terms of getting on well with other people; 25 per cent rated themselves in the top 1 per cent;[16]
- 87 per cent of MBA students at Stanford rated themselves as above the median.[17]

It is natural that we want to think well of ourselves, and we do not take kindly to anyone who attempts to pour cold water on our self-belief. In most firms, 80 per cent of employees or more are rated as above average: this is statistically impossible but emotionally inevitable. In one investment bank, traders are ranked on a scale of 1–10. Given the fragile egos of these high performers it is no surprise to find that anything below a score of 9.8 is viewed as a disaster and below 9.7 means that you may get fired.

So if we are asked to consider whether we have high aspirations, resilience, courage, positive mindset, collaboration, growth and accountability we will naturally consider that we do well on all of these criteria.

In the pages that follow you will discover what these words really mean. The challenge is to move beyond the hype. If you can really live up to what these words mean then you will set yourself apart from your colleagues: you will achieve far more than either they or you think you can achieve now. You will have the chance to turn your dreams into reality.

You will also be able to decide whether you want to become one of the everyday heroes. Chasing your dream sounds like a great way to live. But then you look at the focus, dedication and sacrifice that all top performers in the arts, sport or business make to chase their dreams and you discover the harsh reality of making dreams come true. Endless hard work and repeated failure are the more obvious symptoms of what it takes to succeed.

You will also discover some of the hidden costs of success. Most of the heroes I interviewed were very driven. They all had something to prove, even though it was not obvious what they were trying to prove or who they wanted to prove it to. And behind that drive, there was a spine of steel. Most of them hated the idea that they might be seen to be ruthless, but in their stories it became clear that they would be ruthless when needed. They might hate having to be ruthless, but they would do it anyway.

Fortunately, you do not have to subscribe to the whole package of seven mindsets in order to make a difference. Nor do you have to take them to the extreme that our great leaders have taken them. Take any one or two of the mindsets and build them up slowly. These can be your signature strengths that will let you do more and achieve more.

Perhaps the best news about mindset is that it can be learned. Like learning a sport, we may never play for our country, but with practice we can become better; and the better we become, the more we enjoy it. All our leaders talked about how they acquired the habits of mind that allowed them to succeed. It was a slow and sometimes painful process, but all the mindsets can be learned. At the outset I had doubted that courage could be learned, but leader after leader proved me wrong: even courage can be acquired. Like the lion in *The Wizard of Oz*, we may discover we have more courage than we think.[18]

There are some things that cannot be learned easily: charisma and intelligence are hard to learn, and medical science has not yet invented ways of creating these traits. Height is largely genetic – and helps: a disproportionate number of CEOs are tall.[19] But all of these traits pale into insignificance against mindset, which can be learned. Each chapter will show you how you can build each mindset over time.

You can read this book in more or less any order. Each mindset has its own chapter and can be read as a stand-alone piece. So if you want to focus purely on the accountable mindset, go straight to that chapter. There is nevertheless a logic to the order of the mindsets. High aspirations come first because we cannot achieve more than we hope for, unless we hope to get lucky. But hope is not a method and luck is not a strategy.

Achieving *high aspirations* takes huge amounts of *courage*, to take the risks required to transform and disrupt. With risk comes failure and setbacks: that means you need deep wells of *resilience* to stay the course. That in turn means you need to be relentlessly *positive*: in order to turn every setback into an opportunity to learn and do better. Failure makes you stronger, not weaker.

All the best leaders have high *accountability*. They believe they are the master of events, not the victim of events. But they know they cannot succeed alone. All our heroes are deeply *collaborative*. They are not lone heroes. The way to get 25 hours of work into 24 hours is through other people. The best leaders achieve thousands of hours of progress every day. But they will not blame others or blame events when things go wrong. Instead, they learn from events and grow stronger as they adapt: that is the *growth* mindset.

About this second edition

Since the first edition was published, it has become clear that mindset is a hot topic in management and leadership. When asked to speak at conferences,[20] mindset is regularly the theme which galvanizes the audience. There is a reason for this: mindset makes sense. We can all see from everyday experience that the people who get to the top are not always the most skilled or most talented. They have a special sauce; they act differently because they think differently.

The reaction to the first edition and to the conferences gave me the encouragement to continue the research. There have been two elements to the research. First was to see how people can learn the habits of mind which comprise the mindset of success. The good news is that all the mindsets can be learned. Even courage can be learned, as I discovered when doing field research with the Royal Marine Commandos. By the end of that trip, I was not sure how much courage I really wanted to acquire; they do seriously tough stuff. This second edition shows how you can learn the mindset of success.

The second part of the research is related to the first: how do mindsets grow and change in the course of a career? Throughout the book, I define leadership as the art of taking people where they would not have got by themselves. That means you can be leading from the very start of your career – you do not have to wait until you arrive in the corner office.

What has become clear is that the mindset of success is consistent at every stage of your leadership journey. You need all seven mindsets. But the nature of courage, resilience, being positive and the other mindsets changes subtly at each level. This is natural. When the context changes, you have to change.

For this reason, I have added a major new section to the book which explores your mindset journey. This shows how you can build the right habits of mind to succeed at each stage of your career. *Mindset of Success* is the first, and only, book to show how mindset develops as you develop your career. It is your private map to help you on the path to success.

Summary

There is a gap between the best leaders and the merely very good. Skills can help you to join the merely very good. To become a great leader, you need something more. Mindset is the X-factor that takes you beyond merely very good. The research for this book shows that the success mindset is consistent for the best leaders, wherever they come from. It also shows that anyone can acquire the success mindset with the help of some simple routines and habits.

There is a key to success, and that key is in your head. This book will help you to unlock your true potential.

High aspirations

Dare to dream

Mindset starts with ambition because our potential is limited by our ambition. High aspirations drive us to take more risk, have more courage, show more resilience and be more positive. High aspirations start with a future perfect and work back from there; they are not constrained by today's reality. With a few simple habits, we can dare to dream and make those dreams come true.

Imagine you have a magic wand and you can create the future you want. Create your ideal job with your perfect organization and great colleagues doing great things. Now compare that with your reality today. The difference between your ideal and your reality is your aspirations gap. We all have aspirations gaps: some are larger than others.

For many of us, these aspirations will remain pipe dreams. I wanted to become an astronaut, prime minister, rock star, billionaire, train driver and score the winning goal in the World Cup Final. All on the same day. My modest dreams have been dashed, so far.

But the best leaders don't just dream it: they do it. They imagine a better future for themselves and for others, then they make it happen. They have a way of thinking and acting that makes the impossible become possible. This book looks at how the best leaders consistently weave their magic. Their trick is that they think differently. If we learn to think differently, we will act differently and can achieve far more.

Our magic starts with a dream. We have to dare to dream. Then we have to dare to do it. There are always plenty of reasons why our dreams should not become true. We fear that we lack the skills, time or resources. We will see how none of these are real constraints. If it is important, we can find the time and resources and hire in the skills.

The real obstacle to success is not some malign force of nature. The real obstacle to success is in our own heads. We all have a dialogue going on in our heads, which often turns into a battle between the angels of hope and the demons of fear. The angels will let us dream our dream. They take us to a happy place where we fulfil our true potential and live the future that we want to live. The demons of fear help us and hinder us. They stop us from doing crazy things, but they also stop us doing great things. At their best, they are counsels of caution. At their worst, the demons stop us achieving our dreams and our potential. This book will show how we can make the most of our angels and demons.

Most dreams are just that: they are fantasies that expire on the first contact with reality. But they do not have to be fantasies. So let us take a potential example.

Daring to dream

Martin Luther King galvanized the American Civil Rights Movement with his speech from the steps of the Lincoln Memorial to a crowd of 250,000 on 28 August 1963.[1] His 'I have a dream' speech reminded everyone of the United States Declaration of Independence: 'We hold these truths to be self-evident, that all men are created equal.' In context, the statement was as revolutionary in 1963 as it was when it was first adopted by the Continental Congress on 4 July 1776.

But King's speech nearly did not happen. His prepared speech was floundering until he got heckled by Mahalia Johnson with, 'Tell them about the dream, Martin!' He then preached his favourite sermon: the dream. The speech was at risk, but the dream was never at risk: that is what he lived for, and died for, just five years later.

You cannot change the world unless you dare to dream, act on it and persuade others to act on it.

Imagine you are listening to the radio and it is playing your favourite music. The radio station interrupts the music to do an interview with someone. You are a little too slow in switching channel, so you end up hearing the whole interview. It is a story of someone in an overseas project that gets great graduates to teach in tough inner-city schools. It sounds interesting and the sort of thing that should happen in your own country. So what do you do next?

Most people will carry on listening to some more music and they will forget the interview. Perhaps a few people will remember it and think that someone ought to do something about it. And why should that someone not be you? This is where the demons kick in. They will point out that you have no relevant skills and have not been near a school for 20 years; you have no resources and no time. There are huge practical difficulties: where on earth do you start? And if you start, what will people say? They will probably think you have lost leave of your senses, even if they are polite to your face. It is a recipe for social embarrassment and professional disaster. You quietly put the dream back in its box, along with the dreams about being an astronaut and a rock star.

It does not have to be that way. I called the radio station and got the name of the project: Teach for America (TFA). I called TFA and asked to speak to the CEO,[2] who told me she was too busy but that some consultants from McKinsey had been interviewing her about education in London. So I called McKinsey and explained what I thought we should do: build a similar project to TFA in the UK. We started to get serious.

Then the demons started appearing in person, not just in our heads. All sorts of experts and powerful people popped out of nowhere to give us helpful advice. Did we realize that no top graduate teaches in the schools we wanted to serve? Why on earth would they want to join our madcap scheme? How would we train them? We had no money so where would the funding come from? Why would any school want such raw talent in such challenging circumstances? Have we talked to the unions, who are bound to hate it? Each of these experts sowed the cancer of self-doubt in our minds, encouraging our demons to stop us. But they were not saying *we* could not do it: they were saying that *they* could not do it. And they were right: they lacked the imagination or aspiration to create the future. They did not dare to dream, let alone act.

Ten years later our programme, Teach First, became the largest graduate recruiter in the UK.[3] Before we started, no graduates from Oxford or Cambridge wanted to teach in the schools we serve, now nearly one in ten final-year undergraduates from Oxford and Cambridge apply to get on the programme.

The opportunities are always there: we do not have to look hard. They are being presented to us all the time, even in the middle of a rock show on the radio. Our normal response is to ignore the opportunity or to think that the idea is for someone else. And that is our real opportunity. If everyone thinks that someone else will do it, then no one will do it. The field is left open to us to take up the challenge.

High aspirations are not simply about having a dream. They are about having the courage to act on your dream. This is the starting point for all the best leaders who contributed to this book. We rise or fall to the level of our aspirations. Low aspirations are self-fulfilling. If we set out to achieve little, that is exactly what we will achieve.

The book starts with high aspirations because they are the glass ceiling in our minds: they set the limit on what we can achieve. If we want to achieve more, we have to shatter the glass ceiling. High aspirations drive many of the other mindsets: resilience, courage, being positive, accountable and collaborative. Dreams without action are just dreams: they become real aspirations when we drive to action. That takes hard work and a very particular mindset, which anyone can learn.

In this chapter we explore:

- What high aspirations are (and are not).
- Why we get blocked from having high aspirations.
- How we can develop the mindset of high aspirations.

We have to know what good looks like, how to develop it and what the traps are for us. At every stage throughout this book we will draw on the real-life experiences of our everyday heroes: people like you or me who simply achieve more consistently.

High aspirations: what they are, and what they are not

'High aspirations' is a much overused phrase in business. It is commonly used to encourage people to try harder and do better. It comes in two main forms. The first is the guilt trip: 'You need to raise your aspirations.' The second form is the speech that includes references to high aspirations, commitment, values, excellence, passion, customer focus and all the other identikit phrases that are jumbled up to form the standard executive speech. This means that high aspirations have become devalued.

But for the best leaders, high aspirations are at the heart of how they think. Leaders who took part in this book thought about high aspirations differently from the merely very good in four ways, as shown in Table 1.1.

A good leader will work with the normal aspirations listed in Table 1.1, which are sensible and safe, and are a recipe for a good career. The best leaders' aspirations are in a different league. Let's explore the four main differences:

- Create the future versus work on today's reality.
- Transform and disrupt.

Table 1.1   The nature of aspirations

Normal aspirations	High aspirations
Work on today's reality	Create the future
Improve, seek perfection and excellence	Transform, disrupt
Focus on self	Focus on the mission
Be reasonable	Be unreasonable

- Focus on the mission.
- Be unreasonable.

Create the future versus work on today's reality

Perhaps the worst advice to give to a manager is 'first things first'. That implies you work on today's issues and you move forward incrementally. The best leaders do not start at the beginning and

The power of the dream

Martha was in a rut.[4] She had been CEO for several years, but was losing her enthusiasm. She saw her role as routine: setting and managing budgets, dealing with staff, and (given the nature of the business) lobbying civil servants and government ministers. It was the non-stop lobbying that really ground her down: people and priorities were always changing, and it felt like she was chasing shadows.

Over a weekend she sat down to think about what she really wanted. What she really wanted was to transform young people's lives, and her organization could make that transformation happen. She worked out what needed to happen over the next five years.

On Monday, she returned to the office as a new person. Budgets were no longer routine: they were about focusing resources to change her world. Working with staff was the way to build momentum to achieving the dream. Lobbying was no longer a chore: it was the key that would open the door to funding and the future.

Her role had not changed at all, but the way she thought about it and behaved was completely different. By daring to dream, she rediscovered her enthusiasm, commitment and purpose.

What's your dream?

move forwards from there. They start at the end. They have a dream, a picture of what they want to achieve in the future. They work back from there to identify what they need to do today in order to get there.

As managers progress through their careers, they have to think and act on different time horizons. At the start of your career you were probably set tasks that would take a day, or perhaps a week or two to complete. By the time you hit middle management, you start to think in terms of monthly and quarterly reports and you have to start working on the annual budget cycle. By the time you hit top management, you should be thinking well over a year in advance: where do you want to take the organization in future, and so what are the investments and activities you need to put in place now in order to get there?

Focus on the future does not mean you lose sight of today: you still deal with the day-to-day trench warfare of management: tight deadlines, mini-crises, budget discipline, staffing challenges and more. But all of these things are pure noise. Failure to deal with them causes chaos, but if all you do is deal with the noise you are not making progress. To make progress, you have to focus on the signal you want to make, not on the noise of today. In the words of one CEO: 'Get out of the weeds and onto the balcony.'[5] Even senior managers find this hard to do. They are so involved in dealing with the noise of management that they never focus on the signal. Do not confuse activity with achievement. Dealing with the noise may avoid disaster, but it does not move you forward.

Transform and disrupt

Focus on the future is not enough: the future has to be different from today. And this is where the best leaders separate themselves from the rest. Good managers will, of course, seek to improve things. They will be good stewards of their organization. Improving things is seriously hard work, because the baseline of performance in any organization is not level: it is declining. Things do not stay as they are: skilled staff leave, competition attack, suppliers increase their prices, customers want more for less, random fate intervenes to mess up the best-laid plans. In this world, managers run hard to stay still.

The best leaders reach beyond today to create a future that is not just better: it is different. As one said: 'I want to build St Paul's not a cheap flat.'[6]

The best leaders do not seek to improve: they transform. They do not let today's reality constrain them as they chase their dream. For example:

- History's great leaders from Alexander the Great to Ghandi achieve more than is reasonably possible.[7]

- Great entrepreneurs do not just compete; they change the terms of competition against the odds.

- Great head teachers are not constrained by circumstances.

The leadership difference is very clear in schools. State schools have their children's exam results published, and there is huge pressure on head teachers to show they are doing well. Many head teachers do what many managers would do in the same circumstances: they game the system. They enter children for the easier qualifications. They focused time and effort on the marginal candidates in order to get them over the key performance threshold. They 'teach to test', which means in effect that the children go through endless dress rehearsals for the exam. None of this actually improves the education of the child. It may not help the child, but it helps the head teacher and staff by delivering good public exam results.

Dame Sue John, head of a school in a tough area of London, did things differently. She ignored the easy way out and focused on delivering excellent education all round and putting children into the toughest exams. She did not game the system, which meant that the school performed poorly in the published league tables. Eventually, the government stopped the gaming and schools had to deliver. Suddenly, the excellence of her results were visible, and the heads who had been gaming the system were exposed.

Focus on the mission

It is the mission that motivates the leaders, makes them take risks and put in the extra hours. Take the example of Will,[8] who was working for the UK's Secret Intelligence Service (SIS, more commonly known as MI6). Working in central Africa his mission was to bring a warlord to the negotiating table.

Will was still in his twenties at the time. He set off alone by car and then foot to track down the warlord. Every mile he went he realized he was one mile further away from any friends or any support. Half his mind was shouting at him that he was crazy and he should just go back. But he kept going and eventually found his warlord. When he got there, the first thing the warlord said was, 'Hey, whitey, do you milk cows?' (cows in that part of the world represent wealth).[9] Will said no, and so the warlord told him to 'f*** off back to where you came from'.

Will duly f***ed off back. And then he learned to milk cows, a skill he had not anticipated having to learn as an SIS officer. He returned to the warlord. This time, he milked the cow and drank the fresh, unpasteurized, non-homogenized and unsterilized milk. A couple of days later, before dawn, the warlord kicked Will awake. He was holding a walkie-talkie in one hand and a Kalashnikov in the other. He asked Will, 'So, should I send the boys in?' He was about to launch another round of massacres, genocide and ethnic cleansing.

Half-awake, how would you answer an invitation to murder? The dumb thing would have been to tell him not to do it: that would have just encouraged him. Instead, Will agreed that in the warlord's position he would want to do the same thing... but there is the problem of these pesky foreign powers and the international war crimes court and well... A couple of hours later, the boys were called off and the massacre was averted.

Two things kept Will going, and stopped him listening to the voice of reason that was telling him he was putting his life at risk and he should just turn back. The first was the mission: countless lives were at stake. It was a mission worth staking all for. The second was fear.

There are many ways of dealing with fear, but one way is to have an even greater fear to avoid. As Will put it: 'The culture we learned from the SAS is that it is better to return dead than return stupid.'[10] Peer group pressure is powerful. To fail is one thing, not even to try but to abandon the mission is far worse: it destroys everything you stand for and live for.

The greater the mission, the greater the commitment. People risk more and achieve more for a great mission than for a minor mission. If the mission is to beat this month's sales target, decent sales people will make a decent effort. But they are unlikely to learn how to milk cows and to put their lives at risk for such a mission.

Setting an extraordinary mission, provided people buy into it, leads to extraordinary outcomes. President Kennedy, in a speech at Rice University, promised 'to go to the moon in this decade.'[11] It appeared to be mission impossible: the nation did not have the technology, know-how, organization or resources to fulfil the dream. But it was perceived to be essential: the Soviets had beaten America into space and the fear was that the Soviet Union would end up owning space. They had to be stopped or bettered. On 20 July 1969 the mission was accomplished, just seven years after the Rice University speech.

We all rise or fall to the level of the mission we are engaged in. Our mission anchors our commitment and behaviour. The greatest leaders are all engaged in the greatest missions. Churchill was a truly exceptional wartime leader. His mission was to save the nation and save the world from fascism. Before the war he was seen as a maverick; as a prime minister after the war he was utterly forgettable. The mission brought out the very best in him.

Throughout the research for this book, I found that the best leaders did not simply accept the mission that was given to them. They actively sought out missions that make a difference, which live up to Kennedy's words: 'We choose to... do these other things not because they are easy, but because they are hard, because that goal will serve to organize and measure the best of our energies and skills.'[12] He knew that the harder the goal, the more it tests us and brings out the best in us.

In each of the cases above, the leaders (Churchill, Kennedy and 'Will') achieved great things not out of personal ambition. They were not promoting themselves. If they achieved greatness, it was because they put the mission first – and the mission made them great. This distinction sounds trivial, but it is not. We all know people who are ambitious for themselves. They can succeed in their own narrow terms of pay and promotion, but the best leaders go beyond themselves and do not focus on pay and promotion: they appeal to a collective ambition.

Be unreasonable

Management is based on reason. The dawn of modern management arguably came about with the publication of Frederick Taylor's *The Principles of Scientific Management* (1911).[13] It was a work based on close observation and measurement of what made workers more or less productive: he was applying scientific practice to the workplace. This is a heritage that infuses business schools to this day: they churn out cases and theories based on evidence and reason. In practice, they are not scientific: they use evidence to support a hypothesis rather than to falsify it, which is the opposite of the scientific method.[14] And this is how anyone in business uses evidence. We use evidence like drunks use a lamp post: for support, not illumination.

Nevertheless, reason permeates business. To be called unreasonable is an insult. And yet the world was never changed by reasonable people. If you want the quiet life, be reasonable. If you want to make a difference, be unreasonable.

For instance, at the time of the 100th anniversary of Philips, the company was on its knees under the onslaught of Japanese competition. It was about to go bust. Jan Timmer, the president of Philips, issued a simple instruction: reduce costs, headcount and working capital by 20 per cent. Immediately, the excuses came flooding in:

- We have already cut by 20 per cent, we cannot cut any more.
- We are growing, we cannot cut growth.

- We already have best-in-class costs, so cutting any more is clearly not possible.

- We are your most profitable unit: cutting us would destroy your main source of profit.

Any reasonable leader would have listened and would have adjusted the targets. So the targets were adjusted: make the 20 per cent cuts or you will be part of the 20 per cent. Eventually, the message got through: cut 20 per cent; no excuses and no exceptions. Philips survived. If Jan Timmer had listened to reason, Philips would have gone bust.

The lesson is simple: when you accept excuses, you accept failure. Each leader in the interview panel was messianic about their mission. For example, when we were creating Teach First, we were told it would never work. That simply strengthened our resolve. If we had listened to reason, we would have given up.

Although the best leaders are unreasonable about the mission, they are reasonable about the means. As one put it: 'If you are sailing from Dover to Calais and the wind is blowing in the wrong way, then if you follow your strategy of sailing with the wind you will never get there. You have to adapt to the weather, but know where you are going.'[15] The shortest distance between two points may be a straight line. But when you are sailing against the wind, the quickest way between two points is a zigzag. The best leaders know how to zigzag. To outsiders, it may look like they are just changing direction: but they are steadily making progress towards their goal, despite the adverse winds.

Although unreasonableness is a key feature of the best leaders, so is adaptability, as we shall see in later chapters. This is the exact opposite of junior staff who expect to work to reasonable goals and apply a fixed process. Anyone who has had the frustration of dealing with a disempowered call-centre worker who cannot deviate from the scripted policy will understand this difference.

Our brief look at the nature of high expectations makes for uncomfortable reading for leaders stuck in their comfort zone. For the best leaders, high expectations mean:

- create the future;
- transform and disrupt;
- focus on the mission;
- be unreasonable.

These are not the sort of people you want to disappoint. They have very high expectations. As we shall see, they are very willing to sacrifice friendships and long-term professional relationships if that is what is needed to achieve the goal. Loyalty to the mission trumps loyalty to colleagues.

What blocks us from having high aspirations?

No one sets out to have low aspirations. But the glass ceiling that separates the good from the great is made of aspirations. To break through, you have to find high aspirations that most of your colleagues do not have. This is the good news – and the bad news. It is hard to have genuinely high aspirations, but if you can then you set yourself apart from the rest.

Any self-respecting manager will believe that they have high aspirations. We all tell ourselves a story that gives us our self-respect. Study after study shows that we rate ourselves as above average relative to our peers for driving, popularity, sense of reality, intelligence and more. Corporate evaluation systems reinforce this bias. I am yet to find an evaluation system in which half the staff are rated as average or below: any organization that is this honest would have a very demoralized workforce. A desire to avoid bad news and to flatter drives most evaluation systems to rank dishonesty. As a result, our comfortable belief in our own excellence is never seriously challenged. When a boss dares to suggest that we are less than 100 per cent perfect, they tend to sugar-coat the message with the jargon of 'development opportunities' (weaknesses) or occasionally 'development challenges' (crushing weaknesses).

There are several ways that good, but not great leaders, convince themselves that they have high aspirations. Here are the four main factors that stop us having high expectations:

- high standards;
- achievement focus;
- context;
- entropy.

Let us explore each one in turn.

High standards

High standards and high aspirations pull in different directions. High standards are about excellence. That means perfection in what you do, be it playing the piano or running a service team. There is clearly much that is good about this excellence focus. As customers, we would rather have excellent service than lousy service.

First, we shall look at why high standards and excellence are useful. Then we will look at the alternative: high aspirations.

As a good manager you should have high standards for yourself. The result of high standards is often reflected in long hours and stress. The problem for professionals is when high standards meet ambiguous work, and most professional work is ambiguous. If you work on a car production line, or at McDonald's, you can maintain very high standards without stress. The work is well defined and quality is baked into the process. Follow the process and you achieve the standard.

In the professional world of lawyers, architects, consultants, bankers and teachers the work is much more ambiguous and varied. If you are asked to produce a report, it could be 10 pages long or 200 pages long. Whatever its length, there is always another fact to find or check; another view to canvass, another angle to cover. If you have high standards, you will drive yourself to make the report as good as possible, and hence the long hours and the increasing feeling of stress as the deadline looms, while you know there is more you could do for your report.

With high standards you can rise to the very top of being a good manager. But to break through the glass ceiling and become a great leader you need to do more.

The problem with excellence and high standards is that you are working within the system as it is today. Excellence focus is often risk averse. You do not want to try radically new things, because you risk failure. So you focus on optimizing the system, not changing it. This is worthy, but it is not what the best leaders do.

High expectations are not about accepting things as they are. High aspirations mean creating a future by disrupting, challenging and innovating.

High standards are a safe comfort zone to operate in. Having high aspirations is not safe. It takes people into uncharted waters. High aspirations will accelerate your career: you will succeed fast or fail fast. More likely, you will fail several times, learn from your setbacks and then succeed to a greater extent than anyone thought possible.

Achievement focus

There is a paradox here. To succeed, you must achieve. But if you focus too much on achievement, you trap yourself in a box of underachievement. How is this? The problem comes with incentives and how we think about ourselves: our mindset.

The problem starts with praise. It is normal to give praise for a job well done. Surprisingly, this is very dangerous.

Schools have found that expecting and praising achievement has strong negative impact.[16] When a child learns that praise comes from achievement they also learn:

- Do not take risks, because you might fail.

- Stay within your comfort zone.

- If I fail at a task, I have failed as a person.

- Follow instructions closely and avoid creativity.

Instead of praising the outcome, it is often better to praise the effort.[17] That way, children learn that effort, creativity and learning are good and that 'failure' is simply another step on the learning journey.

At this point, you may think: 'But I am not a child and I would never fall into a trap like that.' Unfortunately, it is a trap that ensures for many managers: promotion means failure. The trap is often formulated as the Peter Principle,[18] which states that people get promoted to their level of incompetence. Look at your own organization and you will find that the Peter Principle works.

The Peter Principle works where promotion is given based on competence at the lower level, not on expected competence at the higher level. This can be a disaster because the tasks at each level are very different. The person being promoted may not even realize that the rules of survival and success have changed. This quickly turns into a tragedy. The newly promoted manager works harder to justify their promotion, but under the old rules.

Some elegant research shows that the Peter Principle is so pervasive that not only is it 'unavoidable, but also it yields in turn a significant reduction of the global efficiency of the organization': it would be better to promote at random than to promote on the basis of achievement at the lower level.[19]

The difference in role is neatly captured in the classic consulting or legal career of grinders, minders and finders:

- Grinders: entry-level graduates do the real work.
- Minders: manage the work of the grinders.
- Finders: the partners who are the sales force bringing in the work.

The three roles are completely different: success at one level is no guarantee of success at the next level. High attrition at each level shows that even smart people struggle to adapt to new rules of survival and success.

As we shall see in Chapter 3, the best leaders fail and continually fail. Their overnight success is often 20 years in the making. But their failures are also their chance to learn and to adapt.

For the best leaders at all levels, the practical alternative to achievement focus is adaptability, learning and growth. This flies in the face of the management mantra of excellence. Excellence and perfectionism are the extreme ends of high standards. They are worth pursuing in the stable context of process industries such as making cars, burgers or computer chips. But they are deadly in the context of developing as a great leader. There is no single magic template for what makes a great leader: Nelson Mandela and Admiral Lord Nelson were very different sorts of leaders for different sorts of contexts. You have to learn, grow and adapt to your existing context. And eventually, if you create the future you will also be creating the context in which you flourish.

Context

Here is a quick quiz. What do the following people have in common? Economist John Maynard Keynes; authors George Orwell, Ian Fleming and Aldous Huxley and poets Percy Bysshe Shelley and Thomas Gray; former King of Thailand; kings of Jordan, Belgium and Nepal; Oscar-winner Eddie Redmayne; actors Hugh Laurie, Dominic West and Patrick Macnee; composers Thomas Arne ('Rule Britannia'), Hubert Parry and Humphrey Lyttelton; scientists Robert Boyle of Boyle's Law and Nobel Laureate John Gurdon; fictional spy James Bond and real spy and traitor Guy Burgess, along with mercenary Simon Mann and numerous rogues and criminals; Brent Hoberman, the co-founder of lastminute.com; Captain Hook from *Peter Pan*; adventurers Bear Grylls and Ranulph Fiennes; two FA Cup-winning teams, nine winners of Olympic gold medals and 37 Victoria Cross recipients; one Thai prime minister and 19 British prime ministers; the Archbishop of Canterbury and Bertie Wooster?

They all went to the same secondary school: Eton College,[20] which is just to the west of London. In that world, high aspirations are the norm. The reality is that most pupils will not land up being exceptional in any way, but there will consistently be a minority who go on to do extraordinary things for better or for worse.

Not far away, Emma teaches at a school in Ealing, which is slightly closer to central London. It was affected by riots in 2011. She decided to organize a school trip for the 14-year-old pupils in one of her classes after she found out that not one of them had ever made the 20-minute train journey to the city. When the pupils were asked what they wanted to do after leaving school, most of the boys said they wanted to be premiership footballers, and the girls wanted to be models or WAGs.[21] But at 14 they were already too late: poor diet and lack of training meant that their dreams were fantasies. Their fallback options were to work at the local supermarket, join a gang or become a hairdresser.

Clearly, pupils from the Ealing school can succeed. But the cards are not stacked in their favour. They don't have the role models to show them what is possible and they often have multiple disadvantages to contend with: speaking English as a second language, chaotic home backgrounds and the daily grind of poverty.

Context is not destiny, but it weights the dice for or against us. If you are surrounded by high aspirations and exceptional role models, it is easy to acquire high aspirations yourself. If you are surrounded by low aspirations then these become the norm. For example, I was visiting a slum school in Delhi. A parent came to complain that her child appeared not to be learning anything. She was distraught: she wanted her son to escape the life she had lived, and education was the escape route. The parent had high aspirations for her child, and was making sacrifices. As she pointed out, a child at school was a child not earning and not putting bread on the table: it was another mouth to feed. After the parent left, the head teacher turned to me and said: 'You see, that is the problem: the child of the donkey will always be a donkey. There is nothing we can do.' The school was busily setting low aspirations, and was ensuring that the child would fall down to the level they expected: the level of a donkey.

As with education, so with careers. The best graduates instinctively seek out the most demanding recruiters. These recruiters do not recruit just on pay. Some, such as Goldman Sachs and McKinsey, pay exceptionally well. Others pay more modestly, such as General Electric (GE), Procter & Gamble (P&G) or Teach First. Graduates know they will be stretched and it will be hard work. They also know they will learn, grow and develop fast. Even if they are eased out after a couple of years, they will be in high demand from other employers who want employees who understand what good really looks like. That, inevitably, draws them closer to the excellence trap: they can become very good leaders but will never become exceptional leaders unless they can break through the glass ceiling of perfectionism to the risky world of high aspirations. They will become conventionally effective, but will find it hard to become great.

The challenge for any emerging leader is to choose the right context. A prestigious organization will inculcate high standards, but can also breed conformity. You may earn highly and strive mightily but you will remain a cog in the machine. But if you choose an organization with low standards and low aspirations, it will be hard to rise above that.

There is an easy way to find a high aspirations context: see how fast people walk. Imagine the difference between a small town and Manhattan, central London or Hong Kong. Fast cultures are more productive, both at a national level and at a firm level.[22] I interviewed an executive who had left a rival firm and asked her what the difference was between the two firms, to which she replied: 'My last firm was a running culture: we ran everywhere, to answer the phone, to go to the bathroom, everywhere. Here is much nicer: it is a walking, ambling culture.' Her new firm was put out of business by the running firm within three years. There is no research on whether this works at the individual level: if you walk faster will you go further, earn more and be more productive? You could try it.

The best leaders have a solution to this conundrum: they create their own context. We have seen that many of the world's top billionaires either dropped out of university or never went there in the first place. Most of them are an MBA-free zone. The leadership panel for the research for this book was drawn up without prior knowledge of each leader's education. It turned out that several of them had also struggled at school: one is dyslexic; another failed exams and left school at 16; a third had parents who discouraged education and found herself putting cherries on grapefruits for a career at age 16. All of them decided to take control of their destiny and create the future they wanted.

Entropy

The journey from bright-eyed graduate ready to change the world to grizzled middle-aged cynic has been taken by too many people. We may not be able to avoid middle age, but we can avoid being grizzled and cynical. No self-respecting graduate actively aspires to become cynical and negative. So what goes wrong?

There is no single disaster that transforms us for the worse. It is a slow and grinding process that, like ageing, we do not notice from day to day. But 10 years later, we look in the mirror and realize that we have changed. Here is Steve Munby, CEO of Education Development Trust, talking about how low aspirations can creep up and catch even the best of us by surprise:

> When I bought a house, we drew up a long list of improvements to make it the perfect house. After a year of hard work, we had got about two-thirds of the way through the list. We did not give up, but we did not keep going. We had got used to lower standards; we had got used to compromises. But great leaders never compromise. They fight endlessly against the second law of thermodynamics.[23] So they always look outside their own organization for inspiration and challenge, to stop themselves becoming complacent.

Avoiding entropy requires constant challenge and constant renewal. Doing this is not easy, which is why many people take the easy route and quietly compromise: they make do with second best and avoid the never-ending battle with entropy. In later chapters we explore how you can develop the resilience, perseverance and self-belief to sustain this challenge for decades.

How to develop and deploy high aspirations

High aspirations are not something you have or do not have. You can nurture it. But vaguely hoping for a better future will not work. Be specific, and then drive to action. Here are five things you can do for high expectations:

- dare to dream;
- seize the moment;
- create the right context;
- act the part;
- choose your destiny.

We will look at each in turn.

Dare to dream

Here are some simple questions to ask:

- Where do I want to be in 10 years' time? Dare to be ambitious: where do you *really* want to be in 10 years? A period of 10 years gives you the time to make a real transformation: from Kennedy's speech to the first moon landing was seven years.

- What are the skills, experiences and support I need to realize my 10-year goal?

- What are the key milestones I need to have achieved in one, two, three and five years to get to my goal?

- So what do I need to do this week to get started? Right now?

These questions are the high aspirations questions: create your future, transform yourself, focus on a mission and dare to be unreasonable in your expectations. This is your critical first step. The level of your ambition creates the ceiling to what you will achieve: few people achieve more than they intend. Aim high: even if you miss by a small margin you will still have gone higher than people who aimed low.

Now test your current reality. How will you remember this year in 10 or 20 years' time? You will not remember it for the number of e-mails sent, or for beating budget by 6.8 per cent or for your 5.2 per cent pay rise. To help you think about what you are likely to remember, try remembering what you did 10 years ago. There are some years where I can remember nothing of note: all I achieved was to get one year closer to death. Life should be lived with the record button on and in full Technicolor. The trick is to make sure that you are not just living for today: you should also be acquiring the skills and experience that will make the next 10 years even better than the past 10 years. Invest in your future: it is the best investment you can make.

Seize the moment

George Orwell wrote: 'To see what is in front of one's nose needs a constant struggle.'[24] We are surrounded by opportunities, but often we do not even see them. Professor Richard Wiseman did a dramatic and extreme test of this. He asked a group of volunteers to count the number of times a basketball team passed the ball. As they passed the ball, a man in a gorilla suit walked into the middle of the group, thumped his chest a bit and then walked off. Quite a few volunteers counted correctly. But only 5 out of over 20 volunteers noticed the gorilla.[25] The same applies to our professional lives. We are so focused on keeping score and managing day to day that we do not notice the endless opportunities that are in front of our noses.

Most of the leadership panel did not expect to get to where they are today. But they saw an opportunity and they seized it. Once they took up the challenge, they became obsessed by the mission it represented. This is your antidote to your 10-year plan. The plan does not lead to a fixed destination. It is a journey that opens up new opportunities to you. As you build your skills, experience and track record, more opportunities will open up to you.

Opportunities often come out of adversity. Here are five examples:

- You find that banks are charging medium-sized businesses far too much; they give poor service; they have not innovated for 20 years and they make excess profits. It is the sort of situation that would have the regulators, politicians and competition authorities seething with anger. Your opportunity? Start a bank that is less greedy, less inefficient and offers better service.

- You are at your company offsite. Head-office staff are inflicting cost cuts on everyone. Then you find out that they have quietly put in a 30 per cent increase for their own budget. Your opportunity? Volunteer to lead an effort to bring their costs back in line.

- Your company has a business in Japan. It is not making any money, has no sales and looks dead in the water. Your opportunity? Accept a one-way ticket to Japan for the adventure of a lifetime in which you learn to lead and make a difference.

- You get mugged at knifepoint. You can complain, or you can see it as an opportunity to do something: start a charity that gets offenders to start their own businesses so that they can make money without turning to crime. So far, over 500 legitimate businesses have been started via this charity.[26]

- You hear a radio interview about a project to get top graduates to teach in inner-city schools. Your opportunity? Take the idea and make it work in your country: create the largest graduate recruiter in the UK.

These are not abstract examples. They are real opportunities I stumbled across and took. There are many more I have failed to see. There are opportunities everywhere if we look for them, and have the courage to seize them. Clearly, no one (including myself) has *all* the skills or experience to take on the five opportunities above – but seizing the moment is not about skills and experience: it is about your mindset. Every opportunity is an opportunity to learn and grow. If you wait until you are 100 per cent ready, you will wait for ever. No one is ever 100 per cent ready for a new challenge.

Opportunity in front of our eyes

Imagine you are reading the newspaper and your eyes notice a letter from the Saudi Arabian Ambassador to London, HRH Prince Turki Al Faisal.[27] The prince is asking the media to stop blasting Saudi Arabia at every opportunity.

By this point your eyes are probably already looking for another letter, or the sports or fashion pages, according to your taste. If you choose to read further, you will find that the prince is arguing that Saudi Arabia has not yet existed as a nation for 100 years – and asking as a point of comparison how long had it taken the UK to give women the vote. He says that Saudi Arabia, like every country, has challenges, but those challenges have to be dealt with at a pace appropriate to the culture. He then asks for the UK to work with and help Saudi Arabia to evolve.

Anyone and everyone who read that letter moved on to more interesting things, like breakfast. Well, not quite everyone. Mark Evans had lived in Saudi Arabia and decided to write to the ambassador saying how much he had enjoyed his time there. The ambassador wrote back and invited Mark to tea.

They talked about what could be done to shift attitudes. Out of that conversation Mark set up the University of the Desert,[28] with support from the prince at a launch in the British Museum. For 13 years the programme has taken young people and future leaders from different cultures into the desert to learn from each other. From there, Mark has set up the very successful Oman branch of Outward Bound.

Opportunities are staring us in the face all the time, if we care to look for them. Every problem is an opportunity, so every newspaper is full of opportunities: it is just that some opportunities are harder to solve than others. What opportunity will you find today?

Create the right context

If you work in a place with dull and duplicitous colleagues, with low prospects and a nasty boss, who is responsible for that? You are. It is easy to blame our colleagues, employer, boss or environment for all our troubles. It is easy, but wrong.

Here are five tests to determine if you are working in the right place for developing high aspirations, which are also good tests to use on assessing any job opportunity:

- Am I learning and growing? Above all, this is about getting the right experiences. 'Right' means the sort of experience that challenges you, develops you and takes you out of your comfort zone. You should be gaining the sort of experience and skills that you can use and reuse in the future that you want to make for yourself.

- Are there opportunities today and tomorrow? Are you in the right role with a supportive boss now, and can you see other opportunities and other bosses who can help you on your journey of growth and development? Or are you stuck in a rigid career system with few degrees of freedom?

- Do I enjoy what I am doing? You only excel at what you enjoy. There is a reason for this: doing well takes time, effort and commitment. Sustaining the required effort for years on end is not possible for something you do not enjoy. Enjoyment is not self-indulgence: it is vital to success.

- Are there good role models for me? We learn through experience, both our own and others'. When we see someone do something well, we try to copy it. When we see someone blow up, we make a quiet note not to step on the same landmine ourselves. You need the role models who can show you what high aspirations really look like, and how you can achieve them.

- Can I find the right support? For some people this means hiring a coach who will challenge and push you; for others it may be finding good mentors at work, ideally at least two levels above you, who can guide and advise you; for some it is about having a supportive spouse. Build the network you need. Remember: if you don't ask, you don't get.

As you reflect on your context, you may be lucky and realize you are in a good context. Make the most of it: proactively seek out the right opportunities and right network.

What do you do if your context is not so rosy? Be patient. The grass always looks greener on the other side of the hill. But remember that it is greenest where it rains the most. All organizations have their fair share of mediocre bosses, dull work, internal politics, lack of resources and stress. Many people do not leave their job: they leave their boss.[29] Remember that the corporate carousel keeps on turning: bad bosses are not for ever, and if you move to a new place your wonderful new boss will not be there for ever either. If you move, make sure it is for the right reasons. See how well your new role will satisfy the five challenges above.

Act the part

Imagine you have a colleague who meets the tests of high aspirations: he or she creates the future, transforms and disrupts, and is unreasonable in the goals they set. But at least they are on a mission. Now imagine an organization full of such people. It would make a chimpanzee's tea party look calm and orderly.

Fortunately, high aspirations are for the few, not the many. Few people actually live up to the hype and propaganda of high aspirations. This means that if you act on high aspirations you will stand out. Your challenge is to stand out in a way that does not make you public enemy number one among all your peers.

You can help senior bosses in two main ways. The first is to minimize the amount of noise they have to deal with. Occasionally, senior managers find that their role is to be pooper-scooper in chief. It is not a role they relish. Make sure it is not your poop they are scooping. Minimizing noise is low aspirations but vital to success both for you and your organization. This is the daily routine that may absorb most of your time.

The second way you can help your bosses is by helping them to maximize their signal. Everyone has an agenda that is important to them, especially the CEO. Lift up your head from your routine and take time to understand what matters at the top. Listening to a CEO speech can be tedious, not least of all because CEOs are often lousy public speakers. But listen past the drone to the substance. Your CEO will be telling you what he or she thinks is important. Most people shrug their shoulders, go for their coffee break and carry on as usual. If you are one of the few who listens and acts, you will stand out in a positive way. Show that you can act on the top agenda and you will get noticed at the top table.

For example, one bank CEO decided to focus everything on improving the customer experience. The risk managers were perplexed. What on earth had customer focus got do with them? They were there to avert fraud, disaster and folly. Most of them figured out that the CEO was really talking about other parts of the bank and so they focused on doing what they were meant to do: managing risk. But one risk manager took a different tack. He decided to spend at least two days per month visiting customers, which involved working with relationship managers. He looked at a different sector each month: construction, agriculture, small businesses, retail and so on. As he went out, he started to notice how risk procedures were jamming up the process; many of the procedures were either not needed, or duplicated elsewhere or were just too complicated. And some vital bits of information were routinely being missed. His behaviour and his findings soon got noticed. In a short amount of time, the CEO decided he had found his new head of risk, who went about fundamentally changing the way that risk was managed in the bank.

In another case a large consulting firm decided it wanted to increase teamwork. As facilities manager, what would you do to increase teamwork? Chuck, the facilities manager at that particular firm, decided that facilities would be at the heart of the teamwork revolution. He approached the senior partner in his magnificent private office, with deep carpets and reproduction antiques. 'If you want more teamwork,' said Chuck, 'the first thing we need to do is to get rid of your office.' The senior partner nearly choked on his fine porcelain cup of tea. Chuck explained the idea: eliminate all the private offices, starting with partners, and move to open plan where everyone can see everyone else. No hiding places, easy to control, improved teamwork and communication and reduced costs. Within six months all the partners' offices were consigned to history, along with some of the more traditional partners who could not deal with Chuck's brave new world. Both Chuck and the risk manager met the tests of high aspirations:

- create the future;
- transform and disrupt;
- focus on the mission;
- be unreasonable.

You do not have to wait until you reach the top to show and develop high aspirations: you can start right now. Even if you cannot work on the CEO's agenda, you can create opportunities to develop your high aspirations mindset. The best opportunities are where you:

- have to make real change;
- are forced to disrupt and challenge;
- will be out of your comfort zone and will learn and grow;
- will be visible several levels further up the organization.

Fortunately, opportunities like this are always coming up in any organization because:

- Crises happen. Initially no one is sure what to do or who should do it. This is your chance to seize the moment and take the lead. Most people regard crises as a problem to be avoided: it is your chance to shine, to make a difference and to learn and grow.

- New ideas need nurturing. Senior executives are always cooking up new ideas. They need help and support to flesh out the idea and to set it up for success, but may not have the budget to assign resources to it. If you join or lead the skunk works with your voluntary effort, you gain a senior executive as a grateful ally, and you will be in pole position to lead the project if it starts up formally.

The key to seizing the opportunity is to strike early. The window of opportunity shuts fast. If you are first to volunteer you may lead the effort. If you are the tenth person to jump on the bandwagon you are likely to have a much smaller role to play, and your ability to transform and disrupt will be less. You may help, but you will not be developing the high aspirations mindset. Be ready to take a risk and take the lead: it is the quickest way to learn and grow.

Choose your destiny

We all have choices and those choices are open to us all of the time. But choices are not always comfortable choices. Your first choice is whether you want to live in a world of high aspirations.

Remember what high aspirations mean:

- create the future;
- transform, disrupt;
- focus on the mission;
- be unreasonable.

This is a high bar that separates the best from the merely very good. High aspirations mean hard work, risk, frequent setbacks and challenge. They also mean personal fulfilment, excitement and meaning. You will create the future you want and be master of your destiny.

You have an entirely legitimate alternative: focus on high standards and develop skills that will be in demand not just with your current employer, but with other employers as well. As with high aspirations this can also involve hard work, setbacks, challenge and stress. Success does not come on the back of working only four hours per week.

Whatever your choice, you have to deal with risk. Having high aspirations creates clear risk: if you attempt to transform and disrupt then you will have plenty of active and passive opposition to deal with. But at least you will see the risk and you can deal with it. If you stick within an organization and choose not to challenge it, the risks are less obvious. But you still face three hidden risks:

- Your colleagues are your competition. They are fighting for the same pot of promotions, bonuses, resources and management time as you.

- Your skills become redundant, or your role is outsourced, offshored, best shored, restructured, de-layered, optimized or best sized. In other words, your employer gets rid of you and you find that you are not in control of your destiny.

- Your employer loses out and is overtaken or taken over by competition. Again, you find that you are not in control of your destiny. You may be a great employee, but that does not help when your firm goes bust.

What was striking about the leadership panel was that they were all positive about the choices they had made. They all told of setbacks and hard times, and they had no regrets. Even in the hardest times, they knew that they were in control of their destiny. None of them could imagine going back to a world where other people controlled their destiny.

The first choice we have to make is around our level of aspiration. Many people make this choice by default: they rise or sink to the level of aspirations around them. Do not default into a choice: know that you have a choice and make your decision.

Summary

Having high aspirations means that you will:

- Dare to dream and create your future.
- Transform and disrupt, not just seek to improve.
- Focus on your mission, not just on yourself.
- Be unreasonable in sticking to goals, but flexible about how you get there.

The major obstacles to having high aspirations are:

- Living in the comfort zone of high standards rather than learning and growing.
- Focusing on achievement in current role, rather than preparing for your next role.
- Working in a low-aspirations rather than high-aspirations context.
- Letting entropy and lower standards creep up unnoticed.

You can develop high aspirations when you:

- Dare to dream: imagine your future perfect.
- Seize the moment: see the opportunities around you every day.
- Work in a high-aspirations context: in a culture that is running rather than walking.
- Act the part: be a partner, not a follower, for powerful people.
- Choose your destiny: know what you want and work for it.

Courage 02

Dare to act

Chasing your dreams takes courage. Without courage, the dream remains a dream. Courage is about taking on personal risk. Fortunately, courage is not a genetic trait. We can all build our courage, and become more adept at knowing when and how to take on risk.

For millennia, leaders have needed courage. Kings, and occasionally queens like Boadicea,[1] led their troops into battle. To this day, traditional societies expect their leaders to have courage (see box). But CEOs no longer have to wield a battleaxe in anger, except perhaps as a metaphor in a speech to rally the staff – which is as brave as the rantings of a keyboard warrior posting their latest anonymous blog.

At first, it seemed that courage should have no place in the mindset of success. And yet, courage was the leadership quality that was most often picked by our leadership panel as being essential to success. It was placed in the top five topics 93 per cent of the time. This chapter explores why leaders believe that courage is a core mindset.

Leadership is the art of taking people where they would not have gone by themselves.[2] And, if the leader has high aspirations, that means doing more than simply improving on better, faster, cheaper. It means transforming, disrupting, setting unreasonable goals and creating a future that is not just better, but different. You can only achieve that by taking risks, and taking risks requires courage.

For business leaders, courage is not about physical bravery. It is about having the courage to take risks. Leaders also require courage to make difficult decisions, to have difficult conversations and to stretch and challenge the organization. If a leader cannot do this, then they are drifting, not leading.

Real risk is not about the business: businesses take risks all the time. The real risk is personal: risking the wrath of your bosses and the quiet mockery of your peers if things go wrong, while knowing they will claim all the credit if things go well.

In this chapter we explore two themes:

- The nature of risk.
- How you can build your courage mindset.

The courage of leaders: lessons from traditional societies

The tribal world has much to teach us about leadership. Leading a tribe is to lead without all the corporate life support systems that enable us and imprison us at the same time: HR, IT, e-mail, phones, lawyers and consultants. And if you mess it up as a tribal leader, you do not lose your bonus, promotion or job. You may lose your life. It is leadership without a safety net.

Over a period of 15 years I did fieldwork with tribes from Mali to Mongolia, the Arctic to Australia via Papua New Guinea and beyond.[3] I would always ask what everyone wanted from their leaders. I always got the same three answers:

- courage;
- contribution;
- responsibility.

Responsibility meant being a role model; contribution meant having the wealth and power to look after the tribe when things go wrong, and courage…?

I was not too sure about courage, although they all had heroic tales to tell of defeating wild animals or wild neighbouring tribes. And then I found myself patrolling the territory of one tribe with a couple of warriors. Suddenly, a pack of hyenas came hurtling out of the bush and charged straight at us.

I did what any sensible coward would do. I hid behind the warriors, who promptly laughed in the face of imminent death. That struck me as one reason why they were warriors and I was not. A moment later, the cause of their laughter became clear: a small child, with an even smaller stick, came charging out of the same part of the bush, chasing the hyenas. The child had been protecting the goats, the entire wealth of the village. And the child knew to protect them at all costs.

In that one moment the child had shown contribution (saving the goats) responsibility (attacking the hyenas, not running away to get help) and courage. If leadership is what you do, not what you say, the child was a natural leader.

We all need courage to face up to danger, to face our demons. What are the hyenas you must chase away?

The nature of risk

When most people think about risk in an organization they think of things such as health and safety, or the risk and issue logs that go with any large project. These are routine risks and firms deal with them routinely. An entire industry exists to help deal with risk: the insurance industry. These routine risks are rational: you can analyse them and cope with them. As we shall see, rational risks are not the sort of risks that separate the best leaders from the rest. The risks that sort the leaders from the pack are around ambiguity and personal risk.

We will look at these three main types of risk in turn:

- rational risk;
- ambiguity;
- personal risk.

Rational risk

Most organizations are set up to deal with business risk. A staple item for most boards is the annual review of the risk register: it is full of risks, issues, mitigating actions and impact assessments. This is the world of rational risk. Done well, it enables businesses to make large bets that are reasoned bets: think of film studios investing in films, many of which will fail; oil majors investing in exploration that may not work; banks lending money that they may not recover. These are big risks, with regular failures. The occasional catastrophic failures, such as the 2008 banking crash or the BP Gulf of Mexico disaster in 2010, are notable precisely because they are exceptional not routine.

Dealing with this sort of rational risk does not take courage: it is business as usual. Although even here, different sorts of organizations have their risk thermostats set at different levels. In the City of London (the financial district), for example, dealers routinely take positions with tens of millions of dollars of value at risk. Just three miles west is Westminster, where risk is like kryptonite to a civil servant. The most insulting advice that government ministers can give to their fellow officials is to say that the minister would be 'very brave' to make such and such a decision. In one place risk is routine, in another it would be as welcome as Voldemort at Harry Potter's birthday party.

Dealing with rational risk is basic management routine: it does not separate out the best leaders from the rest. The level of rational risk that is tolerated depends on the culture of your organization.

It is no surprise that the risk which most often kills an organization is not the known risk: it is the unknown risks. The biggest risk of all is doing nothing: that is a guarantee of being overtaken or made irrelevant by new technology and new competition. As we shall see in Chapter 7, firms that do not adapt, die. Taking risk is risky, taking no risk is fatal. That is true for both firms and individuals. We have to adapt, to grow and to take risks, otherwise we become irrelevant.

Ambiguity

Although most organizations know how to manage rational risk, more or less well, they are not good at dealing with ambiguity.[4]

Most organizations prize predictability and uniformity and dislike uncertainty and variability. The founder of the quality movement, W Edwards Deming,[5] defined quality as reduction in variation: the millionth computer chip should be exactly the same as all the ones that came before. This thinking permeates management, if not always explicitly or well. Many bosses lament that 'no surprise is a good surprise'.

There are good reasons for wanting predictability and consistency: it drives down costs and drives up quality. It also makes management's life easier. In this sort of world any innovation is incremental: finding ways of decreasing variability, costs and time to meet customer needs better. That is the essence of total quality movement (TQM). Incremental improvement does not lead to breakthroughs and stifles real leadership. But it is effective. For example, at Andersen Consulting (now Accenture) the legendary Method One was the system that was used to transform bright young graduates into project managers who could develop and implement large-scale, complex, systems solutions. The entire focus was on defining every need and every step down to the last detail so that there was no uncertainty, no ambiguity. The entire business was built on this method.

Ambiguity and uncertainty is the sort of risk that firms dislike the most. In contrast, entrepreneurs and the best leaders see ambiguity and uncertainty as opportunity. If you want to make a breakthrough, you cannot do it by clinging on to predictability and uncertainty. You have to break free.

In any organization, there are moments of ambiguity and uncertainty. These are the moments that define the best leaders. An average manager will quietly stand back and wait to see how a moment of uncertainty and danger resolves itself. A leader will step up and see the opportunity to take charge. In the words of Sir David Bell: 'Courage is about not following routines and formulas. It is when you go counter-cultural and say "we will not accept the way the world works: we will change the zeitgeist".'[6] The safe and quiet life follows routines, processes and procedures. Leaders rarely settle for the quiet life.

Attitudes to ambiguity and uncertainty reliably sort out the leaders from the managers. As a leader, you have to embrace ambiguity.

That means conquering the fear of the unknown that lives with all uncertainty.

Personal risk: fear of failure

Managers are comfortable with rational risk. But they are not comfortable with personal risk: the fear of being seen to make a mistake, the fear of losing face, the fear of criticism and failure. Fear stops people taking risks, so it makes sense to understand fear. Fear means different things to different people. Some people fear spiders, others don't. Two examples will make the point:

- David Cole, the captain of Scotland's grand slam rugby team, agreed to play a friendly(ish) game against the SAS. In his words: 'They were all asking, "How do you go out in front of 55,000 people? What if you drop the ball or miss a kick?". And I was asking them, "How do you go into caves in Bora Bora looking for terrorists?"'

- It was the weekend, and the CEO of a global bank had a board meeting due the next week. He had also agreed to teach a lesson in a tough inner-city school as part of the bank's support for Teach First.[7] He lost a large slice of the weekend to work and preparation because he was worried. He was not worried about the board meeting: he knew how to deal with global executives. He was worried about the lesson: how would he deal with the kids, what would he say, would he survive? Meanwhile, the teacher who had been assigned to help him recoiled in horror at being asked to do a short presentation about the charity to the board of the bank: how would she deal with the global big shots, what would she say, would she survive?

These two cases show that fear is not absolute or universal. Different people respond in completely different ways to the same situation. Fear is personal. That is our first step to conquering our fear. Instead of saying 'that is dangerous' we should say 'I fear that is dangerous'. The second statement leads us to the correct response, which is:

- How can I reduce the perceived risk and danger of this action?
- How can I reduce my own fears, reactions to this situation?

We need to deal with the external reality and our own internal, emotional, reaction to that reality. As we shall see, we cannot simply dismiss our emotional reaction: we need a more substantive response.

Both cases also show that fear is largely fear of the unknown. The CEO's comfort zone was the boardroom; the teacher's comfort zone was the classroom. Swap the classroom and boardroom around in each case, and comfort is replaced with fear. Neither the teacher nor the CEO had the tools or training to deal with an entirely unfamiliar situation. The insight they offer is that a good way to reduce fear is to make the unfamiliar familiar: training and experience turns the fearsome into the familiar. The response of the SAS to David Cole's incredulity about how they chase terrorists was simple: 'That is just what we train to do'; and Cole's riposte to their fear of playing in front of 55,000 people was the same: 'That [training] is just what we do as well.' Training conquers fear.

How to build your courage mindset

Here are six ways to build your courage mindset. There is no academic theory behind it. These techniques are based on practical examples of successful leaders. The six methods are:

- Train for courage.
- Believe in your mission.
- Create a bigger fear.
- Think courage.
- Find support.
- Manage your fear.

Each of these is explored below. You choose the ones that work best for you.

Train for courage

I was running a workshop and a participant challenged me: 'Courage?' she asked, 'You can't train people to be brave. You either have it or you don't.' From the other side of the room, a county fire chief politely put up his hand. Sensing that the equivalent of the fifth cavalry was about to charge over the horizon with bugles blaring to save me, I gave him the floor.

'First things first,' said the fire chief, 'if any fireman of mine is brave, I will fire him.[8] A brave fireman soon becomes a dead fireman.' We all looked slightly surprised. Another participant asked the obvious question: 'So how on earth do you get them to go into smoke-filled, burning buildings to save people?'

The fire chief explained how he trained new recruits. The first week was spent learning how to dress properly and look after the equipment. After they had mastered these basics, they would go on to using short ladders. They might learn how to put out a fire in a bucket. Slowly, the heights and the fires would get bigger and more complex, but at each stage the chief would check that the recruits were competent and safe with their existing work. Eventually, they would be doing things that you or I would consider to be dangerous and risky in the extreme. To the fire officers it is routine and relatively safe.

The Royal Marine Commandos essentially follow the same process: they start their raw recruits on the basics, including having high standards of kit maintenance and hygiene, and then work on from there. Eventually, they are meant to be able to deal with any situation from urban terror to arctic or jungle warfare.

In your career you can train in the way that the fire officers and Royal Marines train. There is no need to take crazy risks from your first day in the office: if you do, your career is likely to be spectacular but short. Learn to take increasing risk and challenge in small steps. For instance, in popular lore, public speaking is feared more than death.[9] One survey puts fear of public speaking neatly between hell and fear of being buried alive. But even the most inexperienced and nervous speaker can become accomplished fast with training. In a classic test, Ann Brennan who had never spoken in public before, was asked by a television company to make her first-ever speech at a political party's annual conference in front of thousands of people. She was a complete success, with repeated applause and an ovation. The *Guardian* was moved to write: 'It lit up the conference as no other speech had done all week.' Deep training and lots of practice trumps fear every time.[10]

Believe in your mission

People who are truly committed to their mission will make extraordinary sacrifices for it. The greater the mission, the greater the potential sacrifice. Down the ages, assorted saints and martyrs have given everything for their beliefs.

More prosaically, entrepreneurs take risks that few others would contemplate, including putting their home on the line to raise money for their venture. They will go further, faster than most would dare. For instance, Sharath Jeevan decided to start a charity addressing education in the poorer half of the world: that is a reasonably ambitious starting point. In the first year he did a pilot in Delhi. In the second year he is doing a second pilot in Uganda and a third pilot in Uttar Pradesh covering 180,000 schools.[11] For a two-year-old start-up – that is ambitious. You only take on that scale of challenge and ambition if you have deep belief in your mission and deep self-confidence.

Mission and courage

Mike is a vice principal of a school in a tough part of London.[12] Here is his story:

Behaviour was poor. The head worried that if we all focused on behaviour we would become prison officers, not teachers; we would lose focus on teaching and learning. So I put in a system for behaviour management anyway. It ran for a week. And then the police called because 100 of our children were fighting on

> the street. The Tactical Support Unit, the police with guns and batons, were going to be called in to disperse the children. The police would have dispersed them, but their way would have been very bad for community relations. So the first thing we did was to stop the Tactical Support Unit going in.
>
> I went there and saw seven teachers just watching; they did not get involved. So myself and the principle waded in armed with nothing more than our overcoats. Three kids had already been stabbed. I thought we were being intergalactically stupid. And we got them to get on their buses and go home.
>
> Over the weekend I mulled over it, and I did not like it. I was asking myself 'what happened?' Any situation with kids can escalate very fast.
>
> On Monday I took responsibility for what had happened on Friday. It meant that we could move forward as a team.

Mike's obvious bravery was in facing down the kids. His second act of bravery was in dealing with the staff: taking responsibility, not finger pointing – and so enabling everyone to move forward. Anyone less committed to the mission of addressing educational disadvantage might have chosen to step back, not step up at the crucial moment.

Everyone on the leadership panel for this book believed deeply in their mission. This drove their behaviour: they were prepared to take more risks; they were more resilient in the face of adversity; they had higher aspirations and they simply worked harder in pursuit of their mission. If your mission is to meet a budget goal, you will doubtless work diligently to that aim. If you work to some form of save the world or save the firm, then you will have a different view of risk, aspirations and resilience.

Create a bigger fear

Let us return to central Africa and our MI6 agent going ever deeper into nowhere, while half his mind was screaming at him to turn back. What kept him going? The fear of going back empty handed.

In the words of the SAS: 'It is better to come back dead than come back stupid.' This sounds extreme, but peer-group pressure is intense. No one wants to be the team idiot.

In another example, David Cole talks about the pressure to perform: 'As amateurs, we would have to go back to the office on Monday morning and face the receptionist and our colleagues. And you got pretty clear feedback from them.' Fear of mockery, exclusion and failure is a huge incentive to do your best.

In doing fieldwork with traditional societies, I found that the biggest sanction that any society could administer was exclusion from the tribe.[13] This was a devastating sanction, regarded as being even worse than death because it brought shame on the whole family. People went to extremes to stay as members of their group, including undergoing gruesome initiation rites that any sane person would avoid at all costs. But these people were sane: for them, fear of exclusion trumps fear of pain.

In business, leaders use this lesson to force through change. No one really likes change and most change is resisted passively and/or actively. To overcome this resistance, leaders will create a 'burning platform', which shows that the risk and pain of doing nothing is greater than the risk and pain of making change. This was how Jan Timmer led drastic change at Philips: cutting 20 per cent of costs and headcount was very painful for everyone, but less painful than going out of business, which was a realistic prospect at the time.

Think courage

When you face a potentially risky course of action, it is natural to consider all the risks and then quietly turn away. That is human nature. It may be something to do with our ancestors learning to survive predation by wild creatures in our deep past. Whatever the origins, it is clear that we react to the risks faster than we react to opportunities. The survival instinct is safe in the short term: we will not get eaten. In the long term, it is dangerous. Look at what happens when you are in a meeting and someone has a bright idea. Often the heat-seeking missiles come out: colleagues quickly point out the risks and ask difficult questions. This shows how smart they are. It also kills the idea and tells everyone that having bright ideas in public is dumb. So a bright idea is missed and no more bright ideas emerge, all because of our risk aversion.

We need to train ourselves to think differently. The default line of thought is:

- Step one: what are the risks and issues with this idea?

- Step two: the risks and issues are too great. End of idea.

Now try the courageous way of thinking:

- Step one: what is good about this idea, how might it help, how big is the prize, what is the best outcome?

- Step two: what would need to happen to achieve the best outcome?

- Step three: how can we deal with the risks and issues?

There are two big differences with the courageous way of thinking. The first is to think about all of the benefits of an idea before any of the concerns. Start by focusing on the best outcome, not the worst. If you do this, you may find that there is a big prize to be won. If the prize is big enough, it is worth taking risks to achieve it.

The second shift in thinking is to frame problems around actions. A simple way of doing this is to start each problem with 'How...'. Table 2.1 shows in the 'normal' column how very smart people were advising us when we were starting Teach First. It was normal but lethal: it is the sort of thinking that kills ideas stone dead. The courageous way of thinking drives to action.

The normal line of thinking makes statements that either close down the conversation or invite argument in which both sides normally just become more entrenched. The courageous way of thinking asks questions, opens up discussion, avoids positions, and encourages everyone to seek solutions and drive to action.

Use the courageous way of thinking whenever you face an opportunity for a new role, a new task or new job. If you focus first

Table 2.1 Courageous mindset

Normal line of thinking	Courageous line of thinking
No graduates will join an unknown start-up.	How can we create a compelling value proposition to attract the best graduates?
You can't train teachers in six weeks.	How can we prepare students in six weeks and then support them properly once they are in school?
There's no money for this.	How can we find sponsors in government and the private sector for this?
The unions will hate it.	How can we talk to the right people in the unions?

on the risks, you may get no further. You will only have half the equation. The rounded view will lead to taking more, considered, risks. You will be able to stretch yourself and grow, and avoid being marooned in your comfort zone.

Find support

When is a risk not a risk? When everyone backs the same course of action.

Even if the course of action turns out to be a disaster, there is no one to blame because everyone was wrong. The real risk is when you clearly lead the way. When you succeed, you will find that everyone else will claim the credit. When you fail, you will find that failure is a very lonely place.

This is why real leaders need real courage. If leaders take people where they would not have gone by themselves, then by definition they will not be following the herd. They will be leading the herd. This means taking decisions that leave them exposed when things go wrong.

In many cultures this sort of leadership is actively discouraged. A Dutch client had two favourite sayings: 'A nail which sticks out must be hammered down' and 'It is better to be wrong together than to be right alone'. Both sayings reflect a common desire in many firms for total conformity. This is not always healthy: the wisdom of crowds is matched by the madness of mobs.[14]

Finding support improves both rational risk and personal risk. More support decreases the rational risk because a well-supported and well-thought-through idea is more likely to work than the actions of an inspired lone hero.

Manage your fear[15]

Fear is real. If you ignore fear, you will fail. We all have an instinctive side to us that triggers a flight, fight or freeze reaction in the face of real or perceived reality. Fight, flight or freeze may work in the jungle; in the boardroom it would be entertaining but inadvisable.

Two techniques can help you to manage fear.

First, work on the worst case. Recognize the fear. This seems counterintuitive; why would we want to contemplate disaster? The answer is that you cannot run away from fear. Fear is an emotional trigger that alerts you to danger. The more you try to run away from fear, the harder it will chase you. Instead, confront your fears. Work out what the worst outcome could be. A common core fear is social: letting down your peers and colleagues by not delivering, or looking like an idiot because of how you act. Once you recognize your fear, you can deal with it. You have two ways of dealing with the fear: accepting the worst case or avoiding it. For instance, let us say the worst case is that if things go wrong you will lose your job. If you depend totally on your current job, you like your firm and you believe you could not get a job elsewhere, then you will be risk averse. But if you have confidence in your talent, then the worst case is that you might have to work elsewhere and elsewhere may be better; that is an acceptable disaster scenario.

Your second step in dealing with fear is to ask why this worst case will happen. It may be because you will forget your lines in a speech, or your data for a report is wrong. Once you have located the source of your fear, you can start to address it: have a written copy of your speech so that you can read it if you have to; find the right expert to validate the data that you are using in your report.

A large part of fear is fear of uncertainty and of the unknown. Once you have recognized and isolated the nature of your fear, you can deal with it. If you try to ignore it, it will keep on coming back at you more urgently with more alarm. Your survival instinct will be hitting the panic button. So don't ignore it: recognize it and then move on to the second technique – the best case.

The best case is a standard technique for top sports performers.[16] Imagine the very best outcome from the situation you are going into. Use all your senses to visualize your role, how you will feel, act and sound. You might also remember when you have done something similar and done it very well: what did you do, how did you feel and act, and what did it look like? Imagine or recall in detail how to perform in the desired way. This mental rehearsal puts you in a place where you are comfortable, confident and know exactly what you have to do to succeed.

Visualization is a very useful way to prepare for public speeches: I arrive early so I can get a sense of the location. I rehearse getting up on stage and moving any slides. And then I can disappear for five minutes to visualize exactly what a great speech will look like. With that image in mind, I then go out and deliver the speech. Fear never gets a look in.

Summary

You need courage to take the risks that separate leaders from the rest: to transform and disrupt.

Three main sources of risk:

- Rational risk, which businesses deal with routinely.
- Ambiguity: seen as risk by managers, as opportunity by leaders and entrepreneurs.
- Personal risk: fear of failure and ridicule, which the best leaders will accept.

Six ways to build your courage mindset:

- Train for courage: make the unknown become familiar and routine.

- Believe in your mission: the greater your cause, the greater the commitment.

- Create a bigger fear: let the risk of inaction be greater than the risk of action.

- Think courage: focus on benefits and outcomes, then work out the risks.

- Find support: share the burden.

- Manage your fear: recognize the fear, then visualize success.

Resilience 03

Stay the course

Resilience follows courage, because taking risks means that inevitably some risks lead to setbacks. The best leaders learn from each setback and grow stronger. Resilience means learning how to deal with adversity, and how to gain strength from it.

Who is this person?

- Aged seven he was forced out of his family home and had to start working.
- Aged nine he lost his mother.
- Aged 22 his first business venture fails.
- Aged 23 he lost his job, failed to get into law school and lost an election.
- Aged 24 his second business fails.
- Aged 25 he lost another election and proceeded to lose another seven elections over the next 20 years.
- Aged 27 he had a nervous breakdown and spent six months in bed?[1]

With this track record, most normal people would settle for a quiet life, if they could get it. But this was no normal person: it was Abraham Lincoln. The difference between failure and success is often as simple as giving up.

Most successful people have hard times. Winston Churchill had 20 years between world wars, which have become known as his 'wilderness years'.[2] He was 65 years old when he finally became prime minister in grim circumstances, as Britain appeared to be on the verge of defeat in May 1940. He spread his resilience to the rest of the nation and history changed its course.

Resilience means never giving up. Neither Lincoln nor Churchill ever gave up. In 1941 Churchill was asked to return to his old school, Harrow, and give a speech. The assembled crowd waited expectantly for another bout of rhetorical genius from the prime minister. Churchill slowly stood up and looked at the audience: 'Never, never, never give up', he said, and then sat down again.[3] That was his entire speech and the audience was stunned. But that was all he needed to say. If all you remember from Churchill is 'never give up', then that can make all the difference.

Nearly all of our leadership panel talked about the need for resilience, and are frustrated by those who lack resilience:

- 'I see people who get knocked very easily. If you panic, that's the opposite of leadership.'[4]

- 'People just give up too easily.'

- 'I am intolerant of precious people who do not cope well with setbacks.'[5]

- 'One head was successful for a few years and was very boastful. But then she had a setback and could not cope at all.'

A theme slowly emerged: success does not breed resilience. Adversity breeds resilience, and resilience can build success. People who enjoy a run of success for a number of years develop brittle resilience: they appear to be strong, but in practice snap at their first encounter with real adversity. This can be particularly hard for the gilded youth with parents who shield them from the troubles of the world. The youth glides through school and university, succeeding at many things. Then they hit the world of work and find it hard to cope. And at the other end of the ladder, we have all come across the senior executives who are full of smug self-assurance, but have very thin skins and do not tolerate any dissent or criticism.

As the leaders talked, it became clear that resilience comes in two flavours: 1) dealing with setbacks and adversity; 2) building resilience for the long haul. In this chapter we explore both types of resilience and see how you can build a resilient mindset that allows you to stay the course and to deal with setbacks successfully. There are five sections to this chapter:

- Dealing with adversity: the example of POWs.
- Dealing with setbacks and adversity: the leader's guide.
- Dangerous ways to build resilience for the long haul.
- Effective ways to build resilience for the long haul.
- Building super-resilience: anti-fragility.

Dealing with adversity: the example of POWs

Friedrich Nietzsche, the German philosopher, wrote: 'That which does not kill you makes you stronger.'[6] This is a theory that sounds good when read from the comfort of a sofa. It would not sound so comforting if you were in a Nazi concentration camp or if you were a prisoner of war in Vietnam, being tortured at irregular intervals. These are extreme situations, and they are also the situations where much of the thinking about resilience has been developed. We will travel to these dark places to understand how people in these situations cope with adversity, before travelling back to our own world and finding out how to build our resilience.

First, put yourself in the shoes of a prisoner of war of the Vietnamese, who have no reason to love you at all: you have probably been responsible for bombing and killing their friends and family. Your welcome from the prison guard is simple: 'Here it is easy to die and hard to live. I am going to show you just how hard.' The account that Senator John McCain gave of his time in prison is harrowing: coercion, beatings, torture, starvation, no medical care but plenty of isolation.[7]

The Vietnamese wanted to break POWs and use them either for intelligence and/or propaganda purposes. One way of breaking them was to make sure they had no control. They had no control over when or what they ate, when they could sleep, when they might be beaten. How are you going to cope, not knowing what will happen from day to day, and not knowing how many months or years or decades you will have to survive such conditions?

The survival strategies created by people in such situations turn out to be good ways of developing resilience not just in prison, but also in the slightly less traumatic conditions of your workplace. Here are their five main strategies:

1 *Gain control.* Their captors could control the POWs' environment and wanted to control their minds. That was the real battleground. So the POWs took control of the only thing they could: their own minds. None of us can control events completely, but all of us can control our reaction to events. The POWs focus of control was based on optimism, humour and social support.

2 *Will to prevail.* James Stockdale spent seven and a half years in Hoa Lo Prison. As the senior officer he was singled out for particularly unpleasant treatment. Here is how he coped: 'I never lost faith in the end of the story, I never doubted not only that I would get out, but also that I would prevail in the end and turn the experience into the defining event of my life, which, in retrospect, I would not trade.'[8]

3 *Face the brutal facts.* Stockdale noticed that the optimists did not survive. They all hoped that they would be out by Christmas... by Easter... by Thanksgiving... As their hopes were dashed time and again, they themselves gave up hope. This became known as the Stockdale paradox: you need some optimism to survive (his belief that he would prevail) but if you have too much candy-coated optimism, hoping that a genie will come and magically make the world better, you will not survive. The difference between the two sorts of optimism is that the survivors took personal responsibility for their situation; the others simply hoped that something would turn up. Hope is not a method.

4 *Use humour.* What on earth is funny about facing torture and beatings? Nothing, and that was the point. If the POWs could still find dark gallows humour in their plight, it was a way of

telling themselves that they had not been defeated. It was an act of defiance against their captors.

5 *Build your support network.* Stockdale and others were kept in solitary confinement for months on end. So they developed a tap code. They would tap on pipes and walls to communicate. Each letter of the alphabet was on an imaginary five by five grid. So one tap (first row) followed by four taps (fourth column) would be a D. With this they would tap out, very slowly, their jokes – but the one thing they had in abundance was time. Your granny's advice that 'a problem shared is a problem halved' rings true.

If there is a worse place than a Vietnamese POW prison, it is probably a Nazi concentration camp. Untold multitudes perished, a few survived. Viktor Frankl was one of the few survivors.[9] Before the war he qualified as a neurologist and psychiatrist. During the war he was first transported to the Theresienstadt Ghetto in 1942 and then to Auschwitz and to an offshoot of Dachau in 1944, before being liberated in April 1945. He used his time not just to survive, but to use his psychiatric training to work out why some people survived longer than others.

Frankl found that even in the most inhumane conditions, some people could find meaning and could find a will to live. He came to a conclusion very close to that of the Vietnamese POWs: 'Everything can be taken from a man but one thing: the last of the human freedoms – to choose one's attitude in any given set of circumstances.'[10] Frankl eventually developed his thinking into a new form of psychotherapy – logotherapy.

Prison and concentration camps are, of course, extreme situations to take as examples. Because we have so much freedom today, we forget Frankl's lesson. Our ultimate freedom is the freedom to choose how we react and how we feel. This is vital in dealing with adversity: we do not have to feel upset, we do not have to be a victim of circumstances. We can choose to take control and to feel how we want to feel.

As leaders, we need to build a practical mindset and tools to help us deal with the sort of adversity we are likely to face from time to time: crises, bad performance reviews, missed promotions and the myriad mini-disasters that happen whenever humans try to work together. There is no single grand theory, although the Penn Resiliency Programme attempts an integrated approach for students.[11] Putting Frankl, the Vietnam POWs, Penn and our leadership panel together, however, we can create the leader's guide to dealing with setbacks and adversity.

The leader's guide to dealing with setbacks and adversity

Eight steps are outlined below as to what leaders should do in such situations:

1 *Take control.* A paradox emerges here: the less things seem to be in control, the easier it is to take control over what is left. When we are in full control, we often face a surfeit of opportunities: do we invest in China or India or our home market, in new products or extending existing products? Making decisions is hard: it is not clear what is best when you can choose from 20 options. When everything is grim, there are often very few options. This is when weaker leaders start to feel powerless. But if there is only one thing you can do, that is what you must do: do not worry about the things you cannot control. For instance, I found myself in Japan with no business, no sales and no prospect of any sales. The situation was hopeless. The only potential lead was from San Miguel, a huge brewery group in the Philippines. But that was an absurd lead: we had no capability there, our cost base was huge and the Philippines is not a rich country. So that meant there was only one thing we could do: convert the San Miguel opportunity into real work. It saved the business. When you can't control everything, control what you can.

2 *Control your own feelings.* The CEO of a headhunting firm talks about 'wearing the mask of leadership'. He learned that getting angry is pointless. If you are angry or upset, your little cloud of gloom will spread like a major depression across the rest of the office. If you remain positive, you have a chance that your team will remain positive: moods are infectious, especially the leader's mood. Separate the event from your reaction: just because an event is bad, it does not mean you are required to be angry or upset. How you can achieve this is covered in greater detail in Chapter 5.

3 *Stay positive.* This is Stockdale's 'will to prevail'. Believe that you can find a way through and that adversity is your defining moment where you will grow and learn. Look back at your own career. What have been the times you remember most and grew the most, when you had the chance to shine and make a difference? Was it when you were working in easy street, or when your back was against the wall and you had to fight your way out? To paraphrase Dickens, the worst of times are often the best of times,[12] even if only in retrospect.

Mike Tobin, recent CEO of Telecity, started out in sales and got used to plenty of rejection. How do you deal with endless rejection? Here is how he treats each rejection:

> People look at defeat in many ways. If you are a door-to-door salesman, you know on average you will sell one broom per hundred doors you knock on. So every time someone closes the door on you, you are one step closer to success, so your smile should grow each time a door closes on you, because you just got one door closer to success.

4 *Gain perspective.* This is a staple of the positive psychology movement, and it works. Here are three ways to gain perspective:

– Count your blessings. I was interviewing Choi Ma, an elderly nomad in her yurt (tent) in Mongolia. She had virtually nothing, just the bare essentials of life for a nomad. At the end of the interview I asked her if there was anything I could do for her, or if there was anything she needed. She looked astonished. 'What more do I need?' she asked. 'I have everything I need: my family, my friends, my health.' Now look at your own life: what is the first good thing that happened to you today? Waking up in a warm bed is a good start... If we take our blessings for granted and curse every setback, we will never stay positive.

- Know your place. Your situation may be bad, but there are always others in a worse place. The Middlesex cricket team toured First World War battlefields and Auschwitz for pre-season training to remind them how lucky they were.[13] On a personal note, I was going into hospital for a gruesome operation that I was dreading. At the hospital I saw the other patients, many of whom were far worse off. Suddenly my gloom lifted as I realized how self-indulgent I had been. In a similar fashion, the writer Clive James, close to death, said: 'If you hang around a hospital long enough, you'll see things that'll remind you that you've had a lucky life.'[14] Perspective helps to the end.

- Imagine the best and worst outcomes. The chances are that even in the worst outcome you will live to see the sun rise again. Act with the confidence and knowledge that you will survive. And now imagine the best outcome: what do you need in order to make the best outcome happen? Get on with it.

5 *Draw on experience.* You have two sources of experience to draw on: your own and the experiences of others. Drawing on experience helps to build perspective, but it also should give you some hints about what will work and what will not work in your current situation. All the leaders in our panel talked about various disasters with great energy: this was their experience bank that they drew on in challenging times. Ask yourself some simple questions:

- Where have I met something like this before: what worked and what did not work?

- Have I seen other people deal with this before, successfully or otherwise? What can I learn from that?

- What would my mentor/role model do in this situation?

6 *Use humour.* Humour is a good way to keep perspective. At Teach First we created the Cock-Up Club: we would invite eminent business people to talk about their business, but instead of their normal propaganda we asked them to talk about the biggest cock-up they were responsible for in their career. We soon discovered that behind every glittering career there are fantastic disasters. I suspect I am a life member of the Cock-Up Club for my many mistakes. The next time you are at the centre of a disaster, console yourself that you are becoming a full member of the Cock-Up Club. And if that does not work, find another way to laugh in the face of misfortune. Misfortune mocked is misfortune defanged.

7 *Be adaptable.* Mike Tyson, the world heavyweight boxing champion for many years, said: 'Everyone has a plan till they get punched in the mouth.'[15] The best leaders are totally fixed about their end goal, but completely flexible about how they get there. You cannot sail straight into the wind: you have to tack and gybe to make any progress.

8 *Get help.* Lone heroes may save the world, frequently, in the movies. Back in the real world, lone heroes become dead heroes fast. Do not carry the weight of the world on your shoulders. Reach out for help and advice. As a coach I see clients struggling with apparently impossible burdens. They then talk for a while and they discover the answer: I do not have a magic box full of instant solutions. Instead, just the act of talking helps clients to develop perspective, find alternatives and create options. And, somewhere, there is a solution to be found. You do not even need a coach: find willing colleagues, friends and family. Alternatively, set up your own support club. Here are two examples:

- The Social Care Curry Club.[16] In the words of George Julian, one of its two founders: 'Morale is really low in the sector...

If you're married to someone who works in social care you don't want to hear about the moans and the challenges. It (the club) gives people a chance to come and talk without feeling they're boring their friends and family.'[17] Curry with colleagues can go a long way. The club has over 200 active members nationwide.

- Brits not Bankers, set up by Anthony Willoughby in Japan:[18] you can probably guess its two main membership requirements. It provided an outlet and support for expats who could otherwise be very isolated. It mixed alcohol and adventure in remarkable quantities.

The message from these examples is simple: do not wait for help to come to you. It could be a very long wait. If you need help, go and find it. You are even allowed to have some fun at the same time.

When we look at great leaders and successful people we see their glittering careers in all their glory. We do not see what lies behind the glitz, glamour and glory. Normally, we find deep resilience. There is the long-term stamina to stay the course, which we cover in the next section. However, we usually find repeated setbacks and failure. Michael Jordan, perhaps the greatest basketball player of all time, reflecting on the other side of his success says: 'I have missed more than 9,000 shots in my career. I have lost almost 300 games. On 26 occasions I have been entrusted to take the game-winning shot, and I missed. I have failed over and over and over again in my life. And that is why I succeed.'[19]

The more you face adversity, the better you become at dealing with it. You avoid the brittle confidence of people who have never had a setback: you develop deep confidence that can take you through the hardest of times. You live up to Kipling's challenge in the poem If—:

If you can keep your head when all about you
Are losing theirs and blaming it on you,
If you can trust yourself when all men doubt you...

Adversity is not to be avoided: it is to be embraced. It is our chance to shine, to make a difference, to be remembered, to learn, to grow, to build our resilience. They are the times we live life with the record button on; they are the times we will remember for many years. If we step up when others step back, we can advance. Others may prefer the safety of their comfort zone, but they will never scale the heights.

The more you encounter adversity, the better you will handle it. You will find your own way through the valley of death, and eventually it will lose its fear. You will be the exceptional leader who goes where others fear to tread.

It is easy to tell people to fly into the face of adversity, but it is harder to do it. We all have survival instincts that tell us to back off when danger looms. And most of us fear failure, in particular being seen by peers, friends and family to have failed. The emotional hit is hard to bear. It takes real courage to go where others dare not to tread. Fortunately, as we saw in Chapter 2, courage is not something that is either in your DNA or not – courage can be learned.

Building resilience for the long haul

A career is a marathon, not a sprint. Succeeding requires deep reserves of stamina and persistence. Cyclist Chris Froome, winner of the 2013 Tour de France, describes the challenge of climbing Mont Ventoux – a 1,600-metre climb, often in ferocious winds – after a 200-kilometre stage: 'I kept telling myself, "OK, if you are feeling terrible, feeling horrible with nothing left and needing to get off the bike and stop, I'm sure other guys are going to be feeling just as bad"... it is a very big mental challenge as much as it is physical.'[20]

Your race to the top of your mountain will be like Froome's: it is as much a mental challenge as it is physical. You have to develop the ability to keep going while those around you get off their bikes – remember the relentless setbacks and failures that Abraham Lincoln endured.

The scale of your challenge can be measured by the idea that it takes 10,000 hours to become expert at something. The idea, popularized by Daniel Goleman,[21] is disputed. The 10,000 hours concept was originally developed in 1993 by Anders Ericsson, a professor at the University of Colorado. Ericsson argues that the quality of practice counts, and that 10,000 hours is not a magic number: it may take more or less.[22] Others, such as David Epstein, point out that natural talent helps.[23] For instance, the best baseball batsmen have 20/13 eyesight: they can see at 20 feet what others can only see at 13 feet. That gives them a big advantage, which no amount of practice can replicate. And you do not find many short basketball players in the professional game. Yet what they all agree on is that becoming expert takes a huge amount of effort. This is where you have to decide if you want to put in the effort to climb your mountain.

The most successful leaders, such as those on our leadership panel and top sports people such as Froome, are very driven. They do not enjoy work–life balance: work is life, and that is how they gain fulfilment, meaning and purpose. Psychologists like Maslow would call that self-actualization.[24] Maslow's basic idea is that we are all needs junkies: once we have satisfied our basic needs (food, water, shelter) we move on to ever-higher needs (belonging, recognition) and eventually seek self-actualization. In Maslow's words, 'What a man can be, he must be': we all seek to fulfil our greatest potential. This means that many leaders are very driven: achieving one thing is simply evidence that you have yet more potential to be fulfilled. You only know you have gone far enough when you have gone too far;[25] so these leaders, like true needs junkies, are always searching for their next fix, their next challenge.

So how do leaders keep going year after year? From interviews and observation, the leaders have a range of tools and techniques that they use. But first, it is worth covering two things that do not sustain them: money and work–life balance.

Building resilience for the long haul: the dangerous dead ends

Making money and achieving work–life balance are attractive, if contradictory, goals. Making money provides an incentive to keep going; work–life balance ensures you have a sustainable career and life. Neither are good ways to build long-term resilience.

Making money

Academics look down their noses at money as a source of motivation, until they hit the jackpot of a successful book and television series. Typically, they claim that money is a hygiene factor:[26] getting it wrong demotivates people, getting it right helps them. The truth is slightly more subtle. Money buys status, and people crave status. For instance, we were redesigning the compensation scheme for a life-insurance sales force. It was a nightmare and everyone had views on which products should attract what sort of bonus. The talks were going nowhere. Then we said, 'OK, if you take the package as it is, we will give everyone a (very modest) upgrade to the company car.' Suddenly, everyone loved the package. In terms of the status attached to this, let's just say that our neighbours do not normally discuss private matters such as sex or money, they do not know how much you earn – but if you return one day in a slightly better car, they will assume that you are doing very well. Money and status are closely linked.

Money quickly becomes intensely competitive. Watching a team of 10 alpha males at one investment bank at bonus time was enjoyable and terrifying. It did not matter that each one of them was earning a seven-figure income. What they all wanted was to do better than their peers, and money was the measure of their success. Out of 10 wannabe alpha males, the bonus season would mark out just one as the real alpha male. Inevitably, bonus season was ugly. An old joke runs: 'If I can't have a pay rise, can Smith have a pay cut?' Ignobly, we like to beat our colleagues.

Money also becomes a treadmill. If success means that your family gets used to the champagne and caviar lifestyle, you will find it hard to ask them to adjust to the beer and chips lifestyle. In theory, the hedonic treadmill works both ways: we get used to changes in circumstances whether they are positive or negative. In practice, however, most people find it easier to adapt to a better standard of living.

Money is a proxy for status, it is highly competitive and it is a treadmill. It may not be the highest of callings, but it can make people work hard and long. From imperfect observation, it is better at building great careers than at building great leaders. Great leaders are not driven by money when they start out: sports people want to be great at their sport, politicians want to change the world and entrepreneurs want to see their ideas vindicated. Fortunes may be made later, but normally that is not what drives such people from the start.

If you want to chase money, that is fair enough. Be aware that you will never have enough unless you know what enough is. That means you will be on a treadmill where enough, satisfaction, and fulfilment is always just one more pay rise away. Know what you want – and you may find it.

Achieving work–life balance

When did you last hear a work–life balance guru advocating more work? Work–life balance has become a euphemism for finding excuses to work less. This is surprising because the evidence shows that not only are we the wealthiest generation ever, we are also the idlest. Work by Robert Whaples of Wake Forest University implies that the average working week for full-time employees (adjusted for holidays, sick leave, overtime) has fallen from around 65–70 hours per week at the height of the Industrial Revolution to around 35–40 hours per week now.[27]

Of course, averages obscure variations. Successful leaders expect to work longer in order to achieve their goals. Even so, you may want to ask yourself: when did you last get stuck in a rush-hour jam at 8 o'clock on a Sunday morning? How many meetings did you go to last month starting after 6 pm?

We may or may not actually be working harder, but we certainly feel that we are working 24/7. Part of the problem is that we find it hard to compartmentalize our lives. In days gone by, the man with a briefcase probably had nothing more than a sandwich and a crossword inside it (and it was nearly always a 'him'): when he left the office, he left work. Now we wear with pride the electronic ball and chain of e-mail and mobile phones. We are expected to deal with anything at any time, anywhere. The office never leaves us.

All of our leadership panel worried a little about work–life balance: they were not worried about the effect on themselves, but they did worry about the effect on their families. For the best leaders, the work–life balance question was not 'how do I work less?' but 'how much more can I work without destroying my family?' Work is only to be avoided if you do not enjoy it: the best leaders all enjoy what they do.

If you are troubled by work–life balance, ask yourself: 'Am I actually enjoying what I do?' 'Can I find any way to compartmentalize my life better, to give myself downtime?' If your answers to both questions are negative, you may either want to consult a work–life balance guru, or find another job.

Effective ways to build resilience for the long haul

Given below are five ways that our leadership panel built resilience for the long haul.

Enjoy what you do

Work is meant to be serious. Leadership is meant to be very serious: serious people making serious decisions with serious consequences. If you listen to CEOs making speeches, they are all serious. And in private they like to complain about how hard they work and how far they travel and how it is lonely at the top. And they love it: they love every moment of it. The prospect of retirement looks like a living hell to them. They want to keep playing, stay relevant and make a difference.

You only excel at what you enjoy. To excel at anything takes a huge amount of time and effort. You will not put in all that extra effort unless, ultimately, you enjoy it. We can all put in extra effort for a few months out of duty, but to sustain that for years takes more than duty.

Everyone in the leadership panel enthused about what they did. Some of them talked explicitly about enjoying things that most normal people would hate. Some examples:

- Would you be nervous about having to perform in front of 55,000 people while opponents are out to crush and kick you into defeat? David Cole's response was: 'I wanted to enjoy every moment.'

- How would you feel about taking risks such as tracking down a central African warlord? 'Some people are forced to take risk, I enjoy it', replied Will.

- How would you like to stare over the abyss as the dot.com boom bombed, possibly taking your business with it? 'It was then I realized I enjoyed the entrepreneurial world', was Sharath Jeevan's response.

These are not things that everyone will enjoy. And that is the point: there are no rules about what you should enjoy. All that matters is that you find something that you enjoy, and then you will be able to last the course.

Discover your mission

We live in an age of cynicism. A quick look at the comments section on any news story will show that many cynical people exist and like to vent their anger. In such a cynical world, it is hard to believe that anyone actually believes in a moral purpose. But many of the most successful organizations in the world are based on moral purpose. The Catholic Church has survived roughly 2,000 years longer than most businesses, and still has over a billion members; the armed forces have low pay for which people are ready to risk their lives; Teach First offers modest pay for a tough challenge and recruits many of the best graduates.[28]

When people have a higher mission, they are willing to give everything for it, including their lives. Moral purpose drives ambition. For instance, we set up STIR Education to identify successful educational micro-innovations and to build a movement of teacher change makers.[29] We started with a pilot in Delhi and found that it worked. So what next? UNESCO found that in 250 million primary schools worldwide children are in school but not learning.[30] In year two our next pilot took on 180,000 schools in Uttar Pradesh, which is absurdly ambitious for a young charity. But the quietly spoken CEO, Sharath Jeevan, has clear moral purpose: if you are serious about the problem, you have to address it at scale.

Our leaders in the private sector were also clear that they were not just building a business: they were building successful communities that provided a valued service to society. They wanted to make them be the best they could.

Mission drives resilience

David Bell was Director of Education in Newcastle.[31] He knew that if the system was going to improve, he had to make leadership changes in the schools. 'I knew that this meant people, people I knew well, were facing the end of their careers. It would have been easy to duck the challenge. But what was driving me was the need of the children for a better life. When you face difficulties, you get a lot of noise. That is when you have to be clear about what counts.'

If you are unsure of your mission, it is easy to compromise. When you have clarity, you will deal with even the hardest challenges.

What's your mission?

Will to win

Winning is good for you. If you win, you live longer:

- Players inducted into the Baseball Hall of Fame live 10 per cent longer than those who just miss out.[32]

- Winning an Oscar adds 3.9 years to your life compared to the near misses.[33]

- Nobel Prize-winners live 1.4 years longer than those who are merely nominated.[34]

Research shows that happiness comes not just from doing well, but from doing better than others. For us to win, it helps to know that someone else is losing.[35] Brain imaging research at the University of Bonn showed that the happiness of volunteers depended not only on how well they did in a simple test, but on how well their partner did. They were most satisfied when they did better than the partner volunteer, who was a complete stranger. Research of 12,000 UK adults showed that the happiest people were those who were richer than their neighbours: being moderately affluent in a rich neighbourhood just leaves you feeling poor and excluded. Relative wealth counts more than absolute wealth.[36]

The winning motivation is clearest in sport. David Cole, who led Scotland to a grand slam rugby victory against all the odds in 1990, says: 'I realized I did not want to just put on the shirt. I wanted to win. So I was very driven, and I was not prepared to compromise standards in training, irrespective of how tired I was. Do the drills when you are tired, so you can execute them in the game when you are tired. I was always last to finish. You have to set an example.'

Winning, like money, is a treadmill. One victory simply leads to another contest. And it tends to be addictive. In the research for this book I found that the best leaders were often highly accomplished outside their main job. Even though they worked exceptionally hard, they still found time for pastimes and took them to a high standard. For instance, here are the pastimes of three CEOs on the panel:

- Sport: National Fives champion (game of handball in a hard court).

- Gardening: knows all the Latin names of all his plants on a large estate.

- Music: created, maintains and conducts a choir and a youth orchestra.

The will to win, to be the best, was a shared characteristic of all the best leaders on the panel. They focused this will on the mission of their organization, but there was no doubt that they wanted to lead the mission.

Finding the will to win

'My sister and I both started work at 12. It was real work: every evening and all weekend. From 14 we both had to pay our way at home. At 16 I failed all but two O levels.

My mum was always poorly, emotionally and physically. She always liked cuddly toys – for her, not for us. Our parents never took us anywhere. So at 15 my sister and I saved up and bought a moped. It was illegal. But it let us go everywhere. My mum had been collecting Green Shield stamps. And when she had enough, she told me to go and collect a massive stuffed dog with the stamps. So I went on my moped and got the stuffed dog for her. On the way back I thought that O levels were just like Green Shield stamps: they let you get whatever you want. So I decided to go back to school to get O levels and A levels. I had got a job learning catering at Trust House Forte at the time. I was putting cherries on grapefruits. I did not want to spend the rest of my life putting cherries on grapefruits.

I had to persuade my dad, who just wanted me to pay my way at home. I had to persuade my illiterate mum and tell her what O levels and A levels were. And I had to persuade my school to take me back, despite my results.

> When I finally made it to music college, I only had one spare set of clothes and a dressing gown. I did not even have a proper suitcase. My dad only let me go because he had a girlfriend nearby. After he dropped me off, I heard another mother telling her daughter not to mix with that sort (me) because I had a dreadful accent.
> So that is where my resilience comes from.'[37]

The will to win becomes dangerous when we all believe we will win. Everyone is in favour of competition, provided we do not lose. This problem can be seen when graduates rush to join the major consulting firms, all convinced that they are exceptional people who will make partner in due course. They are exceptional people, but the maths are not in their favour. Depending on how fast the firm grows and how long it takes to reach partner, typically somewhere between one in five and one in twelve will make it to the top. Put the other way round, at least 80 per cent or 90 per cent will drop out. This means that competition is intense, which is useful for the employer: each employee strives to do better than all the others. It is pretty unforgiving for the employees.

If you really want to compete:

- Know what you want to win.
- Know your odds and know your competition.
- Be ready to put the effort in.
- Take risks: put yourself forwards.
- Seize opportunities when they emerge.

Cope with stress

Stress is real, and we have to cope with it. It helps if we understand what stress is and what it is not. Stress is not about pressure. If you look back at when you have been at your best, was it when things were quiet and easy, or was it when you were under pressure to perform? Most people react quite well to pressure.

The difference between pressure and stress is control.[38] When we are under pressure but in control we can perform well. When we are under pressure and we have no control, then life becomes hard. We have all had times when we face a brick-wall date: we have to deliver by the deadline. But we depend on inputs from other people who are delivering late, not at all or not to standard. Suddenly, our stress-o-meter starts swinging wildly into the red zone.

So the first way to deal with stress is to take control. It is no surprise that CEOs are normally less stressed than middle managers: CEOs have more control over their destiny than middle managers.[39] Research on monkeys shows that being in the middle of the pecking order is far more stressful than being at the top or bottom, and that this is likely to be replicated in the workplace.[40] If you can't control everything, control what you can.

So how do our leaders deal with stress? Here are four ways beyond taking control of your situation and your life:

- 'I always have a plan A, a plan B and a plan C.' This is an effective way for this head teacher to retain control: she knows that under nearly any set of circumstances she will have a way forward. This is a simple lesson that can be applied to meetings and most of everyday life: if plan A does not work out, what is my back-up plan?

- 'I have a happy place I go to.' It turned out that this CEO had two happy places. The first was in his head: when in a tough situation he would calm down by bringing up happy memories. His other safe place was home, where he made sure that work disappeared. In extreme cases, he said, 'I go home and cry – and then I feel better.'

- 'I know how to unwind.' Many of these leaders had very active, and often unconventional, lives outside work: restoring vintage cars, for instance.

- 'I climb down the mountain', said one entrepreneur, comparing stress to altitude sickness. 'I vary the intensity of work. If I know one month is going to be hard, I make sure the next month is going to be easy.'

Classic signs of stress include: being irritable, drinking, finding it hard to sleep, poor concentration and constant anxiety.[41] It pays to recognize the symptoms and deal with them, including consulting your doctor. Everyone has to deal with stress from time to time: long-term stress is not the road to success.

Stay healthy

Much is made in the media about the superhero chiefs who are also super fit. But you do not need to be super fit to be successful. Churchill was in his mid-sixties, overweight and a heavy drinker when he became prime minister in 1940. Most of European history has been created by people who may have been drunk or in pain. Because the water was dangerous, people drank short beer or wine: the alcohol killed the germs.[42] And given the lack of medical and dental care, most people were probably in pain.[43] That did not stop an array of geniuses from emerging – from the good and the great to the mad and the bad. You do not need to take up triathlon training to be a good leader.

But there is one aspect of physical health that is surprisingly important: sleep.

Imagine for a moment that you come into the office in the morning and you see two of your associates. One is drunk and the other has just worked all night. What is your reaction? Do you fire the drunk and reward the all-night hero? You have an important meeting to go to: which one do you take with you?

The answer is you should take neither: sleep deprivation and alcohol both impair decision making and reaction times. A controlled study by Williamson and Fryer showed that after just 17–19 hours without sleep, cognitive and motor skills were the same as moderately intoxicated people with up to 0.1% blood alcohol content (BAC).[44] A US Department of Transport study showed that driving performance collapses with tiredness: they estimated that 1,544 deaths were needlessly caused by driving while tired.[45]

Not everyone needs a full eight hours of sleep per night. But do not believe the propaganda of great leaders who say they only need

2–3 hours of sleep per night.[46] Churchill was said to sleep as little as this, but that ignored his midday nap (for which he used to get into pyjamas) and his frequent cat naps during the day.

Sleep well.

Building super-resilience: anti-fragility

Most of the work on resilience focuses on remediation. It assumes that resilience is all about dealing with adverse events and that adversity is a problem. But there are clearly many people who actively seek out adversity. This can be extreme or mild adversity. At the extreme, there are plenty of adventurers who will put their lives on the line to climb Everest, explore hostile environments or sign up for hazardous careers, such as the elite armed forces.

At a milder level, you will also find plenty of people who want to play tough sports, with the prospect of losing as often as winning. And at work, there are many people who actively choose to work with the most demanding employers in the most demanding situations.

The evidence shows that many people do not see adversity as a problem to be avoided. They see it as an opportunity to be embraced. In many cases, the greater the adversity, the better.

The research on these people is still embryonic.[47] But the early work indicates that their mindset is different. Like other mindsets, it can be learned to a greater or lesser degree. Four emerging hypotheses about these people are:

- They are very driven by a mission. The tougher the goal, the greater the sacrifices you have to make in achieving the goal. But they embrace that adversity as an essential stepping stone on the path to success.

- They have a high need to prove themselves, mainly to themselves. This means they always have to push and test new limits. Risks are an opportunity to prove themselves. They follow the advice of poet William Blake: 'The road of excess leads to the palace of wisdom… You never know what is enough until you know what is more than enough.'[48]

- They seek comfort in the company of like-minded people. This means that they are always seeing and hearing of people who have pushed themselves harder and further. Achieving respect of the peer group means pushing yourself even harder and further. They live in a bubble where ever-greater adversity is the norm, not the exception. Peer group pressure is powerful: take care in who you choose as your peers. If all your peers make a show of working 16 hours a day, seven days a week, it becomes hard to escape that norm.

- They see uncertainty and ambiguity as opportunities, not threats. Uncertainty and ambiguity create freedom; when no one is sure what to do, you can create new rules and new ways of doing things. They actively chafe against conformity and predictability, because they do not offer freedom. They regard adversity as a small price to pay for freedom – this makes them natural entrepreneurs, not employees.

The work on anti-fragility suggests that there are two sorts of adversity: objective and subjective. Objectively, there is no doubt that a concentration camp represents extreme adversity. But lesser forms of adversity are as much in the mind as in reality, as the examples below show:

- Teaching rowdy children in an inner-city school.
- Climbing Everest.
- Training with the elite armed forces.
- Being a shepherd outdoors in midwinter.
- Working all hours for a top investment bank.

To some people, these would be examples of living hell. For others, these are their life ambitions.

Most of the anti-fragile mindset are habits of mind which we can all learn. We can choose a greater or lesser mission; we can choose to be with an ambitious or less ambitious peer group; we can see ambiguity and uncertainty as risk or opportunity; we can decide how we balance our desire for freedom with our desire for security.

Summary

Resilience is about never giving up, in the face of short-term setbacks or in the long haul. The best leaders take risks, have setbacks and need resilience.

Dealing with adversity: the POW example:

- Gain control: the less you can control, the more you should control what is left.
- Will to prevail: keep your final success in mind.
- Face the brutal facts: cope, don't hope.
- Use humour: laughter is the best medicine.[49]
- Build your support network.

Dealing with setbacks and adversity: the leader's guide:

- Take control, don't worry about what you cannot control.
- Control your own feelings. You always have a choice about how you react and feel.
- Stay positive: focus on your goal.
- Gain perspective: count your blessings, look at the best and worst outcomes.
- Draw on experience, from yourself and others, in order to find a way forward.
- Use humour: mock misfortune.
- Get help.

Dangerous ways to build resilience for the long haul:

- Making money, which becomes an accelerating treadmill.
- Finding work–life balance, which is normally a code for working less.

Building resilience for the long haul:

- Discover your mission: the greater your mission, the greater your resilience.
- Enjoy what you do: you only excel at what you enjoy.
- Will to win: dangerous because beating others is great, but losing is not.
- Cope with stress: find control.
- Stay healthy: sleep well.

Positive 04

Believe in better

The positive mindset is about creating energy, focusing on the future, seeing opportunities where others see problems and becoming the leader others want to follow. It will also help you to live longer. The positive mindset is the opposite of the risk-averse corporate mindset. The positive mindset can be learned through a few simple routines and habits.

Being positive might not just save your career, it might save your life.

An increasing amount of research is showing that being positive helps you to live longer and better. And research with leaders shows that being positive is an essential part of the mindset of success.

This chapter shows three things:

- Optimists live longer, live better.
- Why positive leadership works.
- How you can build and use your positive mindset.

Live longer, live better

If you faced the risk of getting dementia and dying young, you might want to take evasive action. Fortunately, there is a relatively easy remedy that involves no drugs and no operations. Simply be positive and avoid cynicism.

Research shows that hostile cynics are likely to have more stress, more conflict, less work satisfaction and have a negative view of work relationships.[1] Then it gets worse. Further research shows that hostile cynics are more likely to get dementia.[2] At least cynics get put out of their misery: they are more likely to die early than the rest of us.[3] If nothing else, this knowledge should cheer you up next time you are dealing with the office curmudgeon. You might want to test yourself on your cynicism score, with the same questions that researchers used to spot the cynics. How far do you agree with the following two statements?

- Most people would lie to get ahead.

- It is safer to trust no one.

If you disagree, you may be naive but you will probably live longer and better than the 'realists'. In contrast to the cynics, optimists do well.[4] In particular, optimists do best when things are bad: they can see their way through and believe they will get through. In the words of the academics: 'Optimists are significantly more successful than pessimists in aversive events and when important life-goals are impaired.'[5]

In work and in life, the optimists do better.

Fun or duty?

Nuns can show us how to live. They are ideal for research because most of the variables have been removed: they have the same diet, same routines, same access to health care, similar beliefs and the same lifestyle.[6] When they entered into service, they all had to write a letter outlining why they wanted to become nuns. Some wrote about their calling to serve, their belief and their duty. We can call these the 'duty' nuns. At the other end of the scale were those who wrote about how lucky and excited they were to have this opportunity and about how they were looking forward to being nuns. We can call these the 'fun' nuns.

Decades later, the researchers looked at how the nuns were doing.

By age 85, 90 per cent of the fun nuns were still alive compared to just 34 per cent of the duty nuns. By age 94, 54 per cent of the fun nuns were still enjoying life, while just 11 per cent of the duty nuns were hanging on. On average, the longevity difference between the two groups was 9.4 years.

Why positive leadership works

Let's start with an exercise that you should probably avoid. Make a list of the following:

- All the faults and mistakes of your boss or bosses.
- The failings of your peers and colleagues.
- The problems that you have, and are likely to face, on your most important initiatives.

By the time you get half-way through the exercise you will probably resign, go for a drink or seek solace in a cream cake. You will not feel motivated to do much more than give up. Negative thinking is not a good way to lead.

Now think about the most negative and most positive bosses you have worked for. Which one would you prefer to work with again? Positive leadership works for at least six reasons. With it you can:

- turn crises into opportunities;
- create belief in your team and motivate them;
- create new and bigger opportunities;
- attract support;
- perform better;
- get lucky.

Being positive sounds like one of those potions sold by quack doctors in the Wild West, which promised to cure everything from rheumatism to your love life. The difference is that being positive is free, and it actually works. We will explore each effect in turn.

Turn crises into opportunities

At the heart of positive leadership is the art of looking forward and working towards the best possible outcome. This sounds obvious – doesn't everyone do that? Now look back on when things go wrong in your organization. How many people start an inquest, quietly try to shift the blame and analyse where it all went wrong? That is the opposite of positive leadership.

Imagine you are a head teacher. You run a large school in a tough area. Most of the children have English as a second language and over 60 mother tongues are used by them. One day an arsonist burns down one wing of the school; luckily no one is hurt. What is your reaction? Here was the head's reaction: 'This was a blessing in disguise. We desperately needed new facilities, and so with the insurance money we were able to build a new wing which was fit for purpose.' No looking back, no anger: just looking forward to a better new world. To the best of my knowledge she was not the arsonist.

Create belief in your team and motivate them

In the dark days of 1940–41 Britain stood pretty much alone against the overwhelming force of the Nazis. There were plenty of leading politicians, such as Lord Halifax, who had given up and were ready to do a deal with Hitler. Churchill had other ideas. He did not talk like a middle manager: 'It may be bad but it's not my fault and I told everyone this would happen...' Whining excuses were not what the nation needed. Instead, he reached his rhetorical peak: 'Never in the field of human history has so much been owed by so many to so few... their finest hour... we will fight them on the beaches... we will never surrender... I have nothing to offer but blood, toil, tears and sweat.' He left no doubt that we would fight to the end and we would prevail. The doubters were banished to mutter in the corners.

Followers prefer to follow positive leaders, not negative ones.

Create new and bigger opportunities

When has a negative person ever volunteered or delivered a big new idea? If you want to be a transformational leader, you need big ideas and you need the self-belief to back them.

Sharath Jeevan is the leader who decided to start a charity addressing global education disadvantage. If he had been rational, he would have given up before starting. In his words: 'When I told others, they said "You must be delusional." They were right, in a way. Being a social entrepreneur you need to be crazily self-delusional to believe that you can change the world the way you want to shape it.'

All leaders need a positive mindset to see past the doubters and detractors. The bigger your idea, the more you will hear from the doubters. In the words of Steve Munby: 'Cynicism is the cancer of an organization. It spreads and kills it.'[7] If you don't have belief in your idea, no one else will. As the leader, you have to be spreading the antidote to cynicism: enthusiasm, energy and excitement.

Attract support

A leader without followers is not a leader. Even if you have followers, how many would want to follow you to a new role? The best leaders do not have to rely on the assignment system for their team. They are able to attract and retain the best talent.

Research shows that optimists attract.[8] Only 3 per cent of people were attracted to pessimists, and even then only if they had a dark sense of humour to go with their pessimism; 50 per cent expressed an active preference for optimists. Followers want to live with hope. The best leaders not only have hope, they give hope to others. Just as cynicism is infectious, so is optimism and being positive. Your mood as a leader will be reflected in your team. If you wonder why your team is grumpy and negative, look in the mirror.

Perform better

It is notoriously hard to compare performance across executives because their roles vary so much. However, sales forces are ideal for comparisons because everyone is doing the same job. So we will use sales data as a proxy for performance.

Martin Seligman conducted a study on the effect of optimism on sales.[9] He tracked 15,000 new MetLife sales people over three years. The sales people had taken two tests. One was the standard MetLife screening, the other was Seligman's test for optimism. The findings were startling:

- The most optimistic 10 per cent outsold the most pessimistic 10 per cent by 88 per cent.

- The consultants in the top half of optimism outsold those in the bottom half by 37 per cent.

- Recruits who just failed the MetLife screening, but were deemed highly optimistic, outsold the regular but pessimistic recruits by 57 per cent.

He was able to replicate these results elsewhere with other sales teams. In 1995 he found that across industries, optimistic sales people outsold pessimists by 20–40 per cent, and that the most optimistic real-estate agents were up to seven times more productive than their more pessimistic colleagues.

We can argue that sales is uniquely suited to the world of the optimist. But most executives, and even CEOs, ultimately become sales people. Their role is to sell colleagues and stakeholders new ideas, to persuade people to back them, to use their influence to align agendas and promote their priorities. The evidence from Seligman implies that the optimists will do this better than the pessimists.

The simple message is that optimism beats skills in predicting performance. This matters in how you recruit: MetLife was recruiting 5,000 agents annually at a cost of $30,000 each over two years in training and hiring. It also matters because, although it is relatively easy to train skills, few firms can train for optimism or being positive. The purpose of the next section is to show how you can train yourself to think and act more positively all the time.

Get lucky

Professor Richard Wiseman has researched luck.[10] He found one woman who was exceptionally lucky. She was always winning holidays, cars, competitions and cash. Her luck was helped by entering over 100 competitions per week. The more competitions she entered, the better she became at classic tie breakers such as 'Complete in not more than twelve words Sudso is wonderful because...'

Luck comes down to four Ps:

- *Persistence*: the more often you try the more likely you are to win. Robert the Bruce, who did much to secure Scottish independence, was initially heavily defeated by the English. He fled and hid in a cave, where he famously saw a spider repeatedly trying to weave its web. 'Try, try and try again' became the motto attributed to him.[11] He did keep trying and eventually secured a decisive victory against the English at Bannockburn in 1314.

- *Practice*: 'The harder I practice the luckier I get' has been attributed to golfer Arnold Palmer, but also to fellow golfers Gary Player, Tom Watson and others. It is a popular and relevant saying. With practice, the 50/50 chance becomes a 70/30 chance and the 70/30 chance becomes a 90/10 chance. In other words, practice turns luck into skill.

- *Preparation*: if you do not know what you are looking for you will not find it. For instance, the head of a primary school went to a dinner with a bank sponsor. She was ready to explain some recent poor results. The sponsor offered her an exciting role in the bank. The principal duly launched into her explanation of the poor results. Another diner nudged her: 'I think he just offered you a job.' The head was now in a panic: perhaps she had just missed her big opportunity. Fortunately, over dessert the banker repeated his offer. This time, the head was listening and duly accepted.

- *Perspective*: make a list of all the bad things that happened to you today: how many traffic lights went against you, which news stories annoyed you and how have colleagues irritated you? Feeling lucky? Thought not. Now make a list of all the good things that have happened to you today, from the moment you woke up in a warm bed in a decent house. Hopefully, you are feeling luckier. Wiseman's research shows that lucky people are not always luckier than most: they simply feel that way.

Knowing what you are looking for[12]

Imagine you are driving along the Libyan coast, by the Mediterranean. In days gone by you might have been looking for Roman ruins; today you may be on the lookout for trouble. You would be unlikely to notice some cabbage fields. Even if you did, you would not care much: compared to the prospect of a Roman ruin or getting kidnapped, cabbages do not rank very high.

MI6 were fairly convinced that Colonel Gaddafi was trying to develop nuclear weapons. A rogue state with nuclear capability on the Mediterranean was a nightmare scenario. The finger pointed to North Korea as Gaddafi's nuclear partner. Despite huge amounts of effort, no one could find any evidence. One of MI6's officers was driving along the coast road and happened to notice the cabbages. It was his eureka moment.

Cabbages were notable to the MI6 officer because they are not a normal crop to grow in Libya. The climate is not great for them, and the locals do not much care for cabbage. But North Koreans love cabbage, which they ferment to make endless varieties of kimchi. He figured that where there are cabbages, there must be North Koreans; where there are North Koreans, there must be a nuclear facility.

With a lot more effort, the details were established, Gaddafi was confronted with the evidence and he eventually agreed to abandon his nuclear programme – all because of cabbages. Knowing what you are looking for makes all the difference.

How you can build and use your positive mindset

I checked into a hotel and the receptionist was clearly having a bad day. After shoving the room keys at me, she suddenly remembered her corporate training required her to be positive and passionate about her work. So she snapped 'Have a nice day' at me while clearly thinking 'Please drop dead'. Being told to be positive is about as helpful as being told to be happy, enthusiastic, intelligent and charismatic. It does not help at all.

Equally, if you live the mantra of 'don't worry, be happy' you may end up living in a tepee in Vermont cooking organic greens on a wok. That is no doubt good on a fine day in August but less good after fourteen days of snowstorms in February. The positive mindset is not just about having fun and being happy – there is substance and power to the positive mindset.

So what does the positive mindset look like? James Toop, CEO of Teaching Leaders, says: 'You have to model being positive, enthusiastic and excited. Every day you get up, it should feel like Christmas Day. You really have to care about what you do.' How on earth do you cultivate a mindset like that?

The most important route to a positive mindset is to choose your thoughts. That sounds odd, because we assume we always choose our thoughts. But that is not the case. We all have self-talk, which we need to train so that it helps rather than hinders us. Buddhist meditation is one way, but that can take a lifetime to master. Hard-pressed leaders need something practical that they can master faster.

Most of our self-talk arises naturally in response to what we are experiencing at the time. If someone shouts at you, it is natural to feel threatened, annoyed and upset. It may be natural, but there is no law that requires you to feel that way: you choose to feel that way. If a colleague lets you down, you have a right to feel angry and frustrated. But again, there is no law to say that is how you must feel: that is your choice.

Here are three steps towards choosing and conditioning your thoughts:

- Recognize that you have a choice.

- Challenge your thoughts.

- Copy your role models.

Recognize that you have choice[13]

You can try this exercise in the office. Every time a negative thought comes into your mind, note it and mentally raise a big red card at it: banish it to the sidelines of your mind. You can make this more impactful by wearing a rubber band on your wrist. Each time a negative thought arises, lift the rubber band and let it flick back: the little sting will slowly condition you to associate negative thoughts with bad outcomes. You may find you have quite a sore wrist inside an hour.

Challenge your thoughts

Self-talk can become destructive black and white thinking, with two classic traps: personalizing and universalizing bad experiences. Classic warning words that should start red lights flashing in your mind include: always, never, disaster, ruined, impossible and terrible. These words make universal and absolute a single event, which is unhelpful to you. When these words start trotting across your brain, challenge them before they take up residence and hijack your way of thinking:

● Does this always happen? Really? What can you learn from this?

● Will it never be possible? Are there alternatives?

● Is it really ruined, forever with no options and no choices?

● Is it a disaster from which there can never be a recovery?

The second set of warning words are those that personalize any setback:

● I am no good at financial matters.

● My boss hates me.

● I never get any support or recognition.

Again, challenge your thoughts:

● 'I am no good at financial matters.' This can become: 'Finance may not be my strong point, but there are plenty of financial people out there to help me, which lets me concentrate on being the best marketing person I can be.'

- 'My boss hates me.' This can become: 'My boss did not like that last report, because it was late. She is happy when there are no surprises, so I will make sure she is not surprised again.'

- 'I never get any support or recognition.' This can become: 'I am doing good work; I simply need to make sure that my bosses see it more clearly.'

Two simple tricks will help you to challenge your thoughts productively: first, be specific. Challenge your universal, absolute or personal statements and ask whether they are really true under all conditions. Second, ask yourself: 'So what can I do about it?' Figure out what a better future looks like, and what you need to do to get there.

Bad events happen to all of us. How we react to them differs. The differences can be summarized, as shown in Table 4.1. You cannot change the past, but you can change how you react to it.

Table 4.1   Pessimistic versus optimistic mindsets

Pessimists	Optimists
Permanence: this always happens	Temporary: this is a one-off
Personalization: blames self, feels worthless	Sees external causes
Helplessness: nothing can be done about it	Self-efficacy: I can change this and learn from it

Copy your role models

You have two perspectives here, and two questions you can ask yourself:

- How would my ideal role model act and think in this situation? If your ideal role model is Vlad the Impaler, who impaled anyone who incurred his displeasure, you might want to choose another role model. You will have had a mentor, or boss or colleague who you admire: think about how they would react.

- How should I react and think if I want to be a good role model to my team? As a leader you live life in the goldfish bowl: everyone can watch your every action. Think of leadership as a performance where you are the lead actor or actress, because that is what leadership is. Enjoy the limelight and act the part. Preferably, choose not to act like Darth Vader or Hannibal Lecter.

Conditioning your mind takes time and patience. This is frustrating to the alpha overachievers who want instant results. Remember the time you learned any new skill, from riding a bicycle to playing a sport or musical instrument. It takes time, but even a little practice makes a big difference. Keep at it.

Other ways to help build your positive mindset

Thought conditioning may take time and effort, but there are other things you can do simply to help build your positive mindset. If you are impatient to make progress, here are some techniques that you can apply fast and get results:

- Focus on the future.
- Count your blessings.
- Help others.
- Drive to action.
- Take small steps.
- Relax and smile.

Each of these is explored in more detail below.

Focus on the future

The best leaders on the leadership panel were all relentlessly future-focused and optimistic about it. Steve Munby, CEO of Education Development Trust, says: 'Great leaders have huge barrels of hope; they have an ability to weave an optimistic vision of the future. They will create the future in their mind's eye, and convince you to get there.' It is this vision of the future that drives them forward, and helps them to drive their team forward. Some managers drive into the future by looking in the rear mirror: they are always analysing reports and discussing what has happened. The best leaders can do that as well, but then they turn the focus onto how they will move forwards.

Future focus helps in the short term as well as in the long term. In a sticky situation it is tempting to ask, 'What went wrong?' The best leaders leave the inquests for another day. Instead they ask, 'What do we need to do next?' The first question leads to analysis, the blame game and politics. The second, positive question, drives to action and brings the team together. This is obvious and simple, and is routinely missed in the heat of the moment.

Count your blessings

In the section on luck, you were invited to make a list of all the good and bad things that have happened to you today. Focusing on the bad things will convince you that today is a bad day. Focusing on the good things may persuade you that life is not so terrible after all.

Even if you only have thirty seconds to spare as you walk into the office, you can use that time to reflect on what is going well. It is not a panacea, but it may help you spot the silver lining to the clouds of gloom that hang over some offices.

Counting your blessings

I had got used to waking up in the middle of wars, and famines, disasters, crises, lying politicians and greedy businessmen. It is called waking up to the news. It is not a good way to start the day.

On one field trip I found I was waking up in the middle of a minor war between two tribes. I was happy to escape back to civilization. It was a hotel with mud walls and a corrugated iron roof. The rain thundered on the roof. I collapsed asleep in a filthy, uncomfortable bed. The next morning I stumbled towards an equally filthy washroom. And then a miracle happened. I turned on a tap and cold water came out. I did not need to walk five kilometres to the nearby crocodile-infested river to collect water, as I had done on the field trip. A moment later another miracle happened. I turned on another tap and warmish water came out. I did not need to go and collect firewood to heat the water.

Now, when I get up at home I wake up to music and rediscover two miracles in two minutes: running hot and cold water. It is pretty hard to have a bad day when you start with two miracles and a little music.

In workshops I ask people what was the first good thing that happened to them in the day. I realize I am slow in counting my blessings: many people are just happy to wake up in a warm bed, in a nice house, near their family. Everything else is a bonus.

We can choose how we wake up; we can choose how we feel. Choose well.

Help others

There is plenty of research to show that helping others is a good way of helping yourself.[14] This is the puzzle for economists: why do people volunteer their time for no obvious gain? The gain is not measured in money: it is a social and wellbeing gain. Helping others increases our sense of self-worth.

In addition, helping others has two practical benefits to leaders. First, it encourages reciprocity. Professor Robert Cialdini demonstrates that humans have a strong need to reciprocate. He gives a small personal example: 'When I was at the Mandarin Oriental, I pulled out this stationery and my name was at the top. They had given me a gift that wasn't designed to promote the hotel. It didn't have their name on it – it had my name on it. I've never stopped recommending that hotel to anyone travelling to Hong Kong.'[15]

You do not need to volunteer at an orphanage to help others: you can just help your colleagues. And you do not have to spend days helping them. Even small things such as opening doors and fetching drinks will lead to reciprocity, eventually.

Second, reciprocity is good role modelling for your team. If you take time to help your team members by coaching and supporting them, they will value you. And you also role model how you want them to manage their teams.

Drive to action

Positive thinking is action-focused. Do what it takes. Mike Tobin, recent CEO of Telecity and part of the leadership panel, was recruited into a business that had shrunk from £400 million to £4 million market capitalization, which was less than the £6.5 million of cash they had in the bank. They were burning £2.5 million cash per month. Mike takes up the story:

> So I crashed the first board meeting. I was not meant to be there. I told them we would be out of business in two months. It provoked quite a reaction. So we had to turn it around. We got headcount down from 400 to 80, we refinanced and got new investors... we have now relisted again.

You can discuss the problem, or you can deal with it. A good way to start is to focus on what you can do or what you can influence. There are plenty of things you may have no control over: discard those and do not waste time and effort on things beyond your control. Focus on what is possible, and if there is only one course of action possible (reducing headcount from 400 to 80, for instance) that is what you do.

Take small steps

There is an old joke that occasionally cropped up in Christmas crackers (it is that bad): 'How do you eat an elephant? One mouthful at a time.' It is probably better not to eat elephants. But the joke shows exactly how to deal with any complex problem: one mouthful at a time.

Faced with a huge task, it is easy to feel overwhelmed. It is worse if it is a task you do not relish. If you are a leader with high aspirations, you will want to take on a huge task that will make a difference. But you will not want to feel overwhelmed.

The solution is simple: break down the large task into small steps. If you have 100 sales calls to make, focus on making the first five. And hold out the prospect of rewarding yourself at the end of the five calls: allow yourself to go and get a coffee and a biscuit.

Do the same with your team. Do not set them a huge task and wait for them to fail. Sit down with them and work out together what all the key steps will be. Break the project into small, discrete elements which they can deliver with confidence. 'A march of a thousand miles starts with a single step',[16] and often the first step is the hardest. As the leader, you have to start the march and break it down into achievable stages for your team.

Relax and smile

Try a simple exercise: try to smile and feel angry at the same time. Now try grimacing and feeling happy. Although not impossible to do, these are deeply unnatural acts. Our thoughts may condition our posture and appearance, but the reverse is also true: our posture and appearance can influence how we think and feel.

If you do full relaxation exercises, you may find yourself lying on the floor. That does not always work out well in the middle of a tense board meeting. Fortunately, there are plenty of things you can do even in the middle of the toughest meeting: no one will notice anything except that you appear to be the one calm voice in the room. You will have an air of authority that others may be struggling with as they become ever-more stressed.

The easiest way to relax is to breathe deeply and evenly: when we are tense our breathing tends to become shallow and rapid, and we start to breathe from our shoulders, not from our diaphragm. Typical breathing patterns in a healthy person will be about 10–12 breaths per minute.[17] Try breathing deep into your diaphragm. Feel your stomach contract as you breathe in and expand as you breathe out. Concentrate on your breathing for a few moments: feel the cool air coming in through your nostrils and the warm air going out. You only need to do this four or five times and you will feel the tension and stress float out as you exhale. Research evidence is consistent in showing that good breathing reduces tension and stress.[18]

In addition to breathing exercises, you can also try to relax your muscles, discretely. The best way is to start at your toes and work upwards. You can quietly wiggle your toes and no one will notice; then stretch your calf and slowly work up until you reach your shoulders: drop your shoulders and stretch your neck. If you are in a hurry, just work on relaxing your shoulders and then sit up straight: slouched in a chair or hunched over a table is not conducive to staying alert and calm.

If you are in a tense situation, change the situation. One team member had a way of making me relax when we were tense: he would ask me to go for a walk in the park. I would leave feeling grumpy. By the time I got back, sanity would be restored and the problem would have evaporated. This bizarre method also helped disarmament at the height of the Cold War. In spring 1982, Nitze and Kvitsinski took their famous walk in the woods: in these relaxed surroundings the US and Soviet negotiators etched out the framework for reducing nuclear missiles in Europe.[19] If they had been facing each other over a conference table with flags and back-up teams, they would have been protecting their positions, not making progress.

It does not matter what your method is, as long as you have a method that works for you.

Summary

Being positive will help you to live longer and better. As a leader it will help you:

- Turn crises into opportunities: focus on the future, not the past.
- Create belief in your team and motivate them: inspire hope.
- Create new and bigger opportunities: see and seize chances.
- Attract support: followers want positive, not negative leaders.

- Perform better: optimists outperform more-skilled pessimists.

- Get lucky: practice, persistence, patience and perspective leads to winning more.

The positive mindset starts with controlling your self-talk:

- Recognize that you have a choice: how you feel and think is up to you.

- Challenge your thoughts: check every negative thought you have.

- Copy your role models: think and do as they do.

You can condition your mindset to be positive with a few simple techniques:

- Focus on the future: do not dwell on the past too much.

- Count your blessings: focus on the silver lining, not the cloud.

- Help others: encourage reciprocity and feel better about yourself.

- Drive to action: act on what you control, do not worry about what you cannot control.

- Take small steps: break daunting tasks into small steps, reward your progress.

- Relax and smile: find the method that works for you.

Accountability   05
Control your destiny

The best leaders are never victims. They are confident that they control their own destiny, for better or for worse. They are not constrained by the formal frameworks of where they work. They even take responsibility for one thing that many people struggle to control: their own feelings. Building this level of control requires changing the way we talk to ourselves and think about ourselves.

The best book you never need to read is called *Control Your Destiny or Someone Else Will* (2005).[1] The reason you never need to read it is because the message is in the title. If you don't control your future, someone else will.

Any leader who actually leads will believe that they are in control of their destiny. You cannot shape future events if you believe you are a victim of events. All our leaders had strong belief that they were responsible for shaping the future. Many of them came back to the sign that President Truman kept on his desk at the White House: 'The buck stops here.' It may sound corny, but they believed it strongly. Here are some examples:

- *Taking the blame, sharing the praise*: 'Never pass the buck. If we don't hit target in one region, it is my responsibility to work out how we recover overall. I take responsibility for big things, for external matters and for negative things. But I distribute responsibility widely for success.' (James Toop, CEO, Teaching Leaders)

- *Taking responsibility in all aspects of life*: 'The buck stops here. I can't say "My PA didn't do this or that". That applies to every single aspect of my life.' (Anita Scott, partner, Brunswick Group)

- *Standing up for your team*: 'I am always clear with staff that I carry the can, the buck stops with me and that encourages staff because they know that someone will stand up for them. Some leaders are quick to blame others when things go wrong. What upsets me most is when they say things like "You let me down". No good leader ever says that. You have to tough it out and take responsibility.' (Dame Sue John, head of Lampton School)

- *Taking initiative*: 'The buck starts with me. I have to make things happen. That's what leaders do.' (Mike Tobin, recent CEO, Telecity)

As with much of what the leaders talked about, this idea of controlling your destiny seems obvious. Who would not want to be in control of their destiny? Yet while we may all want to be in control of our destiny, it is equally clear that many of us are not. Our destiny is shaped by our boss, our colleagues, our organization and ultimately by the forces of competition, money and technology.

We can feel like small cogs in a machine that we do not control. This is a problem that has been growing more or less since the start of the Industrial Revolution. Before then, the peasant farmers had some degree of control over their lives, subject to the unpredictable forces of nature, disease, famine and war. Factories may have removed the random forces of nature, but they also removed control from their workers who came to depend on the factory. Charlie Chaplin portrayed this haplessness in his 1936 film *Modern Times*, where he becomes a victim of an out-of-control factory line: he has to screw nuts at an ever-increasing rate on an accelerating production line. It was an eloquent protest against scientific management and Taylorism.[2]

The tyranny of the accelerating production line was mirrored by the tyranny of the authoritarian organization, which was essentially modelled on the military: they were the most effective known forms of organizing large numbers of people prior to the Industrial Revolution. Some authoritarian organizations turned out to be benign, such as the Quaker families who set up chocolate firms (Cadbury of Birmingham, Rowntree of York and Fry of Bristol) that sought to provide well for their workforces: housing, education, health care and even limited welfare. They were mini welfare states in their own right. Whether the organization was benign or not, the workers essentially became dependants. They had very little personal autonomy. They certainly did not control their destiny.

In theory, we should be moving to a more enlightened era where employees have more autonomy and can control their destiny much more. In some areas, such as professional services (law, consulting and medicine) this is how things are evolving. Elsewhere, it is not clear that employees or managers are really in control of their destiny: they are still a cog in a machine.

Try the exercise set out in Table 5.1 to discover how far you are really in control. For each activity listed, rank them as high (H), medium (M) or low (L) priority for your idea of a good leader and for your boss. Use time spent on each activity to assess real priorities. So if you think your boss spends a large amount of time managing upwards, rank that an H in your 'boss' column; if you think a good leader should spend little time doing that, put an L in the 'good leader' column.

The first seven activities listed in Table 5.1 are where most managers spend most of their time. They are dealing with the noise of the organization, but they are not adding much value. These are not the activities of people who are in control of their destiny. Like Charlie Chaplin in *Modern Times*, they are simply feeding the machine. Like Charlie Chaplin, we find the machine demands more and more. For us, instead of the technology being a production line, rather it is e-mail, PowerPoint, Word and mobile phones. In practice, office technology does not reduce workloads: it raises expectations. Whereas 30 years ago a big presentation might be 10 pages long and specialist staff would have produced it, now a big presentation may be 50 slides long, plus appendices, and we have to produce it ourselves.

The bottom half of Table 5.1 (rows 8 to 14) is what we normally expect of good leaders. A leader who is focused on these activities has the chance to make a difference and be in control of their destiny. They are not simply responding to the routine of the machine: they

Table 5.1   Leadership activity checklist

Activity	Your boss	Ideal leader
1 Managing upwards		
2 Checking progress of team		
3 Preparing presentations		
4 Completing forms and reports		
5 Checking e-mail		
6 Attending routine meetings		
7 Gaining approvals		
8 Coaching team members		
9 Setting and clarifying direction, goals		
10 Communicating required information		
11 Removing obstacles, dealing with problems		
12 Finding support and resources for the team		
13 Recruiting and keeping the best team		
14 Delegating and empowering team		

where progress is made (handwritten annotation bracketing items 8–14)

are setting and delivering an agenda that makes sense to them in their area of the organization.

If you are feeling brave, now complete Table 5.1 with a third column: where do you spend your time? Are you feeding the machine or are you in control of your destiny? We may all want to be in control of our destiny, but for many of us it is very difficult to achieve this goal when we have to feed the machine that employs us.

To develop the accountability mindset, we first have to understand what it is. Then we have to find a way to develop the mindset. This is covered in the three sections of this chapter:

- Define three mindsets: accountable, corporate and victim.
- Explore the beliefs of the accountable mindset.
- Develop your accountability mindset.

Three mindsets: accountable, corporate and victim

Look at Table 5.2 and see where you come out. Most people in a corporate setting rightly think they have the corporate mindset: they focus on what they are meant to do, and do it well. That is a recipe for a functioning organization and a good career. It is the world of the RACI chart,[3] where everyone knows what they are meant to do. It ensures that all the cogs in the machine mesh rather than crash. But it means you are one of those cogs in the machine. These cogs have the illusion of control, because they are controlling

Table 5.2 Three types of mindset

Factor[4]	Corporate mindset	Accountable mindset	Victim mindset
Locus of control[5]	You believe your control is defined by your formal authority and the corporate framework.	You believe you can control your destiny and your environment.	You believe that you are shaped by events around you, over which you have little control.
Self-efficacy[6]	You will focus on performing well within your defined area of responsibility.	You will have confidence to perform well in a variety of situations and will be confident about taking on new challenges that will let you learn and grow.	You tend to avoid new, difficult and challenging situations and prefer to work in a stable, familiar role that you know.

things. In practice, they depend on the machine: they are not fully in control of their destiny.

The best leaders reach beyond the machine and the corporate mindset. They seek to control their environment, rather than be controlled by it. They will take on new challenges and reach beyond their formal authority where necessary. As we saw in the previous chapter, Mike Tobin crashed a board meeting where he was not meant to be, because that was needed in order to save the company. The accountable mindset shapes the world, rather than being shaped by it.

The opposite of the accountability mindset we can unkindly call the victim mindset. Victims have what has been called 'learned helplessness'.[7] This is where we believe we cannot change things, we learn to become dependant on others and we give up in the face of challenges. This is not just bad for your career, it can kill you. In one test, staff at a nursing home encouraged residents on one floor to look after themselves as much as possible; on the other floor the staff did everything for the residents.[8] On the high-care floor, 71 per cent of residents got worse within three weeks; on the self-care regime, residents actually got better. The more you take control, the better you do. In the words of the researchers, 'A feeling of helplessness may contribute to psychological withdrawal, disease, and death.'

In most organizations, victims are either weeded out or marginalized, which helps the organization but tends to confirm the victim's world view. The real challenge is to rise from the comfort of the corporate mindset to the leader's mindset of accountability. This is a mindset based on a series of beliefs, which we explore in this chapter. We can also nurture our accountability mindset through a series of routines.

The beliefs of the accountability mindset

The accountability mindset runs deep, and is based on core beliefs about how you see yourself in the world. Here are the top six beliefs you need to grow for your accountability mindset:

- I control my own destiny.
- I am accountable for what happens to me.
- I am accountable for my own feelings.
- Challenging tasks are an opportunity to learn and grow.
- I see others as role models, not as competitors.
- I have the talent to succeed.

As you look at those beliefs you will probably agree with them and believe you have them. As we shall see, however, many people inadvertently fall short on each statement and fall into the victim mindset, greatly aided by the nature of modern organizational life.

Challenge yourself to see where you really come out on each belief, as set out below.

I control my own destiny

This is a core self-efficacy belief. Research shows that this belief drives health outcomes,[9] in terms of:

- adherence to medication;
- nutrition, diets and weight control;
- physical exercise;
- use of seat belts;
- addictive behaviours.

If you have high self-efficacy you will believe you can control your own destiny: you are more likely to stick to diets, to medication and to challenging work tasks in the belief that you will succeed, even if it takes effort.

This is the sort of behaviour that organizations claim to encourage: the rhetoric of management talks about the importance of initiative, innovation, challenge and leadership. But the reality is different. Look at Table 5.1 earlier in this chapter, which invited you to look at what you actually do all day. A large amount of management time is spent on compliance work and routine: monitoring, communicating, dealing with e-mails. High levels of reporting, measurement and control are typically low-trust worlds inhabited by people who learn to conform and depend on the system they serve.

This belief is driven by a combination of habit, experience and role models. That means you should:

- Develop productive routines and habits that are important for you: exercising, using seat belts, work routines to finish work well. We are creatures of habit, use habits to your advantage.

- Put yourself in a position where you are surrounded by successful role models: peer pressure is a very powerful motivation for the good (high standards) and the bad (substance abuse).

- Find some small and easy wins that will show you that you can succeed: reflect on where and when and why you have succeeded, and build on that experience to do more of the same.

I am accountable for what happens to me

The victim mindset believes that we are victims of a cruel and uncaring world. This is a form of helplessness. In its strongest form, it means we can learn nothing and do nothing about our fate.

Shakespeare's Hamlet expressed the victim mindset when he tells Horatio:

There's a divinity that shapes our ends,
Rough-hew them how we will.[10]

The strong-form victims don't even believe that they can rough-hew their ends.

The accountable mindset recognizes that what happens to us is a result of our choices and actions. If you have a lousy job and work for a lousy boss, who is responsible for that? If you do not get the promotion or bonus you believe you deserve, who is responsible for that?

In contrast, the victim mindset goes into blame mode when anything bad happens: blame events, blame other people. This is where we find that the victim mindset is an epidemic in many organizations.

Taking responsibility requires deep inner confidence: you have to believe that you will learn, grow and come out stronger from any experience. The victim mindset is fearful of further adverse consequences from taking responsibility, such as criticism from peers and bosses. In poor organizations, taking responsibility for bad outcomes can be a career-limiting move. But in most organizations when the leader takes responsibility, suddenly everyone else breathes a huge sigh of relief: they are excused the blame game and move forward.

Spot the victim

I was walking home from work late one night. A shadow moved and suddenly there was a knife against my throat. A voice from behind asked for all my money. He did not even say please. But he did spell out the consequences of what would happen if I did not comply.

It was not the mugger's night. He probably thought that Christmas had come early because he had found someone in a suit. Surely suits have wallets and money, don't they? Being mean, all I had was a £10 note and some loose change. He was not interested in the coins, but he took the £10.

Some hours later at the police station I realized just how lucky I had been. I heard whispered conversations in the corridor about some poor victim. I slowly realized that they were talking about me. I was shocked. I may have been mugged, but I never thought of myself as being a victim of anything other than my own folly.

While no one should be mugged, if you choose to walk down a dark and lonely street at night in a suit, then you are rolling the dice and they may not be weighted in your favour. If you get unlucky, then how did you put yourself in a position where the luck could go against you? In the end, I got a memorable experience and a good lesson in accountability for just £10. It was money well used.

I am accountable for my own feelings

We have encountered this belief in previous chapters. It is the belief that many executives struggle with the most. But if you become angry, upset or depressed then that is a victim mindset. You are letting your emotions be controlled by strangers, by colleagues and by events. As we saw from the stories of the Vietnam POWs, their last freedom was their freedom to think and to feel as they saw fit. If we surrender that final freedom, then we have become victims.

The best leaders understand that they can choose how they feel. At minimum, they learn to wear the mask of leadership: it is a mask of cool, calm control. Understanding you can choose how to feel is the first critical step to freedom and self-control: you do not have to be at the mercy of others and events.

Challenging tasks are an opportunity to learn and grow

The victim mentality shrinks from new and challenging tasks in the belief that they will fail. Victims assume that tasks are harder than they are. And when they encounter obstacles they are more likely to give up and less likely to learn from what happened. The victim mindset is fundamentally about helplessness. For victims, a challenge is not an opportunity to succeed. It is an opportunity to fail.

The accountable mindset sees a challenge as an opportunity. There is an inner belief that they will succeed at the task, and that in any event they will learn from it and become stronger as a result.

This belief creates an ever-growing chasm between the victim and the accountable leaders. The victims don't try new challenges, so they do not learn and do not grow. That makes them even more fearful of new challenges, because they lack the experience or success in taking on new challenges. Meanwhile the accountable leader is growing stronger all the time. Even if they have a setback on a challenge, they still learn and grow. Most of us learn most from our mistakes: the more we try, the more mistakes we make and the more we learn. The victims do not have the same rate of learning as the accountable leader.

I see others as role models, not as competitors

How we see others helps to frame how we see ourselves. The brutal reality on the ground is that, for many managers, the real competition is not in the marketplace but is sitting at a hot desk near you competing for a limited pot of promotions, bonuses, budget and management time. Even if you are competing with your peers, comparing yourself with them does not help. They are different and will have different strengths. There will always be someone else who is better than you at something. The end result is to acquire an inferiority complex. In small doses this can be healthy. In the words of Alfred Adler: 'It is rather a stimulant to healthy, normal striving and development. It becomes a pathological condition only when the sense of inadequacy overwhelms the individual and, far from stimulating him to useful activity, makes him depressed and incapable of development.'[11] Don't let yourself be awed by others. Everyone else may be better than you at something, but everyone else is also worse than you at something. This runs all the way to the top, as CEO and McKinsey alumnus Brett Wigdortz noted: 'One of the great lessons of McKinsey is that CEOs are not great. They do not know what they are doing. So don't hold back, you are at least as good as they are.'[12]

The alternative way of looking at peers and others is as role models from whom you can learn and develop. And this is how most people learn about leadership in practice. In workshops I do a quick exercise where I give attendees a list of six possible sources of learning. You have to pick the two most important sources of your learning about leadership: books; courses; bosses (good or bad lessons); role models; peers; experience.

No one ever chooses books or courses, which could be awkward for an author running a course. Everyone chooses direct experience or second-hand experience: learning from others. If you learn from others rather than judge yourself relative to others, then you are on the road to the accountable mindset.

So what is the point of books and courses?

If most people learn about leadership from direct and indirect experience, then what is the point of books and courses?

If we only learn from experience, then our learning journey is a random walk. We bump into good experiences, bosses, role models and peers and we accelerate our learning and our careers. If we encounter bad experience and bosses, we hit the buffers or land in a dead end. A random walk is not a good way to manage your career or manage learning.

You cannot expect to finish a book and emerge as a brilliant leader on the final page. The purpose of books and courses is to take some of the randomness out of your random walk of discovery, to put some structure on your learning, to help you make sense out of the nonsense you experience, and to give you insight that will help you to accelerate your learning and career.

I have the talent to succeed

Everyone has strengths. We normally think of these as technical skills, and occasionally people skills. These are important and for the most part organizations measure and recognize these well. But you will also have some signature strengths that are about who you are. Martin Seligman developed a list of 24 signature strengths divided into six areas:[13]

- Wisdom and knowledge: creativity, curiosity, judgement, love of learning, perspective.
- Courage: bravery, perseverance, honesty, zest.
- Humanity: love, kindness, social intelligence.
- Justice: teamwork, fairness, leadership.
- Temperance: forgiveness, humility, prudence, self-regulation.
- Transcendence: appreciation of beauty and excellence, gratitude, hope, humour, spirituality.

You can test yourself to see where your signature strengths lie by trying the Values In Action Survey at the University of Pennsylvania Positive Psychology website.[14]

Too many organizations push in the wrong direction in developing talent. They focus on development areas (weaknesses) not on opportunities. No one succeeds by focusing on weaknesses. You would not ask an Olympic athlete to work on their weak synchronized swimming skills if their talent is weightlifting. A strong organization will have a mix of skills and specialities and will deploy them accordingly.

The accountable mindset requires recognizing your signature strengths, as well as your technical skills. And then you have to find or create the environment where those strengths can flourish and you can build on them and develop more strengths.

Develop your accountability mindset[15]

Accountability is not one of those mysterious qualities, like charisma, that pops out of the ether or is coded into your DNA. Like most things, you can develop accountability with practice. As with anything new, at first it will feel awkward. In time, it should become as natural as breathing.

Below are seven routines to help you build your accountability mindset. Do not try them all at once. Try one that makes most sense to you, and turn that into a routine habit over a few months. Then take another, and then another. Day to day, no one will notice the difference. Within two years, you can have worked a transformation.

Read through each routine, and then pick on one to work on:

- Celebrate success.
- Face the brutal truth, and learn from it.
- Learn from others.
- Look to the future.
- Learn, don't judge.

- Mind your language.
- Choose your reactions.

As you look at these routines, several will sound familiar by now: most of the routines appear elsewhere in this book as ways of developing other mindsets. They are powerful routines, so use them. Here, the routines are focused specifically on helping you to grow your accountability mindset.

Celebrate success

Any mindset is about habit. Our minds become used to reacting in certain ways. This can be harmful when it leads to addictive behaviour, from drugs to drink and beyond. You can also turn habit to your advantage. The best place to start is to focus on positive habits. If you try to eliminate the negatives by tackling them head on, then you are in for a painful struggle that is hard to win. If you focus on the positive habits, then the positive will swamp the negative. So accountability does not start with the burden of taking responsibility for failure. It starts with the positive of taking responsibility for success.

Celebrating success is not about feeling smug and patting yourself on the back. It is a practical tool to learn and grow in two easy steps:

- Step one: recognize what you have done well today, this week or this month. Even on a bad day, find the silver lining to your cloud. You can do this by thinking about your successes, or you can keep a journal to record your successes. As time goes by, you will see how much you achieve.

- Step two: take one or two of your successes and ask what you did to make them a success. This is where you really develop accountability. You recognize that success was not a random stroke of luck. It was the result of things you did well. Once you know why you succeed, you can start to do more of the same. Build on that. Know your strengths and play to them: make sure you find roles that use your strengths, and build a team that is strong where you are not so strong.

Slowly, you will learn to do this simple reflection after every event – after each meeting, ask yourself: what went well? Why? What could I have done even better? Too often, we only reflect on when things go wrong, which means we never learn from success. Learn from success to be more successful.

Face the brutal truth, and learn from it

This is the flip side of celebrating success. We all have setbacks, every day. When something goes wrong it is easy to dismiss it: it was the fault of someone else, or of external events or luck. That is classic victim mentality: believing that we are not in control of our destiny. However much someone else may have let you down, you should still reflect on what you did (or didn't) do to let that happen.

When coaching people, I find it is standard for clients to get upset about how they have been let down by colleagues who are unreliable, idle, deceitful or dishonest. Of course, the client believes that he or she is honest, hard working, loyal and reliable. We have to accept that other people are not perfect, nor are we. They have other priorities. And, of course, we like to believe we could never be seen negatively by anyone else. So it helps if you can coach yourself through setbacks. Here is how:

- Blame everyone else. Emotionally, you need to get this off your chest. Vent and rage about the 'slings and arrows of outrageous fortune'.[16] Using reason to deal with anger is like fighting fire with fuel: entertaining, but dangerous.

- Ask why. Why did things go wrong, why did they behave that way? To start with you will still vent: 'Because they are dishonest low life...' That is classic victim mindset: blaming the world. Try to look at it through the other person's eyes. There will be a reason they let you down or crossed you. In the end, there will be a reason that you let them behave that way. This is the critical step: recognize that you let them behave in a way that hurt you. Once you understand this, you can look at a positive way forward.

- Ask: what could I have done differently? Even if they were dishonest, then what could you have done instead? Could you have dealt with different people, got more support, kept closer tabs on progress, talked to them more often?

- What will I try next time? The emphasis here is on trying new tactics. Do not expect to wave a magic wand: you have to try different approaches and then find out what works for you. When you find a success, you can start reflecting on that and learning from it.

In practice, most of us are poor at learning from success: we assume that our success is natural. For the best leaders, their most intense learning comes from their most intense failures. Don't sulk over setbacks: learn from them. Use each setback to make yourself stronger.

Learn from others

The victim mindset is always judging others. Often this is judging colleagues negatively when they let us down. That does not help. Equally unhelpful is judging colleagues who are successful. That is a good way to make yourself feel inferior and helpless.

Stop judging people. Instead, learn from them. Learning from personal experience is powerful but painful. It is also slow. A quicker way to learn is by watching your peers, bosses and colleagues. One leader remarked on being astonished at a lecture where someone copied his own phrases, gestures and intonation.[17] But he then realized that he had causality the wrong way round: he was listening to his old boss. He had unconsciously learned to copy the habits of his boss.

You can learn from others without thinking. To start with, you may want to make this a conscious habit. Like learning from success or learning from setbacks, you can keep a learning journal. Or you can use five minutes near the end of the day (when waiting for a train or sitting in a car, perhaps) to do some structured reflection. Start by reflecting on three simple questions:

- What have I seen others do well or poorly: what can I learn from that?
- What have I done well and what can I learn from that?
- What could I do differently or better in future to deal with challenges?

Once you switch from judging and blaming to learning, you are on the road to growth and accountability.

Look to the future

This is a key mindset to use in the heat of the moment when things are going wrong. The victim mindset resorts to variations of the blame game: analysing what went wrong, spreading blame, justifying their own actions. None of this helps the situation. It makes it worse: once one person starts the blame game, everyone else joins in. It becomes like a game of pass the parcel, where the parcel is a bomb. No one wants to be left holding the parcel of blame.

The best leaders look to the future when things are tough. Two examples will make the point:

- You are in a heated discussion. The victim mentality is to prove that you are right and they are wrong. Indignant self-righteousness may make you feel good, but it does not move things forward. It is better to win a friend than win an argument. Once you have both calmed down, you will be in a better position to find a way forward. In the heat of the moment, ask yourself: 'Where do I want the other person to be at the end of the conversation? And how can I get him or her there?' Do you really want them to feel resentful that you have battered them and cornered them? Or do you want them to be willing to work with you?

- A crisis has blown up. No one is quite sure what happened or who is responsible. The first heat-seeking missiles have been launched as team members start the blame game. The victim mindset launches a few anti-missile missiles, and a few outbound missiles for good measure. The leader mindset ignores the blame game and sees a chance to take control, make a difference and to shine. The leader does not ask 'What went wrong?' Instead, the leader asks: 'What do we have to do to move forward and fix the crisis?'

If your reflex thought is to ask 'How can we move forward?' then you are thinking like the best leaders.

Learn, don't judge

The accountable mindset is not judgemental. This sounds odd: surely, if we are accountable we are always judging how we are doing? The problem with judging is that it can very quickly become a victim mindset that stops you moving forward. Try answering the two questions below:

Q1: when do you apply for a new role?

A: I am 100% ready for the new role

B: I am 50% ready for the new role and will learn the rest in post

C: I am 10% ready but the role looks great so I will go for it

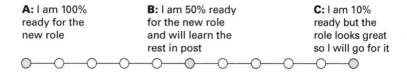

Q2: how do you react if you do not get the role?

A: I was not ready or good enough

B: How can I do better next time?

C: They made a big mistake

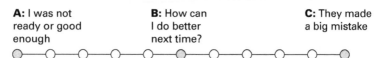

If you answered close to A on either answer, then your judgement is holding you back. First, no one is ever 100 per cent ready to step up to a big new role: there is always an element of the unknown that you have to discover. If you judge yourself too much, you will never have the confidence to progress. And if you are rejected, then an A-type answer sets you back: it will confirm to you that you are not good enough and will knock your confidence even more.

The C-type answers show the opposite problem: a complete lack of judgement. And even when such people are rejected, they simply believe that the selection panel made a mistake. In other words they adopt an aggressive form of the victim mentality: they blame others.

Qualitative research indicates that there is a gender bias here.[18] Females tend to answer closer to A, while males answer closer to C. In other words, men are more ready to go for it when only partly ready, blag their way in and hope to learn fast in the role. Women may be more honest and critical about their abilities, which is not always to their advantage.

The accountable and growth mindset avoids the judgement extremes. Instead it is focused on capacity to learn: to learn the job in role, rather than waiting to be 100 per cent ready and to learn how to improve after any setback.

Mind your language

This is about controlling your self-talk. We have looked at this in some detail before. Here are some of the power words to look out for: *never, impossible, always, everyone, must, should, can't, mustn't.*

The best leaders struggle with the English language: they seem not to understand the word 'no' and they appear never to have heard of the word 'impossible'. As my best sales mentor once told me: 'A no is simply a prelude to a yes.' Never accept a 'no' unless you want to accept defeat. Leaders know that 'no' is a no-no.

When you hear yourself use the power words: stop. Then challenge yourself with some basic questions:

- Why is this impossible, or never or always or why should I?

- What is the ideal outcome I would like here?

- How can I move towards the ideal outcome?

Language shapes our thoughts and beliefs.[19] If we let the power words go unchallenged, then those thoughts become our beliefs over time. If we challenge ourselves, then we open up new worlds of opportunities and new and better ways of thinking.

Choose your reactions

We are accountable for how we feel and how we react. This is a level of accountability that many people struggle with, in practice if not in theory.

If someone is being offensive to you, slighting you and undermining you, then you have the right to feel upset and annoyed. But there is no law saying that you have to be upset and annoyed. That is your choice. Many of our reactions are hard-wired and unthinking: the fight, flight or freeze syndrome of any animal in a corner. The way to deal with negative feelings is the same as the way to deal with negative thinking, as outlined in Chapter 4:

- Recognize your feelings and that you can choose them.

- Challenge your feelings: is that how you want to feel and be seen?

- Follow the example of your best role model: how would they behave?

The theory is easy, the practice is hard when you are in a tight corner. In practice, each leader has their own way of dealing with these moments of truth. One imagines the other person in a pink tutu: it is hard to get angry with an overweight 55-year-old when you see him in a pink tutu. Other low, but effective, techniques include:

- Imagine that you are a fly on the wall: observe yourself and how you would like to be seen.

- Ask yourself what impression you want to make on anyone watching you.

- Count to three before replying.

- Take a deep breath and relax.

- Retreat to a happy and safe place in your mind: relax.

It does not matter what your method is, as long as you have one that works for you: it should give you space to react in the way you want to react, rather than letting instinct take over.

Summary

Identify what mindset you have – accountable, corporate or victim:

- Accountable: control your destiny and shape the world.
- Corporate: perform within a framework, cog in the machine.
- Victim: helpless in the face of the world.

Core beliefs of the accountable mindset:

- I control my own destiny.
- I am accountable for what happens to me.
- I am accountable for my own feelings.
- Challenges are an opportunity to learn and grow.
- I see others as role models, not competitors.
- I have the talent to succeed.

Develop your accountability mindset:

- Celebrate success and learn from it: always ask why things went well.
- Face brutal facts and learn from them: don't blame, see the world through others' eyes.
- Learn from others: borrow their experience, both good and bad.
- Look to the future: don't get sucked into the blame game.
- Learn, don't judge: avoid being too self-critical and knocking your confidence.
- Mind your language: challenge negative and absolute self-talk.
- Choose your reactions: know you have a choice and choose well.

Collaborative mindset

Succeed through others

The days of heroic leadership are over. Success comes with and through others. The collaborative mindset is about learning how to gain the trust and respect of willing followers, without chasing popularity.

How many productive working hours are there in a day? This has become an ever-more pressing question as work becomes longer and more intense. There is a limit to how much more work we can squeeze into any 24 hours.

The correct answer to the question is clearly not 24. It is: 'As many hours as you want.' Individually, we can only work so much. But as a team, the number of hours is limited only by the size of our team. If we are to succeed, we cannot do so alone because we cannot work more than 24 hours a day. If we are to succeed, we have to succeed through others.

If we have to work together, that raises questions about *how* we work together. One way of looking at how we work with our peers is in the diagram overleaf. Where do you come out on the spectrum?

How do you relate to your colleagues?

I want to be
liked by
my peers

I have to
compete with
my peers

Both answers are common, plausible and justifiable. But neither represent the collaborative mindset of the best leaders. Let's look at each in turn.

I want to be liked by my peers. Who doesn't want to be liked? Few people try to be disliked. Socially, popularity is attractive. In business, however, it leads to weakness. The easy way to popularity is to compromise: accept the wishes and excuses of your team and your peers. Table 6.1 shows the differences between a manager who wants to be popular and one who wants to be effective. The effective manager not only achieves more, but in the long term attracts the best team. Weak staff are attracted to weak managers; strong staff are attracted to strong managers.

Table 6.1 Popular versus effective managers

Popular manager	Effective manager
Makes life easy for the team	Sets high standards
Solves all the team's problems for them	Coaches the team to help them solve their own problems
Sets easy goals	Sets stretching goals
Socializes with the team	Works with the team
Accepts excuses	Expects performance

I have to compete with my peers. This is true. Organizations are set up for conflict. This comes as a surprise to business gurus who like to think that organizations work harmoniously for a common goal. It is no surprise to anyone who has battled over budgets, argued over promotions and fought for resources. Priorities are set and resources allocated through competition between departments, all acting within a broad strategic framework. Competition can be healthy or unhealthy. Here are two forms of unhealthy competition:

- *The politician*: always happy to spread a little poison, create doubts and to brief against you. They want to weaken everyone else so that they look good by comparison: that in itself is a damning indictment of their true capability. They gain few allies because no one trusts them. When you hear a colleague malign another, do you trust them or do you wonder what they are saying about you behind your back? Because few people trust them, they remain weak and rarely go far. But they cause damage.

- *The autocrat*: autocrats can be successful in their own way. They are the power barons who run their own show, and even the CEO finds it hard to influence them. They may fiercely protect their own team, but they expect 100 per cent loyalty. And if you are not on their side, expect no mercy. They are not working for the greater good. They are working for themselves.

So what does healthy competition and collaboration look like? It is time to revisit the trade-off we saw at the start of the chapter, but with one vital addition:

How do you relate to your colleagues?

| I want to be liked by my peers | I need the trust and respect of my peers | I have to compete with my peers |

The sweet spot for working with peers is neither competing nor seeking popularity. It is about being trusted and respected. Think of your own career, and of the bosses who have helped you most to grow and develop. The chances are that you trusted and respected them. This is confirmed by previous research,[1] which showed that one of the most important things followers wanted from leaders was honesty. Digging further showed that honesty meant being able to trust and respect the boss. It was also the most divisive leadership quality. Bosses who were not trusted were slated for every other leadership quality: motivation, decisiveness, judgement and more. To be seen as a good leader, you have to be trusted. If you have ever worked for a boss you do not trust, you will understand why this is important.

The single best predictor of whether the boss was seen to be any good was this one: 'My boss cares for me and my career (agree/disagree).' Bosses who scored well on this, scored well across the board. Bosses who scored poorly on this, struggled elsewhere. If there is only one thing you do, show that you care for your team.

Time and again our leadership panel came back to the need for a great team, which several of them referred to as the hardest skill. Why is collaboration so important and so difficult for leaders? It is important and difficult for the best leaders for the same reason: the best leaders are disrupters.

If a leader is to be truly disruptive, then he or she cannot change the world alone. You have to build a team: behind every great leader there is a great team. The myth of the great leader changing the course of history was always a myth. Behind every giant of history, such as Napoleon or Churchill, you will find exceptional leaders at every level achieving exceptional things. The generals needed Napoleon, but Napoleon needed the generals: collaboration. As the world becomes more complex, with global supply chains where everyone depends on everyone else, the need for teamwork grows ever larger.

If a leader is disruptive it makes teamwork not only more important, it makes it more difficult: 'A good leader is competitive and will want to beat others. But a great leader will see that they are all working to the same goal.'[2] Anyone who has worked their way up through an organization knows that they are competing and collaborating with their peers all the time. Those conflicting instincts do not magically evaporate when you enter the C-suite.

Finally, the problem of the disruptive leader is knowing what sort of team to create. Most of us like to be in the company of people like ourselves. Our social instincts are poor business instincts. At work, a good team is not like us. Think of a truly disruptive leader who is ready to challenge the system, make radical change and is focused on the five-year horizon. If that leader hires 50 people who are just like that, you have a recipe for total chaos: nothing will be done because everyone will be too busy challenging each other and disrupting the system. Teams have to be balanced. A team full of extroverts is a nightmare: everyone will spend their whole time talking over everyone else. A team meeting of introverts will echo to the sound of silence.

A great leader is like the guru who sees the future and sets the direction. Gurus are rarely great managers. Behind the guru you need a small army of kommisars who make sure the trains run on time, the bills get paid and the staff turn up. Great leaders may lead the revolution, but you need great managers to run the world before and after the revolution. The trick is that in a world that is in permanent revolution, you need the gurus and komissars doing a double act to change and maintain the world at the same time.

Succeeding together

Success is a team effort, from top to bottom. Here is the story of Mike Tobin, recent CEO of Telecity:

I first became a managing director when I was 21. I made so many mistakes, shouting at people. I went to Denmark. I was working late and I was the only person left in the building. Then I heard the noise of a hoover cleaning, and it came closer. Then the cleaner came into my office. I said: 'Look, I'm working hard and do not want to be disturbed. Could you come back later?'

And he said, 'You're new. But I rely on you to get it right so you make the sales and keep me in my job. And you rely on me to make your room spotless so it can impress your clients. So I rely on you to do my job, and you rely on me to do your job.' So respect everyone you meet, especially on day one.

Teamwork is much talked about and greatly valued. It is a standard item in appraisals. It makes regular appearances in CEO speeches. Although the rhetoric is long, the practical advice is short. How do you work with people who are not like yourself? The standard answer is to send people to a conference room and put them through half a day of Myers–Briggs Type Indicator (MBTI) training.[3] This will put people into boxes according to their style, which might be summarized as INTJ or some other four-letter abbreviation. MBTI makes team members aware of – and to value – different styles. But it is not satisfactory because:

- MBTI does not tell you how to work with people unlike you.

- Becoming an expert at using MBTI takes years, which destroys its purpose: managers need tools they can use now.

- MBTI pretends that all styles are fine: it is non-critical, which is smart if you want to sell MBTI programmes to everyone. But anyone who has worked for a psychopath will know that not all styles are fine.

- People should not be put in boxes until they are dead.

When we start our careers and we are asked to do something, our natural reaction is to think 'How do I do this?' Leaders think differently. They do not ask 'How do I do this?' they ask 'Who can do this?' or at least 'Who can help me?' The transition from 'how' to 'who' is the key transition from worker to leader.

In this chapter we explore how you can move from 'how' to 'who'. The good news is that the collaborative mindset translates into a series of specific skills that anyone can learn and use.

We will look at four main themes:

- Build your influence across the organization.

- Build your team.

- Maintain and grow your team.

- Be a partner, not a child.

Build your influence across the organization

For some managers, teamwork means 'do as I tell you or you are not a team player'. In the old world of command and control, managers could get away with that attitude. Old-world management was about making things happen through people you controlled. New-world management is about making things happen through people you do not control, and you may not even like. We have to persuade peers in other departments, and possibly in other organizations, to help us if we are to achieve our goals. We have no formal power over them. So how do you make people help you when you do not control them? Welcome to the world of influence.[4] Control was the key skill in the old world of work; influence is the key skill in the new world of work.

Think of the most influential and effective managers in your organization. The chances are that they have influence that goes beyond their formal scope and power. They make things happen through a network of trust and support. Put the other way round, no one wants to support someone they do not trust. Building trust takes time and is not easy.

The best way to not build trust is to say: 'Trust me.' Here is a classic example: 'OK, John, I'm a straight sort of guy... be kind to me... of course I'm an honest sort of a bloke.'[5] How far would you trust this person? Would your trust rise or fall when you find out that this was Tony Blair explaining the absence of weapons of mass destruction following his decision to invade Iraq?

Outlined below are three ways to build trust with someone:

- Listening: the art of alignment.
- Building credibility: no surprises.
- Making it easy: reducing risk and the art of incremental commitment.

Listening: the art of alignment

The best leaders have two ears and one mouth. And they use them in that proportion: they listen at least twice as much as they talk. Most of us feel that we are not listened to or understood properly. When someone takes time to listen, they are quietly flattering us by investing time with us. Do some listening research: go to a coffee bar and watch two people gossiping. Normally, one will be holding court while the other listens. All the listener has to do is to look interested and occasionally say things like, 'Really?!... She said what?!... He didn't, did he?' This prompts the talker to open up even more. Back at work, the more you listen, the more you will understand what your colleagues really think, and what they hope and fear. They are giving you the raw material of influence: information.

One of the most effective influencers I worked with was a paradox. She had no charisma, she was dull and unimaginative and was never at risk of having an original idea. And clients loved her. One day, I found out why. I saw her listening to a client at 11 am. At 7.30 pm, she was still listening to him. By the end of the day, the client had poured his heart out to her. In her words: 'Only when he had emptied his brain, could I start filling it with my ideas – which I was able to present to him as his ideas.'

Listening helps you in several ways, because it:

- flatters the other person;
- lets you build an emotional bond with them;
- helps you understand what they are thinking;
- enables you to present your ideas in a way that aligns with what they need and want.

Listening by itself is not enough. Listening to someone in a pub or bar is a good way to sustain friendship. But we all have friends who we would not trust at work: good friends are not always reliable colleagues. So we need to do more. Above all, we have to show that we can do as we say.

Build credibility: no surprises

Credibility is like a vase. It takes time to build and is easy to break. Once broken, it is hard to repair and never fully recovers. At its heart, credibility is about doing what you say you will do. Few of us go out to deceive by saying one thing and doing another. But even without deception, there will be some people you trust more than others. So why is there often a gap between what we say and what we do?

The first problem is what we say. What we say and what the other person hears may be quite different. It is natural, but dangerous, for us to use weasel words when we are in doubt. Here are some weasel words that we use to hedge our commitments:

- I will try...
- I hope...
- I think...
- I intend...
- I will work towards...

Now turn the tables. When your boss says he or she will try, or hope or intends to work towards your bonus or promotion, we hear a commitment. It sounds like the bonus is in the bag. When your boss comes back and says, 'I tried, but...' you will feel let down. The credibility of your boss will have gone down as fast as your hopes of a nice holiday. Politicians are past masters at not making commitments. Instead of saying, 'We will...' they say odd things like, 'We have an aspiration to...' When it does not happen they can say they never promised it: an aspiration is not a goal or a commitment. Then they whine that no one trusts them.

Credibility starts with knowing what commitments you are making. It does not matter how carefully you pitched something, if the other person thinks you made a promise, then you have made a promise. This means that you must be brutally clear in what you say: avoid the weasel words. If there is doubt about being able to deliver on a project or a bonus or anything else, say so early and say so clearly. Lay out exactly what the doubts are. Agree the conditions on which success depends. And then go on reminding everyone about those doubts and conditions. This avoids the problem of surprises. A surprise is like dropping your vase of credibility from a height: you will be lucky if it survives. Most of us like to avoid difficult conversations, but it is better to have a difficult conversation early about expectations than an even more difficult conversation later about results.

The second problem with credibility is what we do. The aphorism that the path to hell is paved with good intentions is on the mark[6] – good intentions are not enough: we have to deliver results.

Another aphorism says it all: hell is full of good meanings, but heaven is full of good works. There are always reasons why we cannot deliver, or we have to deliver late, or deliver not quite the quality that was expected. For example, schools are used to all the homework excuses:

- The dog/cat/goldfish ate my homework.
- I've left it at home/on the train/on the moon.
- My computer/printer/house crashed.
- I/my mum/aunt/parrot was ill.
- It clashed with other assignments/sport/volunteering/saving the world.

These are about as credible as the reasons your builders and colleagues give for delays and disasters. We've heard them all before and do not believe them. But we also know from bitter experience that when we are let down, it can have a knock-on effect: we then let down someone else.

The antidote to such a surprise is the difficult conversation held early. As soon as you know there is a risk that you cannot deliver, then say so. Be clear about the nature of the risk and what you will do to mitigate the risk.

Credibility means doing what you say, always. It is about small things as well as big. If you promise to send an e-mail with some details, send it. The moment you let someone down, you lose credibility.

Make it easy: reducing risk and the art of incremental commitment

Let us return to trust and the stranger in the street. We trust the stranger to give us directions (sometimes) but we would be fools to trust them with our wallet, passport, phone and credit card details (normally). If we want someone to trust us, we have to build trust in stages.

Trust and betrayal

Intelligence agencies are masters at building trust with foreigners they want to recruit to their cause. Helping a foreign intelligence agency means you will probably be betraying your country. That is high risk. Here is how they go about building trust with a target:[7]

- Arrange a meeting, with the cover as a journalist, analyst, investor etc.

- Listen in order to find out their motivations. Flatter them to make them feel wanted. They will want to reciprocate your generosity in recognizing their hitherto unrecognized genius and insight.

- Arrange a follow-up that requires a small commitment from them: build the idea of reciprocity and commitment from the start. Do something small for them in return. Start with low or no risk: what is risky about sharing your views with a potential investor in your country?

- Over time, slowly increase what you ask and what you give: build commitment in small steps. Don't ask them for the nation's battle plans in your first meeting. If you have understood their real motivations, then money is unlikely to be their main driver. Recognition, revenge, profile, feeling important and wanted are all usable motivations.

- At some point, the target will cross the invisible line of no return: they will have given too much information and will know it. Psychological dominance has been achieved by the agency.

The agency is using all the tools you need to use to build trust: listening, flattery, incremental commitments, reciprocity and working on people's real motivations. If being a mid-level manager seems boring, then think of yourself as a spy building your covert network of support: it will make the humdrum of everyday work feel more entertaining.

The three principles behind 'make it easy' are:

- *Minimize risk and, at least initially, effort.* We are all risk averse, to some extent. The more stress we experience, the more risk averse we become.[8] Specifically, fear of losses have up to twice the power of desire for gains.[9] We will work hard to avoid a loss. In one experiment, a group of teachers in Chicago Heights were paid a bonus up front and were told they would have to pay it back if they did not meet targets. Another group of teachers were told they could earn a bonus in future if they hit targets. The fear of loss drove the first group of teachers to better performance than the potential bonus for the second group.[10] The message is simple: if you want people to work with you, make sure it is not risky and it is not difficult.

- *Reciprocity.* We are taught from an early age to give as well as take: people who never give are seen as Scrooges and outcasts. The power of reciprocity has been shown many times over. In one experiment a student showed people an art exhibition. At the end, the student had to sell some raffle tickets. In half the cases the student bought a soft drink for the target during the tour, in the other half the student did nothing. Buying a soft drink paid for itself many times over in raffle tickets at the end.[11]

  This implies that we should be generous: help others and they will help us. But unlimited generosity is unwise: you will be taken for granted. Apply the reciprocity principle in full: if you get nothing in return, then stop giving. This is equivalent to the winning strategy in game theory: tit for tat. Extensive research shows that this works in everything from international relations, through to prisoner's dilemma and human and other animal behaviour.[12]

- *Incremental commitment.* This is an extension of reciprocity. Do not give everything away to start with, and do not ask for everything. Consultants are good at using this principle. They will offer to do an initial scoping or analysis phase for you at low cost, or sometimes even for free. That seems like a low-cost and low-risk commitment, because you can always kick them out at the end of their scoping phase. But when the time comes, you find they are embedded in the organization, they know all the issues and just happen to have the team that can solve all your problems. A small early commitment suddenly becomes a big commitment.

As you build influence across your organization there is one more art to master. It is one that works with all people at all levels: flattery.

The art of flattery

How many people think they are paid, promoted, recognized and valued too much? Not many. The sad reality is that organizations are full of exceptional people who are not recognized, valued or even used as they should be. To spend years being overlooked and undervalued is an exercise in eternal disappointment. And then someone comes along and recognizes the full extent of your genius, humanity, wit and endeavour. What would you think of a person with such fine judgement? The chances are that you will form a favourable impression of this person.

The aphorism says that flattery will get you everywhere. It is an aphorism that looks like it is true. Research shows that flattery works even when it is insincere.[13] Even more surprisingly, there is no point at which flattery becomes counterproductive. To quote the *Economist*: 'Jennifer Chatman, of the University of California, Berkeley, conducted experiments in which she tried to find a point at which flattery became ineffective. It turned out there wasn't one.'[14] In a praise-starved world, people just cannot get enough praise. This is a very simple route to influence: use it.

You do not have to imitate a grovelling, bowing and scraping courtier in the dazzling world of Louis XIV, the Sun King. Here are some easy ways to flatter:

- *Listen and show interest*: you are investing your time in someone, which implies you think they have something worth saying. If in doubt, let people talk about their favourite subject: themselves. It is a source of endless fascination to them.

- *Seek advice*: this confirms to the subject that they are wise and valuable.

- *Agree*: agreeing with someone is low-grade flattery. If you hint that you had your doubts but now you agree, that is high-grade flattery. For instance: 'I was thinking that would be crazy, but now I realize it is brilliant!' This shows that your target is not only clever, but also has exceptional powers of persuasion and is generally great.

- *Conform*: show that you share similar values and tastes. Avoid competing. If you both like skiing, do not mention that you went to a better ski resort: be suitably impressed about where they went and how they fearlessly conquered the nursery slopes after just one week.

- *Appear reluctant to praise*: this makes the flattery appear more authentic. 'I don't normally say things like this, I really don't like passing judgement, but I have to say that presentation was stellar.'

- *Flatter in public*: praise someone in front of others. It is like cocaine for the ego: it delivers an immediate high.

Build your team

Collaboration is not just about working across the organization. It is about creating a high-performing team to support you. Behind every great leader lies a great team: 'The best leaders develop a strong team and let them fly. They do not look for yes people: they look for powerful people.'[15] Do not assume that the team you inherit is the team you need for the future. Any coach of any sports team knows that one of their main jobs is to find the right players for the right positions. The same goes for you: find the right people for the right roles on your team. Like the sports coach, you then have to train and develop them so they can achieve their full potential.

Building the right team is a balancing act. You have to balance four variables: skills, perspectives, styles and values. Balancing four things at the same time is like trying to juggle four balls at the same time, but less entertaining. You will never achieve perfect balance, and you do not need to. The logical consulting way of working out the balance of your team is to start with the strategy, design your organization structure and then look for the right people to fill each organization box.

Great leaders build their teams differently, in an illogical way that sends consultants and gurus mad. They start by looking at what talent is available. Then they work out how best to assign the talent, based on their differing strengths. If that leaves any glaring holes, then they try recruiting from outside: either poaching staff from other departments or poaching from competitors and the marketplace. The result is often a messy structure, but it works because it is based on great talent playing to their strengths. If in doubt, find the talent first and then worry about how to organize it.

This still begs the question: 'What is great talent and what is the right mix for my team?' The four variables you need to work on are skills, perspectives, styles and values:

- *Skills*. This is fairly self-evident, and most managers work on this well. If you run a business, you do not want to have only sales people or only accountants on your board. You need balance. This is easier said than done. There will always be more functions, skills and people who think they should be at the top table than there are seats available.

- *Perspectives*. The great dictators of history blaze an inglorious path for a while and then crash and burn, often at great cost to their own people. There are many reasons why they self-destruct, but one reason is that they tolerate no dissent. Theirs is the only voice they wish to hear. On a visit to North Korea, for example, if you see any propaganda picture of Kim Jong-un you will see all his cronies with notebooks open, ready to capture his pearls of wisdom.[16] Sustainable leadership depends on having different views and being open to challenge. As the proverb says: 'More than one bird sings in the forest.' Listen to them all. If you run a business, do you have business units, functions, geographies of customer groups at the top table? Or a mix of them? If you run a school, do you have year heads, subject heads or functions?[17] There is no single formula to solve this. In practice you have to decide where your priorities lie, and then organize around that. This means that, over the years, your organization will shift priorities, shift focus and shift form.

- *Styles.* Mention styles and most people think about MBTI. But MBTI only looks at eight possible styles. Humanity is more varied than that. Take a look at the list below, and then add some of your own choice style trade-offs:

  - Big picture versus detail.
  - Numbers versus words.
  - Morning people versus afternoon people.
  - Risk taking versus risk averse.
  - Controlling versus empowering.
  - Inductive versus deductive thinking.[18]
  - Ambitious versus cautious.
  - Competitive versus collaborative.

  The risk is that we recruit in our own likeness. If you are an ambitious, big-picture and risk-taking person you might like the company of people like yourself. But you probably need people around you who will work on the detail and can help you to avoid disaster by being more risk aware. The more different the styles are, the more painful it is to make the team work. Teams with the most diversity of style are often the highest-performing teams, provided you can help them to work together well.

- *Values.* After a long interview, the CEO relaxed. We chatted, and his guard was down: I had put my notebook away. He then casually reflected: 'I find I hire most people for their skills, and fire most for their values.' In that one throwaway remark, he had shown why many teams work or fail. Successful teams need strong values as much as strong skills: honesty, reliability, hard work and openness are better fuel for a team than pure technical skills. John Timpson, who ran a chain of shoe-repair shops, took this to its logical conclusion. He replaced the normal HR recruiting forms with a list of pictures of Mr Men.[19] If you were Mr Messy, Mr Fib, Mr Lazy or Mr Uppity, you would not get a job. Mr Helpful, Mr Tidy or Mr Cheerful were more likely to succeed. Timpson's insight is that you can always train for skills, but you cannot train for values.

When you build your team, recruit to values first, then worry about the skills.

Maintain and grow your team

The big trap is to 'get hung up on the official leadership and organization structure'.[20] Great leadership is not about pulling the levers and turning the dials on your organization chart. You have to unleash the energy of everyone who works for you: delegate like crazy, engage with them, support them and help them to grow. This is not old-style command and control. This is real collaboration and teamwork.

If you want teamwork, you have to help your team to work. We saw earlier that the one question that best predicts how your team will rate you is this: 'My boss cares for me and my career (agree/disagree).' Your starting point is to show that you care for your team. That means you have to invest time to understand each team member: what drives them, what their strengths are, what they hope for and how best to use them. Based on that, you have two critical activities as a collaborative team leader: to delegate and to coach.

Delegate

Weak managers do not delegate, and they have weak excuses for not delegating:

- I'm too busy.
- I can do it better myself.

- I can do it faster myself.
- The team is too busy already.
- My boss wants me to do it.

You can add other excuses you have heard. Behind all the excuses are two fears:

- The team is too good: they will show me up.
- The team is too bad: they will mess it up.

The best leaders delegate like crazy. This allows them to focus on the one or two things that are most important to them and that they are good at. By delegating so much they:

- Show they trust their team.
- Help their team to learn and grow.
- Find better solutions.
- Create more hours in the day.
- Achieve focus for themselves.

There are plenty of resources on the skills of delegating: the purpose of this book is to show that delegating is a vital part of the collaborative mindset.[21] When you face a new role, do not ask 'How shall I do it?' – ask 'Who can do it?' and then delegate as much as you can.

Coach

Coaching marches hand in hand with delegating. Leaders should be very good at delegating tasks downwards. Followers are often highly skilled at delegating problems back up. In the traditional world of command and control, the heroic leader has to act like Kim Jong-un and solve every problem personally. This shows that they are great and wise. It also shows that they do not trust their team, and it stops their team from learning and growing.

The collaborative mindset assumes that you do not have all the best answers. Instead, you focus on helping your team members to discover the best solution. The 'best' solution is not necessarily the textbook answer or whatever is in your head at the time. The best solution is one that your team members discover for themselves: if they think it is their solution they will be committed to it and will make it work, even if that means adapting it as they go along. If you reveal your best solution to them, then they have no reason to feel any commitment to it: they do not own your idea. Worse, they may feel it is not as good as their own idea, so they will happily sabotage yours.

The essence of coaching is to ask good questions and to listen. There are different structures and frameworks for doing this. The goal is not to become a professional coach: the idea is to have a way of helping your team to discover solutions that they own and will make work.[22]

Be a partner, not a child

The best leaders reach beyond the command and control mindset. They apply the collaborative mindset at all levels of the organization. This transforms relationships at all levels.

Hierarchies are based on the parent–child relationship.[23] This is far removed from the collaborative mindset. In a hierarchy, your parent–boss may be a good and caring parent, or abusive and neglectful. They have all the power, and we are put in the role of the child. We think we are quite able to cope by ourselves, thank you very much, and resent constantly being parented by our boss, however well meaning they may be. Not surprisingly, most of my coaching time is spent dealing with highly paid executives who resent this relationship and want to work out how to deal with their parent–boss.

The collaborative mindset busts this relationship. Instead of parent–child, it creates a partnership, or what Eric Berne called an adult to adult relationship.[24]

An adult conversation

I wanted to start a bank. I needed a billion dollars of capital to start it. I checked my bank account. I was some way short of the necessary. So I had to find a partner to stump up a billion.

I found myself in discussion with Halifax (now Lloyds-HBOS). Eventually, I sat down with the CEO, James Crosby. I knew this was important, because we were sitting on sofas facing each other. Really important discussions do not take place at the table, they take place in an informal setting. 'So,' said James after a while, 'how much will this cost?'

'About a billion, but it's mainly success capital – regulatory capital.'

James did not blink an eyelid, 'Dollars or pounds?'

I had been working in dollars, but decided to hike my budget by 50 per cent: 'Pounds', I replied as casually as possible.

We then agreed to get his team working on the details. And I realized that until that point I had not shown him any papers. If I had done that, I would have been like any other junior person or sales person coming to pitch an idea. He would have been judging me rather than working with me. That is not helpful. Partners pitch PowerPoint to each other as much as presidents and prime ministers do: never. If you want to be a partner, you have to act as a partner. As an outsider with no money I had no right to think of myself as his partner: but if you act the role, you will be treated accordingly.

Have courage: act the part.

The partner relationship recognizes that each partner simply has different roles, and that you have to work together to make the most of your respective strengths and roles. The hierarchy will re-establish itself when it comes to appraisal time: even that can be turned into a discussion about learning and development rather than the praising and chiding of a parent to a child.

This collaborative way of thinking also works with your team. The traditional mindset will focus on monitoring, controlling, directing, deciding, reviewing. If you manage professionals, you will know that they hate to be treated this way. They want to be trusted and supported, not controlled and monitored. The collaborative mindset focuses on coaching, delegating, supporting and growing your team. Even professionals will accept that sort of management, and it will bring out the best in them.

Summary

The collaborative mindset is about being trusted and respected, not about popularity. Collaboration is key because managers no longer control all the resources they need for success. The collaborative leader will focus on four activities:

- Build your influence across the organization:
  - Listen. Use the secret weapon of all the best sales people and leaders: your ears.
  - Build credibility. Do as you say, set clear expectations, avoid surprises.
  - Make it easy for others to collaborate: reduce perceived risk and effort, engage incrementally.

- Build your team: do not blindly accept the team you inherited. Achieve balance across:
  - Skills: recruit to potential as well as achievement.
  - Perspectives: avoid a company of 'yes men'.
  - Styles: different styles are the most productive, but hardest to manage.
  - Values: you can train skills, but you cannot train values. Know what you want.

- Maintain and grow your team:

- Delegate: stretch and test the team with challenging work, not just the routine.
- Coach: do not let the team delegate every problem upwards to you.

- Be a partner, not a child:
  - Act the part with senior management. Step up.

Growth

Adapt to thrive

What works today may not work tomorrow – or in another place.
Merely very good leaders can become prisoners of their own
success: they cling on to a success formula until the world changes
and they become irrelevant. The very best leaders are always
learning, always growing and always adapting. They have the
courage to move on. The growth cycle is a simple way for anyone
to keep learning and growing.

The modern City of London is full of medieval guilds, or livery
companies, which you can join if you want to do good works and
have the occasional dinner in a magnificent hall. The livery companies have an order of precedence, based on when they first started.
The earliest started in the 14th century. Here are a few of the livery
companies you can join:

- wax chandlers (wax candle makers);
- tallow chandlers (tallow candle makers);
- girdlers (sword belt and dress belt makers);
- armourers and brasiers;
- coopers (making wooden barrels);
- bowyers (longbow makers);
- fletchers (arrow makers).

In the 15th century, the longbow makers had a vital role to play in
national defence: the longbow was England's secret weapon that
led to stunning victories against England's long-standing ally and
foe, France.

There is not much call for bowyers or fletchers nowadays, although their trades live on as common family names. You can also find plenty of Chandlers and Coopers, whose families can ultimately trace their way back to these ancient trades.

Today's vital skills are tomorrow's historical curiosity. The pace of change is as fast as it ever was. The mythical 'digital divide' is meant to separate a generation that gets the internet and social media, and the generation that has been left behind. Think of the jobs of your grandparents, and how they went about them: it is like entering a different world. Our grandchildren will also judge our ways of working as bizarre and antiquated. Today's leading-edge technology will become as relevant as that of the tallow chandlers.

If we are to survive and thrive in our careers, we have to learn new skills. Otherwise we will end up on the scrap heap.

Changing worlds

The cage went down from the brisk bright outside air to the dark and stuffy confines of the mine 300 metres below ground. We boarded a rickety rail trolley and went two kilometres out under the sea to the coalface. Getting off the rail track, we walked into ever smaller passages: first stooping, then on hands and knees. Finally, we found the coalface and had to get down on our elbows and knees to crawl along it. On one side a huge cutting machine hacked away the coalface, inches from us. On the other side, pit props held up the roof. As they advanced, the roof behind them collapsed. The air was foul. By the time we got back up top, my lungs were full of black soot, which I kept coughing out for a week afterwards.

At the time, the miners were about to go on strike for a wage of £45 per week for face workers. Most people in the country thought that was outrageous and greedy. Most people in the country had never been down a mine. By the time I came back to the surface, I was wondering why they wanted so little. It was dirty, dangerous work they were doing.

The mine was closed 15 years later. It was uneconomic. Most of the miners were still unemployed 15 years after the closure. These were proud people used to working hard. The only work around was stacking shelves for the unskilled, or finding new skills to work in an office. Hacking at coal does not give you the skills for pecking at a keyboard.

The miners were heroes left stranded by the tide of change. No matter how heroic or how hard our work may be, if we are to survive we have to adapt: learn new skills for new jobs, wherever they are.

This chapter covers three topics:

- Why a growth mindset is important.
- What stops us from growing: the prisons of our minds.
- How to build your growth mindset.

Why a growth mindset is important

There are three main reasons why we have to keep on learning and adapting:

- Today's skills will be less useful or relevant tomorrow.
- We will change employer several times in our career.
- The rules of survival and success change at each level of the organization.

Today's skills will be less useful or relevant tomorrow

We have already looked at how skills are changing all the time. Even where a job does not change, the skills required for it will change. There have been farmers since the dawn of civilization, but the job of farming has changed beyond all recognition.[1] Cows now prefer to be milked by robots than by humans because robots are flexible: the cows can be milked whenever they want.[2] Farmers are now tech literate; their most desired technologies include: GPS tractor steering to ensure straight plough lines; drones for assessing how much fertilizer to apply where; cow heat detection devices to manage pregnancy rates; combine yield meters to monitor, store and display grain yields; and smartphones for everything.[3] The days of the peasant ploughman and dairy maid have long gone.

Clearly, office jobs are changing all the time. Technology has changed the way we work, not always for the better. We are shackled by e-mail and mobile phones in a way we never used to be, but we are also enabled by the internet to do things we would never had done before. The bright side of technology is empowerment, access and productivity. The dark side are higher expectations, the threat of offshoring and automation, and being on 24/7. But we have no idea how our work in the next 20 years will change. If we cannot predict the future, then the only way to thrive is to adapt.

We will change employer several times in our career

There was a time, in a mythical golden age not long ago, when you might expect to start work with an employer and then receive a carriage clock from your grateful employer as you headed into retirement after 45 years of loyal service.

Across the Organisation for Economic Co-operation and Development (OECD), average job tenure varies from 8 to 13 years:[4] the more rigid the labour laws, the higher average tenure, which is offset by higher youth unemployment. In the United States, median job tenure is 4.4 years.[5] With increasing pressure on social security, today's entrants into the labour market can look forward to perhaps 50 years of employment. That means they are going to be switching employer many times across their career.

A new employer is not going to want someone with out-of-date skills. This truth has exposed many workers who acquired craft skills in an industry that disappeared or where the jobs were outsourced. In the UK, in 1842 68 per cent of jobs were in agriculture, fishing and manufacturing. In 2011, those industries occupied just 10 per cent of the workforce, while 81 per cent were in services.[6] Major employers have become minor employers in the last 50 years in the UK: shipbuilding, steel making, coal mining and garment making. If you were in a declining industry, you could not use your old skills for a new employer: you had to find new skills for your new employer.

Relying on one employer for a career is dangerous. The FTSE 100 was created in 1984: it comprised the best and strongest firms in the UK. In one generation, only 19 have stayed in the index all the time. All the others have been taken over or overtaken: 251 firms have been in and out of the index.[7] The United States displays equally creative destruction: only 15 of the top 100 firms from the original 1955 Fortune 500 remain in the top 100.[8] In advance, it is nearly impossible to tell which firms will flourish or flounder for an entire career of 40 plus years. Do not rely on your employer: rely on your employability.

The rules of survival and success change at each level of the organization

Earlier, you read that success at one level of an organization can be a barrier to success at the next level. Research shows why this is.[9] I asked leaders at different levels of organizations, what they expect of the best leaders at each level. Table 7.1 shows what they want.

Table 7.1 Expectations of leaders at each level of an organization

Top level	Middle	Front line
Vision	Ability to motivate others	Hard work
Ability to motivate others	Decisiveness	Proactivity
Decisiveness	Industry experience	Intelligence
Ability to handle crises	Networking	Reliability
Honesty and integrity	Delegation	Ambition

The rules of survival and success change as you progress. This is a disaster for someone who does not adapt. When you start your career, you probably have to learn a craft skill: trading, teaching, accounting or even the art of PowerPoint. You are not expected to change the world. But you are expected to work hard, be proactive and reliable, and be reasonably intelligent in how you deal with all the minor crises and setbacks that go with any job. You are also expected to be ambitious, both for yourself and for your employer: that is at the heart of high aspirations.

These expectations are completely different from a leader in the middle of an organization. You are still expected to work hard and be proactive and reliable like a front-line leader. But you have to layer on another set of skills, around managing people and organizations: motivating, networking, delegating and deciding. A front-line leader who relies on their original success formula of hard work and reliability is doomed to fail: they will fail not because they have suddenly become lazy and unreliable. They will fail because they have failed to adapt, failed to learn the new rules of success. In most cases, no one tells them that the rules have changed, and little training is on hand to help you. You have to pick it all up by osmosis, and many discover this when it is too late.

The butterfly leader

A butterfly goes through many life stages. Each looks quite unlike the previous one: egg to caterpillar to chrysalis to butterfly. The same animal takes on very different forms. The same is true of leaders. One career transition is not enough. The same person has to reinvent themselves repeatedly in order to blossom into an exceptional leader. You cannot stay the same: you have to transform yourself at each level of the organization: front-line, middle and senior leadership. The rules of survival and success change at each level, and you have to change with them.

At the top, suddenly you have to have vision. This takes us back to the idea of high aspirations. A vision is not something that a committee dreams up and then spends months arguing over the nuance of each word. It is a simple statement of where you want to get to. The best visions are no more than a story in three parts:

- This is where we are.
- This is where we are going.
- This is how we will get there.

And if you want to make your vision highly motivational, you add a fourth part:

- And this is your very important role in helping us get there.

If you can tell a story, you can create a vision. And if you can make it personal, relevant to each person you meet, then it is compelling. A vision based on customer delight, satisfaction or retention does not mean much to a janitor. But if the toilets are filthy, your clients will not be delighted: if you want to – you can make your vision relevant to everyone at every level. Craft a story that means something to everyone. A vision that is about maximizing shareholder value means a lot to executives whose bonuses are tied to shareholder value. It means not very much to the worker on the shop floor: it is just more meaningless jargon from the bosses.

Let us return to the butterfly. The butterfly goes through miraculous transformations. But the butterfly is still the same animal as the caterpillar. And so it is with the leader. The great top leader will still be the same animal as the exceptional front-line leader. The front-line leader will be developing the potential to transform and progress from the start. Learning the new role does not start when you arrive in the new role: it starts from day one. You may only run a team of three people, but even that should allow you to develop the skills of the top leader:

- Set a vision.
- Motivate your team.
- Be decisive.

- Handle crises.
- Be honest.

The true growth mindset is always learning, and always looking to the future: work out the skills you will need in the future and start learning them now.

The good news is that the growth mindset, like the other mindsets, is not about training to be a superhero. It is about doing some basic things very well. If you can do that, you will stand out from the rest of your peers. Despite all the hype around passion for excellence and being in search of excellence, often success comes from being less incompetent than your peers.

As you look at the expectations of good leaders at each level, you are not being expected to achieve greatness. You are expected to be professional. The expectations of a front-line leader look fairly low. But in reality, these expectations are a good way of sorting the best from the rest at an early stage. Around one-third of people at this level fail to meet each of these expectations (see Table 7.2). They are low hurdles over which many people fall. If you can jump these hurdles, you will be doing well.

Satisfaction ratings get lower with leaders as they progress. But the sense of delusion increases. Over 70 per cent of top leaders thought they were fairly good at motivating their teams. Only 37 per cent of their teams agreed. But few people dare to speak the

Table 7.2 Percentage of staff satisfied with leaders' skills at each level

Top level	Middle	Front line
Vision (61%)	Ability to motivate others (43%)	Hard work (64%)
Ability to motivate others (37%)	Decisiveness (54%)	Proactivity (57%)
Decisiveness (47%)	Industry experience (70%)	Intelligence (63%)
Ability to handle crises (56%)	Networking (57%)	Reliability (61%)
Honesty and integrity (48%)	Delegation (43%)	Ambition (64%)

truth to their boss, so the boss carries on in blissful ignorance. The growth mindset is more challenging: you always should be asking yourself how you can perform better and learn more.

In management there is ambiguity about what good performance really looks like, because there are so many ways of looking at performance. And feedback adds to the ambiguity, which means we do not get the feedback we need in order to improve. Sport is different: there is much less ambiguity about what good looks like. You win or lose. And the feedback is instant. In the words of Heath Monk, CEO of Future Leaders,[10] talking about an exceptional head teacher:

> He is so good at learning because he used to be a sportsman. In sports, you get instant feedback all the time. And there are no excuses. In golf, the ball is stationary: you can't blame anyone else. As a head he is always asking, 'How did I do, how can I do it better?' and then he acts on it. Most people are quite bruised, defensive and even insulted by feedback, even if they do not admit it in public. He was totally accepting of it: he saw it as the best way to raise his game.

Where sports people devote themselves to training, business people avoid it. This helps to explain why so many leaders get such poor ratings from their teams (see Table 7.2). Part of the problem is that training is seen as a sign of weakness: 'If I have to go on a course about motivating people, that shows I must be no good at motivating people.' The growth mindset takes the opposite approach: 'I am no good at this... yet.' For the growth mindset, training is the chance to build capability and perform better. For many of us, the growth mindset gets weaker as careers progress. In the early years of a career no one minds being told that they have a development opportunity – and being offered training. As years go by, managers become more defensive and more embarrassed about 'showing weakness' by going on training courses.

The best leaders display intense curiosity. They always want to learn and to grow. For instance, James Darley leads graduate recruiting for Teach First. Over 10 years, he transformed a small charity into the UK's largest graduate recruiter: it was unthinkable that a charity could outperform all the banks, consulting firms and other prestigious recruiters. But that is what he has done. At that point, you might relax with your leading market position. But this is what James is doing:

> I want to meet ASOS and find out why they are the leading retailer of clothing – because of their customer service – and I want to learn from that, to see how we can raise our customer service. We are already the only employer that does not screen people out. As soon as they start an application they get a phone call from us to see if they want help filling in the form. We are the only recruiter that selects people. Everyone else deselects people; they use screens to offboard people. We want to be better than that.

So when you get to number one, the best leaders do not ask: 'How can I stay here?' They ask: 'How can I do even better?' And they look anywhere and everywhere to find ways of reinventing themselves.

Table 7.3 is a crib to your 40-year career. I use it with newly minted graduates who find 40 years an unimaginable time frame. But it shows the butterfly effect: it shows how everything changes as you progress. Your role changes, your skills change and your time horizon changes. If you want to accelerate your career, learn the top skills as soon as you can. If you can see the world through the eyes of your bosses, if you understand how they think, then you can anticipate and respond to their needs better. By talking in their

Table 7.3 How leaders change by level

	Top level	**Middle**	**Front line**
Role	Take people where they would not have got by themselves	Make things happen through others who you may not control or like	Make it happen
Time horizon (max/min)	Five years/today	Six months/today	One month/today
Skills bias	People, strategy, engagement	People, politics	Technical

language, you will show that you are one of them. You will crack their code and join their club.

To paraphrase Charles Darwin: 'It is not the strongest of the species that survives, nor the most intelligent, but rather the one most adaptable to change.'[11]

What stops us growing: the prisons of our minds

The growth mindset is all about learning and adapting. At first sight, growth seems less demanding than other mindsets such as courage, resilience and high expectations. But in practice, the growth mindset is one that slowly disappears over time. Look at a toddler learning to walk. It will keep on falling over and keep on trying. It is resilient, it is determined to learn and to grow. But even at that young age it will start to show aversion to too much experimentation: unfamiliar foods are greeted with suspicion or outright rejection in favour of what they know they like. And by the time the toddler has become the grizzled corporate veteran, learning has gone out of the window.

We should want to grow and improve, but our minds get trapped in one or more of four prisons that stop us growing:

- The prison of success.
- The prison of the past.
- The prison of performance.
- The prison of fear.

These are deadly prisons because they are invisible prisons of the mind: we do not know that they are there and we do not know that they are trapping us inside. There are two keys to escaping the prisons. The first is to know they are there: if we don't know where they are we cannot escape them. The second key is to have some routines that keep us out of prison in the first place. This section looks at how you can spot your prison.

The prison of success

This is the gilded prison. The more successful we are, the stronger the prison walls become. If you become a CEO with a good track record, you will not take kindly to an expert coming along and telling you that you need to learn how to improve: your track record of reality always trumps theory. But then the world changes: you have to move from growing to cutting and suddenly you find yourself playing a lot of golf. If you cannot adapt, you leave.

We have seen how the rules of survival and success change throughout your career. You have to adapt to thrive. This is best illustrated by the lesson of the leader in the locker room. In many sports the best players rarely make the best coaches, and the best coaches were often pedestrian players. The switch from playing to coaching is the one that we all have to make when we progress into management.

Imagine a soccer player is asked to step up to coaching the team. So he is now playing and coaching. Recognizing his increased responsibilities, he now tries even harder on the pitch: running further, trying to make every tackle and every pass and to score every goal. And then he is fired, because the team is confused, demoralized and losing.

The job of the coach is not to run harder and make all the tackles and score all the goals. The job of the coach is to select the team, choose the tactics, understand the competition and develop the players. On match day, the nearest the coach gets to the pitch is the sidelines, where he can wave his arms, shout a lot and argue with the officials. Playing and coaching are different, and you have to adapt to the new role.

You are, hopefully, successful in your current role. If you want to escape your personal prison of success you need to start preparing for your next role. Understand what you will have to do and the skills you will need to learn. Start preparing and adapting now.

The prison of the past

Most people let themselves slowly fossilize. We do not even realize that we are getting set in our ways. As a test, think about your favourite music, films and books. If we associate music with good experiences, we store up emotional memories. These are precious, and we will keep on returning to them time and again. The ubiquity of personal music players shows how strong these connections are. The more we play our favourite music, the more we are encoding those memories and emotions.[12] But emotions are not a reliable way to remember or to learn. Research shows that emotion hinders observation: witnesses to crimes recall the weapon very clearly (that is the emotional part of the scene) but are often poor at recalling the criminal.[13] We are attached to the past, but the past is a poor guide to the future.

Different generations stick to different sorts of music. Many of our preferences are set before the age of 25 or 30, which gives bands a wonderful second lease of life in their fifties: by then their fans have grown older and more affluent and can afford the time and money to go to their concerts again. You do not have to listen to the latest boy band to show that you have a growth mindset. But if you are learning new skills, taking up new pastimes, pushing yourself into trying new things, then you not only have a growth mindset, you will probably also enjoy life more.

The prison of performance

Performance means different things to different people. Here is one version:

- Meet your targets.
- Stick to the process.
- Don't mess up.
- Give appraisals.
- Ensure compliance.
- Improve.

This may not be the most inspiring culture, but it is likely to be an effective culture. It will deliver and it will perform. But it may not learn or change or outperform very well. It is stable and steady, which is good if it is in a fairly stable and steady environment.

Table 7.4   Performance in different environments

Stable world	Dynamic world
Meet your targets	Outperform
Stick to the process	Focus on the goals, flex the process
Don't mess up	Try, learn, adapt
Give appraisals	Encourage development
Ensure compliance	Build commitment
Improve	Change

There is an alternative view of performance, as set out in Table 7.4 – see where you and your organization are.

Fundamentalists of the growth mindset will dismiss the stable world as a 'fixed' mindset and culture that they disparage.[14] But, in the right context, the fixed culture is exactly what is needed: it creates stability and certainty. If you are administering welfare payments, stability and certainty are keys to fairness. Welfare claimants need to know what to expect. If you are a regulator, then stability is important; you cannot flex the process and change things all the time, unless you are the sort of regulator that mysteriously gets very rich very fast. Then ambiguity is good and you can put it all down to having a growth mindset: you change the rules depending on who is paying you the most.

Most of the world is moving from being stable to being dynamic. This is where the performance mindset becomes a prison with a straightjacket. Performance requirements stop us moving, learning or improving. We get better and better at a way of doing things that is becoming increasingly irrelevant. Swathes of Western industry were decimated in the 1980s and 1990s by the Japanese. The Japanese were not low cost: anyone who has eaten in a Tokyo restaurant will wonder if they are buying the meal or buying the restaurant when the bill finally arrives. They succeeded in consumer electronics, cars, earth-moving equipment, office equipment and more because they changed the rules of the game. They did not just improve, they changed the rules.

For instance, Xerox was invincible in photocopying because it ruled the photocopy room. No one could compete because Xerox had all their customers tied into service leases, and they had all the technology and infrastructure. Canon changed the rules by focusing on distributed copying: they started the move to the small printers that you see on desks near you. They were small, cheap and although slow they were very convenient for printing out two or three sheets of paper. The central copying unit looked like a dinosaur in comparison. The performance mindset is married to the success model of the past, so it would look to improve print speeds on the big central copying machine. Performance might improve, but Xerox nearly went out of business.[15]

The performance prison is beguiling. Focus on performance sounds like what all managers should do. But in a dynamic world it risks making us redundant as competitors change the rules on us. The dinosaurs were staggeringly successful, until the climate changed.[16] We have to stay ahead. We cannot do that by trying harder and running faster. We have to get off the treadmill and buy a bicycle: change the rules so that they are in our favour. In the words of Andy Grove, CEO of Intel: 'Only the paranoid survive' let alone profit from the inevitable groundshifts in the world.[17]

Paranoia is one way to escape the prison of performance: the other is to learn to grow and adapt.

The prison of fear

This prison is nasty enough to be called a dungeon. We all know it is there, but we do not want to admit it. And we certainly do not want to go there. The prison of fear is the fear of failure, which even has its own name: atychiphobia.[18] To see how nasty this is, try calling someone a 'loser'. On second thoughts, if you value your career and your safety, do not try that particular exercise. No one wants to be branded a loser, or a failure. So we do not want to lose or to fail. But that prevents us from experimenting, trying new things, and learning from falling over and getting up again. Fear of failure stops us growing.

There are three sides to this prison: praise, perfectionism, competition:

- *Praise*. Training in fear starts early. Praise can be as damaging as criticism. Teachers know that if you praise the achievement of a small child, the child will keep on doing the same thing: that is how you get praised. If instead, the teacher praises the effort the child has put in, then the child will learn that effort gains praise. Effort is more likely to lead to growth and learning, rather than simply repeating what has worked before.[19] To knock down this wall, praise the effort not the achievement and recognize that this is how you can also grow.

- *Perfectionism*. This can be healthy: Michelangelo did not take any shortcuts in completing the Sistine Chapel or his other masterpieces.[20] Musicians need to perfect their craft. But there is a difference between high standards and extreme perfectionism (normal versus neurotic).[21] Neurotic perfectionism is black-and-white thinking. It accepts nothing less than an A grade; it demands the perfect body shape. Neurotic perfectionism hurts in three ways because it leads to:

  - loss of confidence and self esteem, when you do not achieve perfection;

  - avoidance of challenges, because you may not achieve perfection;

  - grief and tears, for instance when your perfect wedding is spoilt by a trivial problem such as a drunken cousin or the napkins being the wrong shade of pale blue.

- *Competition*. We do not want to lose. As we have already seen, most of us have a superiority complex: we like to think that we are better than our peers. So anything that tells us that we are not as good as our peers can be devastating. Corporate evaluation systems recognize this and routinely rate 80–90 per cent of staff as above average. The result is that we avoid competition and often avoid learning. In schools I see struggling students reject education as a waste of time: they do not care to be seen to fail, so they focus on being a success in other ways. This may involve being the centre of attention through antisocial behaviour. This is self-reinforcing: they fall further behind, which reinforces their belief that education is pointless. Executives may not take to throwing chairs around the room, but they will often avoid training sessions because they are at risk of being shown up as less than perfect.

Knowing that these prisons exist at least alerts us to their risks. If we know they are there, we have a chance of avoiding ending up in them. But to escape the prisons and to keep out of them, we need to establish positive routines for ourselves. We need to hone our growth mindset. The section that follows shows how.

Building your growth mindset

All mindsets are matters of habit, and the growth mindset is no different. You can think of the growth mindset as a cycle of growth, as shown in this diagram. The four steps of the growth cycle are: challenge, test, learn, adapt. We will look at each in turn.

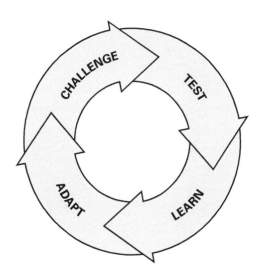

Challenge

The first step is to challenge yourself. This is not about crazy challenges such as climbing Everest on a pogo stick for charity. It is more modest but absolutely constant. Four sorts of challenge will help you to grow:

- How can I stretch to a new goal?
- How can I improve?
- How can I change?
- How can I try something new?

How can I stretch to a new goal?

A good challenge is one that forces you out of business as usual. When I was invited to build a business in Japan without speaking Japanese, it would have been sensible to turn down the offer because I was clearly not competent for the task. By accepting the challenge I stretched myself and forced myself to learn. Doing the same as before was not possible. Yet you do not have to be so extreme. Start by thinking about the ideal role you would like to have in three years' time. It could be where you are now, or elsewhere. Set that as your new goal. Work out all the skills and experience you would need for your ideal role. Now start the process of learning those skills and building that track record.

A goal that is a straightforward performance goal does not help: it fixes you on the performance mindset, not the growth mindset. If your goal is to beat your budget by 10 per cent, you can do that by working hard and perhaps using some smoke and mirrors on your accounts. You will learn nothing new.

Use your high aspirations to imagine your future perfect. Define your goal and then work back from that. You do not need to make a risky or magic leap into the future: you can start quietly assembling the capabilities you need to succeed, once you know what success looks like for you. You do not have to leave your comfort zone immediately: wait until you are ready. Instead of jumping in at the deep end of the pool, learn to swim first. Then you can enjoy jumping in instead of fearing it.

How can I improve?

This is the process of constant improvement, which the Japanese call kaizen.[22] Kaizen is not just about quality, it is about learning to eliminate waste – and that includes the waste of re-work and overwork. In the section on learning that follows, you can find the questions that will sustain you on your personal journey of kaizen.

How can I change?

If improvement is about incremental steps, change is about the big steps. Look widely for sources of inspiration. It might be books, or role models in or beyond work, or it may be other businesses. Recall the story of James Darley looking to take graduate recruiting to a new level by seeing how ASOS, the clothing company, does customer service. The more you look, the more you will find in the unlikeliest of places. I was in the middle of the bush when I realized that tribal people probably knew more about survival and success in harsh conditions with few resources than most of us will ever know. We have corporate life-support systems to enable us, and occasionally to imprison us. Tribal people have no IT department, or HR or anything else. After seven years of research across the world, I was able to write about a new way of looking at leadership.[23]

How can I try something new?

Stop the fossilization of your mindset. Instead of relying on memories of your golden youth, create new memories for your future. Try new things: listen to new music, see new films, go to new places, try new activities, meet new people. You will have moments of delight and moments of horror. But give yourself permission to live life in Technicolor, not in black and white, and certainly not in a sepia-tinted nostalgia for the past. How you live outside work affects how you live inside work. If you dare to have small adventures outside work, you are more likely to push boundaries inside work. And the more you try new things, the more you learn.

Test

Once you have your challenge, you need to find ways to meet your challenge. You will look in vain to find a textbook answer to the ambiguous and messy challenges of life at work. If you cannot design the perfect solution in theory, you have to discover the workable solution in practice.

For instance, imagine you have a grumpy boss, if such a thing is possible. Unfortunately, bosses do not come with a user manual, let alone a guarantee. You cannot turn to the trouble-shooting section on fixing grumpiness. So you set yourself a challenge to see if you can make your boss less grumpy in dealing with you.

The only way you will find out what works is by testing different ways of dealing with your boss. You can find some ideas to test by looking at how other team members or colleagues of your boss deal with him or her. Maybe your boss is less grumpy with other people: find out what they do differently, or go and ask them for advice. Then start trying different approaches. Perhaps you learn never to meet after lunch, or perhaps you have to talk about baseball, or perhaps you have to be more enthusiastic yourself. Keep testing until you find a way that works consistently.

Learn

The growth mindset is about constant learning. That does not mean you have to go to training courses all week. The lessons we value the most are things that we discover for ourselves, rather than things that are revealed to us. But we will only discover what we want to learn if we look for it. We can learn by ourselves or in groups. Either way, there are two basic questions you should always ask yourself at the end of any meeting, important phone call or at the end of the day:

- WWW: what went well?
- EBI: even better if...

WWW is essential in good times. When things go well we tend not to think about it. We assume that is how things are meant to go anyway. In reality, you will have done things that caused the good outcome to happen. Catch yourself doing things well and understand why you succeeded. This is not just about building your self-confidence. It is about building your knowledge of what works, so that you can do more of it and build on your strengths.

WWW is also essential when things go awry. In the face of setbacks, it is natural to focus on what went wrong. That quickly gets into an orgy of depression and blame, which helps no one. Focus on what you did right. Focus on any silver linings that may help you in the future.

EBI is the antidote to the normal inquest question of 'what went wrong'. What went wrong leads to blame. EBI leads to insight and action. It forces you to think about how you could do things better in future. It is a learning question, not an inquest question.

WWW/EBI is not an occasional tool. It is a non-stop tool. The best sales person I knew used WWW/EBI after every call. He was always wanting to learn and to improve. And even though he was a master of his art, he still found that most of his mistakes were elementary mistakes. Staying at the top of your game, let alone improving, requires a constant struggle. Top musicians, sports people and performers never stop practising, never stop learning – just to stay at their peak.

There are different ways that you can go about this non-stop learning. Here are a few:

- Have a coach: use him or her to talk about your learning on a regular basis.

- Set up a system of team debriefs using WWW/EBI after every important meeting. This can be done after the meeting in a corridor, as you walk to the car park. It need not take up extra time: use dead time productively to learn. Make it a habit for you and your team.

- Keep a journal and fill it once a day or once a week: have alternate sheets for WWW and EBI.

- Spend five minutes at the end of the day reflecting on EBI or WWW.

It does not matter what your system is, provided you have a system and it works for you. Once the habit becomes ingrained, you will find yourself doing it all day. You will even end up working out the best way to empty the dishwasher, park the car and mow the lawn. You do not have to inflict this way of thinking on your whole family, just let them enjoy the fact that you seem to be highly effective around the house.

Use the learning approach not just on yourself, but also on your team: the growth cycle is a good way to help your team grow, improve and reach peak performance. That means moving feedback from being appraisal-based to development-based. Appraisals tell people they did well or badly: appraisals never lead to learning. If the appraisal is good it leads to complacency: there is no need to learn. If it is a poor appraisal it leads to conflict. Instead, focus feedback on development. You can use the WWW and EBI model to have a sensible conversation about growth and development.

Adapt

There is not much point in learning unless you put your learning into practice. Knowing that you will put your learning into practice also puts a hard edge on your learning and debriefs with your team. So when you have gone through your WWW/EBI, take your debrief to the next step and ask:

- What are the one, two or three things we will continue to do more of (WWW)?

- What are the one, two or three things we will do differently in future (EBI)?

This sorts the wheat from the chaff. You may have a mixture of radical ideas and easy-to-do ideas. Take on the easy ideas anyway. Build your confidence by finding some early wins: actions that lead to improvement fast.

The temptation is to put the radical ideas into a special file called 'too difficult' or the one next to it called 'too risky'. That is a waste. The biggest ideas may lead to the biggest improvements, but often have the biggest obstacles: time, effort and risk. If you find a big idea, focus on it. Start by looking at all the benefits of the idea: if this idea works the way you want it to work, how much better will things be? Who will gain from the idea? Size the prize: if the prize is big enough, then it is worth putting in the effort to make it happen.

Break down your big idea into small parts. You do not need to bet your career on a leap into the unknown. Perhaps the first steps are to talk to some people in order to test the idea further, or to canvass support from experts and power brokers. Make the difficult simple: it is easier to take many small steps than one big leap.

Once you have adapted your practice and your way of working, you have completed the growth cycle from challenge, through test, learn and adapt. But, of course, the growth cycle never ends. Once you have your new way of working, that is your cue to start challenging it again to see if you can improve it even further.

Summary

Why a growth mindset is important:

- Today's skills will be less useful or relevant tomorrow: offshoring and technology will challenge existing jobs and skills, forcing us to upgrade our skills.

- We will change employer several times in our career: average job tenure (in the OECD countries) is about 10 years (in the United States it is 4.4 years); a career will last 40 years or more.

- The rules of survival and success change at each level of the organization: a success formula at one level is a formula for failure at the next.

What stops us from growing – the prisons of our minds:

- The prison of success: prepare for new challenges and new rules of survival.

- The prison of the past: build new skills for the future, not the past.

- The prison of performance: focus on learning, not just achievement.

- The prison of fear: have courage to try, to fail, to learn, to grow.

How to build your growth mindset – the growth cycle:

- Challenge yourself to improve, stretch, change and try new things.

- Test: try new approaches, discover what works.

- Learn: ask WWW (what went well) and EBI (even better if...) after every key event.

- Adapt: put your learning from WWW and EBI into practice.

- Challenge again: start the next growth cycle.

The dark side

Beware the demons

Success does not mean always being popular. You have to make hard choices and you have to find your hard edge. And recognize that every mindset has a dark side. Knowing the dark side will help you to avoid it, and it also helps you to understand why the positive side of each mindset is so powerful. Learn from the dark side, but do not become part of it.

All the best movie heroes have a dark side. Luke Skywalker's father was Darth Vader; the Sorting Hat thought about putting Harry Potter into Slytherin;[1] the ring in *The Lord of the Rings* exerted power for good and for ill. Most of us do not work for a Darth Vader-type boss, although it can feel like that at times. But every leader has a dark side. No one is perfect.

The demons of the dark side come in two forms. The first is the demon of ruthlessness. The second are the demons of the seven mindsets of success. Turn a coin over and heads become tails. Turn the bright side of any mindset over, and you find a dark side.

You cannot protect yourself from the dark side unless you know what it looks like. It is even possible to put the dark side to use. It is time to take a trip to the dark side.

The ruthless leader

When interviewing the leadership panel they were uniformly kind and generous with their time. Most of them disliked the idea of being seen as ruthless: 'Leaders should not be ruthless. I have met many ruthless people. They are violent and mean and always me, me, me.'[2]

But the members of the leadership panel were not the sort of people I would like to disappoint. There was a hard edge to them. I would not want to be an obstacle on their path to achieving their mission. One described firing a head of science whom she had known for 20 years: 'The head of science was OK – but not good enough and would have held the school back.' So the science head was zapped, along with their friendship. The school head, along with all the other leaders on the panel, strongly denied being ruthless. In her words: 'Ruthless people are just bastards – they pick on someone, blame them and sack them so they can avoid responsibility.'

Leaders may not like to be called ruthless, but they can certainly act that way. If they disliked the word ruthless, they warmed more to the idea of having a hard edge:

- 'Be ready to argue your case, and do not compromise when people fight back: stand by what you believe in.'[3]

- 'There is a hard side to fairness: telling the people the truth so you will not be popular, people will not like it.'[4]

- 'They [leaders] will do the tough things... have the difficult conversations with teachers, parents and children. One of the big weaknesses of leaders is to avoid these conversations.'[5]

- 'The best leaders are both ruthless and compassionate, in the same way a good coach is ruthless and compassionate. They say tough things, but they say it to help you.'[6]

- 'Every single leader is focused and ruthless. You cannot be side-tracked. Even though I like some people here, if they are not delivering, you have to get rid of them.'[7]

- 'Leaders have to have a dark side. It is not about being nice and popular. You have to be ready to do things that you may not want to do, you do not like.'[8]

The leader's dilemma

Penicillin was first produced in stable and industrial quantities during the Second World War.[9] The first batches were very valuable, and there was not enough to go around. In 1943, a large batch arrived in North Africa at a critical moment when the British under Montgomery were fighting the Germans under Rommel. It was known that penicillin was a very good and quick way to treat the clap (gonorrhoea). It could also save the lives of soldiers who had been wounded on the front line, although that required much larger doses of penicillin, with a more uncertain outcome: some of the wounded might die anyway, and others might recover but not be able to fight.

This left the military with a problem. Should they save wounded war heroes, or treat soldiers who had been fooling around in the pleasure palaces of Cairo and Alexandria? Your choice: save the heroes or treat the clap?

They requested advice from London. The message came back from Churchill: use it for 'best military advantage' – get as many soldiers back into action as fast as possible.[10] So the penicillin was used to treat the clap, and the wounded heroes were left to take their chances.

If you are focused on a mission, you will find yourself acting ruthlessly.

The dark side is a difficult and confusing place to be. It is not simply black and white and good versus evil. At one extreme are the socio-paths who make Darth Vader look like a vicar at a tea party. At the other extreme the effective leaders who know they have to be focused and hard-edged. There is no sharp dividing line between categories.

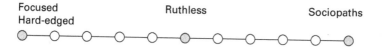

Focused
Hard-edged   Ruthless   Sociopaths

The focused and hard-edged side is essential for any leader. For all the leaders on the panel, their hard edge came from being focused on a mission. They were not focused on their own position. They focused on the goal of the organization as a whole. This is a crucial difference from sociopaths whose sole mission is themselves. Unwavering focus on the mission drives leaders to do things that they know are unpopular, and which they themselves find difficult to do. For instance, in my coaching role I have watched several executives struggle with firing someone for the first time. It disturbs them. They know they are seriously messing with someone's career and life. They do it not to be mean; they do it because their mission depends on it.

There are four areas where all the best leaders need to have a hard edge. They are the four preconditions for you to succeed in your role. If any of these are missing, you will struggle, so you cannot compromise:

- right goal;
- right team;
- right performance;
- right budget.

Right goal

If you have 16 goals, you will win on some and lose on others. You can then trumpet your successes very loudly and keep quiet about the rest. That is good career survival, but it is not leadership. Leaders create focus and clarity. For instance, if you are a head teacher you are inundated with goals and requirements: behaviour, literacy, numeracy, programmes for gifted and talented children or for those with special educational needs and disabilities (SEND), parental engagement, student voice, community cohesion, teaching English as an additional language. The list goes on. Here is how one head teacher responded to all the noise:

> One primary school decided to do just two things, and he put all his energy over two and a half years into just two things: 1) every child

would be tracked and every child's progress would be reported to the governors every half term: there was no hiding place for failure; 2) focus on team teaching and coaching for every teacher.

They went from 53 per cent to 85 per cent pass rate in year one, to 100 per cent in year two at level four[11] (versus a national average of 75 per cent, and they had 100 per cent free school meals).[12] He could have done all sorts of other things such as student voice, curriculum reform, behaviour management. That would have been easy. But he stayed focused, even though he got real pushback from all the teachers who saw their workloads go up.[13]

The right goal is the cornerstone of leading with a hard edge. If you have belief in your goal, that will drive you to do the hard things around your team and performance. If you chase lots of goals, then you can hide behind the ambiguity this causes.

Once you have your goal, you are committed and you need to make sure the rest of your team is committed. Throughout history, leaders have found dramatic ways to commit themselves and their followers. Here are two examples:

- Crossing the Rubicon: when Caesar crossed this river from Gaul to Italy in 49 BC he was breaking Roman law, which forbade generals from bringing their troops to Italy. He and his troops would either succeed or die.[14]

- 'Fight with your backs to the river': the order given by Chinese general, Han Xin, at the Battle of Jingxing in 204 BC[15] – because he had no way to cross back over the river he, like Caesar, had to succeed or die.

As a leader in relatively peaceful times, you should not have to choose between death and glory. But if you are to achieve your goal, you have to commit to it.

Right team

Venture capitalists do not just back a great idea: they back a great team. A B-grade idea from an A* team will succeed because the team will find a way to make the idea great. An A* idea from a B-grade team will wallow and struggle. In the words of anthropologist Margaret Mead: 'Never doubt that a small group of thoughtful, committed people can change the world. Indeed, it is the only thing that ever has.'[16] The right people will turn mountains into molehills; the wrong people will turn molehills into mountains. Since you cannot do it all yourself, you have to build the right team to make it happen.

Weak leaders will stick with the team they inherit from their predecessor. There are plenty of reasons for not changing. Change is risky; it is painful and embarrassing to move people out; we feel a sense of loyalty to those who work with us. Effective leaders have loyalty to the mission and are not put off by pain or embarrassment. They will take the tough decisions to put the right team in place.

As we saw earlier, the right team is a mixture of:

- right skills;
- right styles;
- right values.

The skills are fairly easy to assess; styles are about finding the right balance. Values tend to be the difference between a high-performing team and an average team.

Right performance

Right performance is about having difficult conversations: if someone is not performing you help no one by staying silent. Weak leaders avoid difficult conversations.[17] There is an art form to managing difficult conversations well.[18] The basic principles are clear:

- *Act early*: the longer you leave it, the worse things become.
- *Stick to the facts*: if you are annoyed or upset, that is your problem and keep it to yourself. Focus on what has gone wrong and the impact it has had.
- *Listen*: there may be a good reason why things are going wrong. Don't make assumptions.

- *Show respect*: this is not a contest to prove who is right or who has moral superiority. Take the emotion out of it.

- *Stay positive*: drive to action. Even in the toughest situations there will be choices, even if the choices are not pleasant. Avoid getting bogged down in, 'I said but she said and anyway he said and then I did but he didn't and I thought but she really meant...'. This kind of conversation goes nowhere very fast.

- *Summarize*: both sides need to be clear about next steps: who, what, where, when and how. Avoid any ambiguity. Check to see if they need any help.

What is important is that you find the courage to have these conversations. The more you have them, the better you will be at having such conversations so that they lead to improvement, not conflict.

Right budget

None of the leadership panel talked about money or budgets. Perhaps that should not be a surprise, since we were talking about mindsets. But in reality, you cannot change the world without balancing the books. It is easy for leaders to get confused about money.

Some leaders regard money as the goal: success means a big personal bank account. It is their way of keeping score. Money ceases to be about needs and wants: it is about status. That is why bonus season in investment banks can be so ugly: if I get a million-dollar bonus I may flounce out in a huff (having made sure the bonus is in my bank account) if someone else gets a bit more.

Leaders who focus on the mission, not on themselves, see money as a means to an end, not as an end in itself. But they are as ruthless in negotiating their budget as investment bankers who lobby for their bonus. One of the best managers I ever had was relatively idle, but one of the things he did very well was to negotiate his annual budget. For one month a year he would go into overdrive to prove that he needed lower goals and a higher budget. That meant he could always outperform relative to his peers who accepted the 'challenge' of a tough budget: low resources and high goals.

Each of the charities I have started, has started with nothing. No money, no resources: just an idea, ambition and some great people. This helps. It means you have to focus, and you have to find new ways of doing things. It forces business not as usual: you have to be original. Use the same mindset when focused with declining resources. The best and average leaders respond with different questions to the same challenge of a 20 per cent reduction in resources:

- Average mindset: 'How can we reduce our budget by 20 per cent?'

- Great mindset: 'How can we do even better with 20 per cent less?'

The first mindset leads to the normal arguments over people, property, procurement and all the other budget lines. The organization becomes thinner, not fitter. Eventually, it becomes emaciated and dies.

The second mindset invites everyone to think differently: to change and to improve. It gives them licence to reinvent how things are done. It is a more positive discussion with the potential for a more positive outcome: the organization can become thinner and fitter.

The hard edge of leadership takes us into the darker side of leadership. It is part of the dark side that leaders have to put to use if they are to succeed.

The sociopath as leader

At some point, the hard edge can become vicious. Eventually, it becomes a recipe for being a sociopath. The difference between a hard-edged leader and a sociopath is mission. The hard-edged leader is focused on a mission that is about their organization. The sociopath is focused on a mission that is themselves. Some of the leaders in the leadership panel are clearly wealthy. But for them, wealth is a by-product of what they do, rather than an end goal.

Each one spoke with energy and enthusiasm about their business: they had pride in their organizations.

But the sociopaths are out there. They clearly are the dark element of the dark side. There is no Harry Potter-style spell to deal with them. Instead we first have to recognize them and then find some practical ways of dealing with them.

Here is how to spot a sociopath:[19]

- superficial charm and good intelligence;
- absence of nervousness or neurotic manifestations;
- unreliability;
- untruthfulness and insincerity;
- lack of remorse and shame;
- inadequately motivated antisocial behaviour;
- poor judgement and failure to learn by experience;
- pathologic egocentricity and incapacity for love;
- fantastic and uninviting behaviour with alcohol and sometimes without;
- sex life impersonal, trivial and poorly integrated.

Many sociopaths are clever, will lie convincingly and can attract a cult of loyal followers around them. They will often be the successful power baron who carves out a firm within the firm and no one can touch him (most sociopaths are male).[20] Followers love him; others fear him. You are either on his team, with 100 per cent unquestioning loyalty, or you are against him. Put positively, sociopaths can be valued for their daring leadership: they will take risks that others would not. Look at some of the great dictators of history, and the chances are that most of them will pass most of the tests of a sociopath. If you are a sociopath, you probably will not be reading this. If you are not a sociopath, the question is how to deal with one when you find one.

A simple way to deal with them is to join them. They can succeed and they can go far, as the success of history's dictators shows. But if you choose to follow them, then you are by definition a follower, not a leader. Sociopaths do not like followers showing too much freedom of thought: they want blind obedience.

If you are a leader, then do not fight a sociopath on their terms: they are more aggressive, and are better at lying and cheating because they have had plenty of practice over their lifetimes. The appropriate response is neither aggressive nor passive – which is going into victim mode. The middle way is to be assertive. Table 8.1 sets out the three different approaches.[21]

You can use the assertive path at all times. The more you use it, the more natural it will become. In dealing with sociopaths you may be more robust, and in dealing with victims you may be slightly more thoughtful. But the basic approach will stay the same: be clear about your goals, find the win–win where possible and maintain respect. Bullies and sociopaths feed on people they can bully and manipulate: when they find that you are not an easy meal, they will look elsewhere.

The demons of the seven mindsets of success

Diamonds are pure and brilliant. Coal is dirty and polluting. Both are pure carbon. The same matter can be beautiful or ugly, and so it is with each of the mindsets. In the corporate world, any good idea soon gets trivialized or abused. 'Strategic intent' now refers to anything that an executive wants to do; 'core competence' is anything we are faintly good at. They are grand words that sound impressive. But they are so far removed from the original *Harvard Business Review* (HBR) articles on strategic intent and core competence as to be unrecognizable.[22]

The danger with the seven mindsets is that they go the way of all corporate ideas: they will be abused to the point of irrelevance. This section sets out some of the major traps that lie within each mindset. Think of them as hazard warnings on the road: once you know the hazard is there, it is up to you to avoid it.

Table 8.1   Choose your mindset

	Passive victim	Assertive leader	Aggressive sociopath
Characteristics	Allow others to choose for you; inhibited, set up to lose	Choose for self; honest, self-respecting, find the win–win	Choose for others; tactless, self-enhancing. Play to win, others to lose
Your own feelings	Anxious, ignored, manipulated	Confident, self-respecting, goal-focused	Superior, deprecatory, controlling
How you make others feel	Guilty or superior: frustrated with you	Valued and respected	Humiliated and resentful
How you are seen	Lack of respect; do not know where you stand	Respect; know where you stand	Vengeful, fearful, angry, distrustful
Outcome	Lose at your expense	Negotiated win–win	You win at others' expense

High aspirations

It seems like there can be nothing wrong with high aspirations. In practice, two pitfalls lie in wait for the unwary.

The first pitfall is that high aspirations are about the mission, not about the person. We have all met people who have very high aspirations... for themselves. It is all about 'me, me, me'. These are the sorts of people who either are sociopaths, or are going that way. They believe: 'It is not enough that I should succeed – others should fail.'[23] Personal ambition and a win/lose mentality is toxic. It leads to politics, infighting and division. Personal ambition can lead to personal success and wealth. It can also sustain an organization for a while, but the human price is high. The high aspirations I saw in the leadership panel were all about the mission: each leader cared passionately about what they were doing and who they were working for. Their success is more sustainable and leads to a better workplace with fewer human casualties.

The second trap with high aspirations is that they have to be shared across the organization in order to be effective. This is obvious, but it is a trap that many leaders fall into. They have high aspirations, and then they get frustrated that no one else shares their passion. There are two reasons for this happening, both of which can be managed.

First, it is easier to have high and noble aspirations if you are the CEO, not the janitor or a middle manager struggling with conflicting goals, inadequate resources, competing colleagues and endless ambiguity. The captain of the ship has a wonderful view from the bridge; the engineer in the boiler room does not have such a lofty view. You have to find a way of translating your grand vision into something relevant and exciting to engineers in the boiler room and janitors sweeping the floor.

Second, leaders go on a journey in which they slowly develop their vision. It takes time and effort. In one case, a CEO went through a six-month effort to develop a radical, exciting and innovative new vision. He had involved his executive committee, and they supported it. He then announced it at a big offsite presentation. Six months later he was tearing his hair out with frustration, because no one seemed to 'get it' apart from his executive committee. Yet it was no wonder they did not 'get it': they were given 30 minutes to complete a journey that had taken the CEO and his team six months. Engaging the organization in your vision takes time, effort and endless communication. Another CEO noted that developing the vision was the easy bit; after two years of transformation he estimated that 60 per cent of his time was spent simply communicating the vision. Don't leave your team behind, and don't expect a 30-minute presentation will help them to complete a journey that might have taken you six months.

Courage

Remember the words of the local fire chief, quoted earlier: 'I don't want a brave fireman, because a brave fireman soon becomes a dead fireman.' A courageous leader can be great. A dead leader is useless.

For the most part, we do not expect our leaders to choose between death or glory. But we are still in love with the idea of the heroic leader who leads all to the promised land. This is one reason why we are so cynical about our political leaders: they make promises consistent with being the great hero but then cannot deliver on them.

It is easy to fall into the hero mindset. When you finally arrive in the corner office and find that the carpets are deeper and the flowers are fresher, strange things happen. Suddenly, everyone finds your rubbish jokes to be hilarious; your half-witted idea is seen as a stroke of genius and is acted on; your judgement in everything from strategy to art becomes impeccable. The danger is when you start to believe your flattering courtiers. At that point, the CEO becomes a teenager again: blind to risk and blind to consequences. Unlike Julius Caesar, you may not have the luxury of owning a slave who reminds you 'Remember, you are mortal.'[24] But you need to find someone who is dispassionate and can help you to keep your feet on the ground: coaching can help.

The second problem with the hero headset is the 'go it alone' mentality. Heroes think they can do it all themselves. They can't. In a complicated world, leadership is a team sport. The mark of a good leader is the quality of the team they build around them.

Resilient

Don Quixote famously decided to fight some windmills, believing that they were giants and that their sails were 'arms well nigh two leagues in length'.[25] The resilient mindset will keep fighting; when it goes too far it fights irrelevant and pointless battles. It will not even realize that the battles are pointless or irrelevant. At its worst, the resilient mindset becomes the conspiracy mindset, which believes that Princess Diana was murdered by Elvis Presley and John F Kennedy (I may have mixed up my conspiracy theories). It will keep on going in the face of all evidence to the contrary, absolutely convinced of the righteousness of the cause. The crusade takes over from reality.

Here is a simple checklist to make sure that you are fighting the right battles. Sun Tzu argued that you should never fight a battle unless:[26]

- there is a prize worth fighting for;
- you know you can win;
- there is no other way to gain your prize.

Most corporate battles fail one – and sometimes all three – of these tests. They are pointless.

Positive

'Creatures of the universe – rejoice! On pain of death!' These were the instructions sent out by Emperor Ming the Merciless in the film *Flash Gordon*.[27] Telling people to rejoice, or be happy, or be positive and sincere is pointless. And yet there are plenty of training programmes out there which essentially get staff to fake being positive: staff learn to smile, say the right things and act the right way. The result is an act, not reality: being positive has to come from within. Superficial positivity can be taught in an afternoon; becoming a positive person takes years but lasts a lifetime.

The second pitfall with positive thinking is that it can crowd out reality. One bank chief liked to make a speech about being solution-focused. You can imagine the sort of speech this would be: 'Bring me solutions, not problems: are you a solutions person or a problems person?' So what do you do if you work for this bank chief and a weak economy is turning your loan book sour, and the bad and doubtful debts are piling up? You hide the problem, because you cannot afford to be seen as a problems sort of person. Eventually, of course, the pressure cooker explodes and the bank goes down, only to be saved by endless billions of taxpayer's money being poured in.

The alternative form of being positive actively encourages problems to emerge early. Each problem is a chance to learn, and the earlier the problem is spotted the less damage it does.

Collaborative

The big pitfall here is to confuse collaboration with popularity. Collaboration is based on building trust. It is a professional relationship in which there can be difficult conversations. It is tough but productive. It is not about friendship or popularity.

Popularity is the high road to weakness. If you want to be popular, you compromise. You accept excuses for why staff are late, or fail to deliver, or can't do something. You try to make their life easy. And you are as popular as your next concession, and your team will not respect you.

The collaborative mindset will challenge where it needs to. If anything, challenge forces collaboration. Kennedy's challenge to put a man on the moon forced a massive national collaboration of engineers, scientists, technicians, universities and military.

The collaborative mindset finds a win–win based on mutual interests. The popular mindset simply gives away wins in the forlorn hope that something will come back. Know your interests and promote them with other people.

Accountable

Accountability has three traps for the unwary:

- *The accountability cult.* It was a classic training session. We were sitting in an airless room. At the front, there was a facilitator with a flip chart and a franchised theory. We had to guess what he wanted to write on the flip chart. The place he wanted to get us to was that each of us was personally accountable for everything: global warming, world peace, world hunger and even all world history and the future of the world. You can justify this: if we choose not to do anything about global warming or global poverty, then we cannot complain about the consequences.

And while we cannot change the past, we can be accountable for how we feel about the past. Put positively, we choose what we take accountability for. Accountability, taken to an extreme, becomes a cult.

- *The hero trap.* Accountability falls into the same trap as courage. The boss who thinks they can do it all, also thinks they are responsible for everything. This makes them unable to delegate well; they trust their own skills above others and they make the organization dependent on their own uncertain talents. They end up trying to be the lone hero who saves the organization from disaster, although the disaster is most likely to be one that they created.

- *The word tricks.* If the pen is mightier than the sword, then words are weapons. Accountability can be used as a deadly weapon. It can be used in three destructive ways:

  - The guilt trip: 'You are accountable for that, so why haven't you...' This is an accusatory use of the word, which shifts the blame from the speaker.

  - The blame shift, as above. It is also a way of absolving the speaker from taking any responsibility for finding the solution. Nasty, toxic and often effective in the world of corporate politics.

  - The land grab: 'I am accountable for that...' This is a way of saying 'get off my turf'.

All three word tricks protect the interests of the speaker, but lead to conflict and resentment.

Growth

You can spend a lifetime pursuing personal growth and never achieve anything. A good way to do this is to become an ageing hippy and spend your life touring the ashrams of India in search of enlightenment, drugs and sex. Not necessarily in that order. In the corporate world there are people you find who pursue personal growth. They are often wonderful people to meet, but they are ineffective. They are jack of all trades, master of none; they prefer the safety of writing reports to making things happen. Their ideal job is in a think tank where writing good reports on varying topics is how to make a living.

Growth is not an end in itself. It is a means to an end.

When we set up Teaching Leaders, we realized there were many other training programmes for middle leaders in schools. None had a great reputation. So we did not set up Teaching Leaders to be training-led. We set it up to be impact-led: its mission is to reduce educational disadvantage by developing great middle leaders. That means children's progress, not teachers' progress, is our key performance measure. The result is a growing programme with a good reputation, which helps middle leaders to grow and develop fast. Look at your own training programmes. Are they training for skills, or training for impact? If you train for impact, you still have to build skills, but the training suddenly becomes more relevant, credible and urgent for everyone.

When growth is focused on an outcome, it is more powerful and more effective than growth for its own sake.

Summary

All the best leaders have a hard edge. Four areas where they show their hardness:

- *Right goal*: which is stretching and they focus relentlessly on it.

- *Right team*: build the best, achieve balance and do not tolerate second best.

- *Right performance*: have difficult conversations early.

- *Right budget*: negotiate hard because you cannot change the world without the resources.

Each of the seven mindsets has a dark side to beware of:

- *High aspirations*: should not be about self – focus on the mission and gain buy-in from the team.

- *Courage*: do not be the lone hero. Success is a team effort.

- *Resilience*: avoid pointless battles. Only fight when:
  - there is a prize worth fighting for;
  - you know you will win;
  - there is no other way of achieving your goal.

- *Positive*: avoid denial. Recognize and deal with problems when they arise.

- *Collaborative*: do not chase popularity. Build trust and respect.

- *Accountability*: do not try to do it all yourself.

- *Growth*: learning is a means, not an end. Drive to action.

Mindset and your leadership journey
09

Accelerate your career

*Leadership is not just about the person at the top of the firm.
Anyone can lead at any level. You do not have to spend 20 years
climbing the greasy pole of careers before you start leading. You
have to start leading as soon as you start work.*

The definition of leadership in this book is: 'The ability to take
people where they would not have got by themselves.' You can do
that as an entry-level employee if you have a bright idea and get
people to take it up. Equally, there are plenty of CEOs who are
not really leading: they are simply managing a legacy which they
inherited. There is nothing wrong with that, but it is not leadership.

Leadership is not a destination; it is a journey. It is a never-ending
journey because you can never reach perfection; no leader gets ticks
in all the boxes. But the good news is that you can lead at any
point in your life journey within and beyond work. But as with
all journeys, the landscape changes as you progress. The nature
of leadership changes. Leading when you are a young graduate is
different from when you are a veteran senior executive.

This chapter shows how the mindset of success changes as you
make your leadership journey. To understand how mindset has to
change, first we have to understand how the nature of leadership
itself changes at different levels of the organization.

The simplest career trajectory looks like Figure 9.1.

Figure 9.1 Simple career trajectory

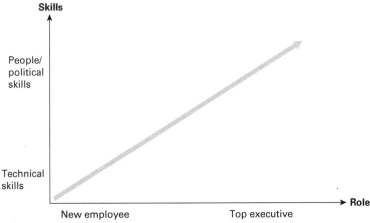

To start with, everyone has to learn some sort of craft skill. The skill might take the form of a qualification, like accounting or teaching. Or it may be a set of craft skills, such as doing PowerPoint, analysing documents and preparing reports. These skills matter and will continue to matter throughout your career. But these skills are not enough to carry you through your career. Over time, you need to layer in another set of skills, which are all around managing people and managing politics. Managing people is an obvious but demanding task. Managing politics is less obvious but equally important. Politics is the art of making things happen across the organization, through people and functions you do not control. That means learning the arts of persuasion and influence; learning how to align agendas, create agendas and occasionally fight battles.

The important thing to take away from this highly simplified career road map is that the skills of success change at every level of the organization. This helps to explain why many people who succeed at one level fail at the next level: you have to keep on learning a new success model as you progress.

So the most important mindset for a successful career is learning and growth. If you stay still, you will fail. There will always be someone who is younger, hungrier, working harder for less money and with more up-to-date skills who will be happy to take your place.

Table 9.1 is a simplified version of how the nature of leadership and management changes at each stage of a career. It shows how the rules of survival and success keep on changing, which means that you have to keep on changing and learning if you want to succeed. It also shows the context in which you have to develop your mindset.

A core theme of this book is that skills are necessary, but not enough, for success. You can learn all the skills for the leadership journey in the figure above, but you need the secret sauce of mindset to stand out from your peers. Just as the context for leadership changes at each stage of your journey, so your mindset has to keep on changing and developing. Progress and change are inseparable.

The eight mindsets of success are present at every stage of your leadership journey. But the nature of each mindset changes. The simplistic notion that you have to have a 'growth' mindset is not enough. It is like saying you have to 'learn'. It may be true that you have to learn or grow, but it helps to know what you have to learn and how you can learn it.

Table 9.2 summarizes how the eight mindsets of success develop during the course of your leadership journey. To succeed, you need to achieve mastery of the level you are currently at, but that is not enough. You also need to be developing the mindset required of the level above you: when you go up a level you want to be ready, rather than starting from scratch. You have to hit the ground running, which means you have to be mentally prepared. And if you really want to succeed, you need to have an understanding of how the more senior leaders think. Once you can understand how they think about the world, you are in a strong position to work with them and influence them well; not understanding them is a recipe for failure.

You can use Table 9.2 to see where you are on your leadership journey, and where you can gain from developing your mindset further.

Table 9.1 Your leadership journey

Leadership level	Managing self: new employee	Managing others: front-line supervision	Managing a function, several teams	Managing a business with P&L	Managing a group of businesses
Time horizon	A day or a week	A week to a quarter	A quarter to a year	Over a year	Long-term future
Main task	Doing: quality, speed, craft skills, work planning	Managing: coach, motivate, performance manage, delegate	Optimizing: improve how things work	Integrating and changing	Leading
Who you value	Self	Your team	Other functions	Staff support	External stakeholders
Financial skills	n/a	Cost management	Budget management: negotiate and control	P&L management: revenue generation, cost allocation	Financial accounting: tax, reporting
Traps and challenges	Disenchantment: dull, boring work	Not changing your game	Not managing politics	From impostor syndrome to hubris	Losing touch

Table 9.2 Your mindset journey

	Managing self	Managing others	Managing a function	Managing a business	Managing a group
High aspirations	See long-term opportunities and ambition	Understand agenda and perspective from above	Stretch and challenge team	Set agenda	Focus on big picture
Courage	Take risks to learn; push yourself	Have difficult conversations	Fight battles where needed	Change and innovate	Let go where necessary
Resilience	Deal with boring work and long hours	Daily war of attrition	Manage ambiguity, stress, low control	Focus: avoid distractions	Go extra mile
Positive	No whining	Motivate others	Stay the course	Create sense of hope and certainty	Be a role model
Accountable	For self and career	Avoid the blame game	Find a claim to fame	Create an accountability culture	Be a role model
Collaborative	Supportive and loyal	Work through others not self	Work across firm: positive politics	Value all perspectives and roles	Reach out beyond your firm
Growth	Learn a craft	Learn to manage others	Learn to work politics	Learn strategy and CEO perspective	Be constantly inquisitive
Ruthless	Focus	Hold others to account	Push your agenda	Build right team; make tough calls	Cut losses early

The rest of this chapter will show how the context and mindset of leadership changes at each stage of your journey, and what you can do about it.

Managing self

Starting a career is a shock. The world of work requires different skills and a different mindset from the world of education.

The first shock is the shock of choice. While in education, the future world is one of endless opportunities and choices. By choosing a career you make a critical choice about what you do, where you do it and for whom. Once you have made your choices, the world of opportunity narrows down fast.

To help you make your choice, employers have probably shown you a rosy future of interesting work with interesting people where you will make a difference and have great prospects. Then reality hits. Much of the work can be dull and repetitive. There are petty rules to be followed, from expense policies to dress codes and the sorts of typeface you have to use on reports. Your colleagues and bosses may be interesting, but they often seem to leave their intelligence and character with their coats at reception, only to retrieve them again on the way out at the end of the day. You may well feel you are working for a boss who is not as smart as you are. If you want to progress, you are going to have to do better than all your contemporaries who put on a good show of being confident, enthusiastic and successful, even if they feel the same way as you do. The rat race has started. The shock is to realize that this may be the rest of your life.

When you start your journey to leadership you are likely to find you have low autonomy: you are told what to do. You have to learn a set of craft skills. These skills may involve a formal qualification or not; your craft may be about analysing reports and preparing presentations. And for the most part, your performance metrics will be short term and personal. Productivity is defined by what you can deliver, not by what you get other people to deliver. All of these expectations change dramatically later in the leadership journey, but to get there you have to make the most of your start.

Given this context, it is easy to see how many people fall at the first hurdle. Some become disillusioned and some find it too hard. Either way, they make their excuses and find an alternative. Others make the most of their opportunity. The difference between the two comes down to a different mindset. The mindset of success is quite distinct for anyone at the start of their leadership journey.

High aspirations

Established leaders see ambition as one of the hallmarks of future leaders.[1] This is not just ambition for self. It is ambition for the unit where you work. The emerging leader wants to make a difference from the start. They are ready to challenge and improve the status quo. This may seem like a low hurdle to jump, but from the viewpoint of senior executives it is clear that many emerging leaders fall at this first hurdle. Too many people at the start of their career become cynical too quickly about their work, their boss, their peers and their firm. Others find it hard to stand up and speak out: they keep their head down and follow the herd. Following the herd is a recipe for survival, not success.

High aspirations means seeing the longer term, both for yourself and for your unit. Emerging leaders may be doing mundane work today, but they do not see that as a life sentence of drudgery and boredom. They see it as a vital stepping stone to a better future. It is a chance to learn a craft skill and to learn from bosses and peers about what works and what does not work. The work may be boring, but the learning curve is steep and rewarding. If you are able to learn constantly then even the most mundane work has meaning.

Courage

We have already seen that courage can be learned, and that the best way to learn it is in small steps. You cannot suddenly become the courageous leader at the age of 50. Courage has to be built up slowly, which means that you need to start early. This is vital. At the start of your career, courage means pushing yourself into situations where you learn and develop the skills you need for the future. For instance, many people have a dread of public speaking. The best time to start learning this skill is early in your career. You may crash and burn, but when you are starting out the stakes are low and people are more likely to be more forgiving. It is better to make your mistakes when speaking to eight people than trying to learn in front of 800 people.

Courage means learning the art of calculated risk taking. Throughout your career you have to learn when to speak out and when to shut up. The easy way is to keep quiet: never challenge, avoid confrontations and duck the opportunities which arise in the middle of crises and ambiguity. Learning to take risks early in your career makes sense; like public speaking, the stakes are lower and colleagues will be more forgiving.

Resilience

The clash between the rhetoric of the recruiter and the reality of the office can be brutal. Entry-level work can be a hard and boring grind. You may well think your boss is an idiot, your peers are unreliable and that your work is dull. That is pretty much what most people think most of the time. And you face the prospect of living and working like that for the next 40 years of your life. But if that is how you think, you will have low reserves of resilience to draw on when a real crisis hits and things go wrong. It will be very tempting to bail out and seek greener pastures elsewhere. If you do that, you will find that it is greenest where it rains the most. You will find it hard to land the dream job unless you yourself have a dream. You have to know what you want.

To become resilient, you need to develop a different mindset from most of your peers. You need to think positively about what you do and who you work with. That means finding meaning in your work. This may be as simple as recognizing that you are building the foundation of skills on which your future will be built; and if you are learning then, the best way to learn is from your peers and bosses. Even if they are not perfect human beings, you can watch and learn from them all the time. When they mess up, learn not to make their mistakes; when they do something well, try to copy them in your own way. Slowly build your own unique success formula.

There are four more things you can do to bake resilience into how you think and work:

- *Take control of what you can.* This is the accountability mindset. Let others do the whining about how unfair and stupid everything is. Find out what you can do to make a difference, and then do it.

- *Build support.* Any leader succeeds through other people: find people you trust and can rely on inside and outside work.

- *Find a life outside work.* You need perspective. Once your work is your identity you create a pressure cooker which will eventually explode.

- *Sleep.* Long hours become a macho display of commitment. But all the evidence is that performance drops when you are sleep deprived.

These are patterns of behaviour and thought which can sustain you not just at the start of your career, but throughout your career. Start as you mean to carry on.

Positive

Leaders are dealers in hope. You do not motivate teams by being negative, cynical and depressed. You can only help others be positive if you yourself are also positive. The start of your career is the ideal place to discover how to be positive naturally. Being positive comes from within, not from a company policy telling people to have passion and be positive.

The good news is that many of your peers will be negative and cynical about where they work. Everyone likes to moan occasionally.

This is your chance to stand out from the crowd. Although your immediate boss will know how well you are performing, everyone else will judge you by how you appear. Others may not see your day-to-day performance, but they can see your day-to-day behaviour. Being positive makes a difference.

Learning the art of positive thinking now will reap benefits for the rest of your career and your life. It is not about changing who you are, it is about cranking up some traits and winding down other traits you already have. At the heart of positive thinking is controlling your self-talk, or internal dialogue. The techniques are simple to state, but hard to learn:

- Focus on the future, not the past.
- Count your blessings, not your setbacks.
- Focus on what you can do, not on what you cannot do.
- Drive to action, do not get paralysed in analysis and thinking 'what if....'
- Build your network of support.
- Do things you enjoy, inside and outside work.

Only if you are positive will you be able to build a positive team as a future leader.

Accountable

Early in your career, you have little power or discretion. You have to do what you are told to do, and often there is little flexibility in how you do it. If you have an enlightened boss, they will help and support you. If you have a self-interested boss, you may find yourself working all hours with little recognition. It is easy to feel disempowered and disenchanted. From there, it is a small step to feeling like the victim of an uncaring and heartless machine. The victim mentality is a recipe for failure. Leaders shape events, rather than get shaped by them. So how do you shape events when you are at the bottom of the pyramid?

The key is to remember that you are accountable for yourself and your career. You always have choices, even if they are not always comfortable choices. Your first choice is about where you work and who you work for. You made that choice. Be clear about why you made that choice and whether those reasons still hold true. If they hold true, focus on making the most of that choice. If they no longer hold true, create some alternatives: find another boss, another role or another firm.

Learning to hold yourself to account is uncomfortable, but it is a vital first step to knowing how to hold others to account. The most valuable lessons in accountability occur when things go wrong. Our first instinct is to blame others, the system, fate or the weather. But ultimately we let ourselves be put in a situation where things went wrong and the finger is pointed at us. Only when we learn from setbacks can we avoid further setbacks. Accountability and learning walk hand in hand in a successful career journey.

Collaborative

The collaborative mindset shows itself in two ways at the start of a leadership career.

First, from the point of view of your boss, being collaborative is about being 100 per cent loyal and supportive. Most bosses forgive most sins, but disloyalty is not forgivable. If you fail to stand up for the agenda of your boss, then you are telling your boss that you are unreliable. Soon enough you will find yourself working for another boss. The rhetoric of modern management is all about flat organizations and empowerment. Do not be deceived by the rhetoric. Your boss may dress down and have a hot desk, but the hierarchy is alive and well. Do not mess with it.

Second, having no power is a wonderful opportunity to learn one of the key skills of all leaders: influence. You need to make things happen through other people you do not control, which means you have to learn the art of influence. Instead of cursing your lack of power, relish it. Learning how to influence people is a skill which will set you apart from others for the rest of your career. Influence covers building professional and personal trust, aligning agendas, managing personal and institutional risk and having persuasive conversations. These are deeply political skills which are not taught in training courses, but have to be acquired through experience. They are vital skills for your future.

Growth

Growth has been a consistent theme throughout this section. The early stage of your career is the best time to push yourself, make mistakes and to learn. You do not want to be learning the basics when you are in a senior position. But it is vital to be learning the right things.

The odds are that you have to learn some basic craft skills as an emerging leader. Most firms put an emphasis on learning technical skills which may be accounting, the law, teaching, doing PowerPoint or research. If you focus just on learning these technical skills, you fall into a deep leadership trap. You are learning to be an expert, not a leader. You can have a good career as an expert, but make that choice deliberately, not by accident.

The skills you need for the long haul are political and people skills, together with a mindset that will carry you through good times and bad times alike. If you focus on building your capabilities, then even mundane work, crises and difficult bosses and peers become an opportunity to grow, not a setback to be overcome.

Ruthless

When you have no power, you have little to be ruthless about. Machiavelli urged leaders to execute a few people to keep everyone else in check. This is not the sort of ruthlessness you have the power to enforce. Although ruthlessness becomes more important later in your career, it still matters at the start of your career as well. Ruthless starts with yourself, in two ways.

First, be ruthless about your commitments. The world of work is ambiguous: for instance, when is a required report complete? There is always more data to be gleaned and another appendix to be added. Given this ambiguity, it is very hard for bosses to judge workload. So they simply keep on asking for more, until you can no longer produce. You need to manage expectations well. This means having a difficult conversation at the start of every assignment about expectations, timing and support. This avoids the need for an even more awkward conversation about missed delivery later on. Knowing how to have difficult conversations early is a valuable discipline to acquire for when you are sitting on the other side of the table as a boss.

Second, be ruthless about your choices. You cannot do everything well. All leaders only succeed in a context which suits them and plays to their strengths. Churchill was useless for most of his career, but heroic for five years; he did not change, but circumstances did change. Discover what you are good at and what you enjoy, and then find roles which play to your strengths. No one ever succeeded by playing to their weaknesses.

Managing others

This is the first, and often toughest, role transition which leaders make. Many people fall at this first hurdle. They fall into the trap of the leader in the locker room. The leader in the locker room is the great football player who is made coach. The player has learned to be successful by running hard and fast, making passes and tackles and scoring goals. When they become coach they try to run even harder and faster, and contribute more tackles, passes and goals. And then they get fired because the team is losing. The job of the coach is not to play well. The job of the coach is to get the team to play well, and that is a completely different skill set.

The leader in the locker room trap is very easy to fall into. You have been promoted because you did well, so it is natural to assume that you should do more of what worked before. But promotion changes everything. As a leader, your job is not to do everything yourself. Your job is to make things happen through other people. The rules of the game have changed, so you need to change as well.

As a front-line leader, you have to learn two vital truths which will stay with you for the rest of your career:

- Your job is not to be the best person on the team; your job is to get the best people onto your team.

- When there is work to be done, you switch from asking 'how do I do this?' to 'who should do this?' How to who is a huge leap.

You have to acquire a new skill set, which you did not learn when starting out on your leadership journey. Your key skills include knowing how to motivate and delegate; managing performance; coaching and supporting your team; managing costs and workloads and directing work. While there is a huge amount of theory and training on what works, most people leaders learn from experience. The challenge is to learn the right lessons. The problem with learning from experience is that it is a random walk. If you get the right experiences, bosses, peers and role models you learn the right lessons. If you get the wrong experiences, you learn the wrong lessons. Discover best practice from books, courses, coaches and mentors.

Alongside a new skill set, you need a new mindset. The heart of the new mindset is learning to make things happen through other people. This is the shift of moving from asking yourself 'how do I do this?' to 'who can do this?'

High aspirations

High aspirations are dangerous for new leaders, if misunderstood. When leading a team for the first time, high aspirations can be translated as being highly demanding in terms of quantity and quality of work. Everything has to be bigger, better, faster. That is the traditional route of macho management. It looks strong and purposeful, but it is simply unreasonable. Soon enough, your team will burn out and drop out. A leader with no followers is not much of a leader.

If you make the team do what it has always done before, but bigger, better and faster you fail the test of leadership. Leadership is the art of taking people where they would not have got by themselves. Simply doing more of the same is not leadership. To lead, you have to change and improve what the team does.

The high aspirations mindset is more ambitious than bigger, better, faster. High aspirations does not look down into the team, but upwards to senior management. Your challenge as a team leader is to understand the agenda of your boss and bosses two or three levels up. Once you understand that, then you need to show how your team can help management achieve their agenda better. For instance, a risk manager in a bank heard that the bank wanted to be customer focused: what on earth has risk management got to do with customer focus? The risk manager decided to start visiting branches to see how risk operated at the front line. The result was to find that risk policies were causing real problems; they could be simplified and made more robust at the same time. He changed the way the team worked. They did not have to work harder, but they were far more effective and the team leader was quickly noticed and promoted by senior management.

High aspirations starts by looking up, not down. Understand top management's agenda and make it relevant to your team.

Courage

Many new leaders want to be liked, especially if they are suddenly in charge of peers they have been working with previously. This is a disaster, because it leads to weakness. You can become popular by avoiding unpleasant decisions, by not delegating unpleasant work, by avoiding difficult conversations, and not demanding high performance. You will be popular but ineffective, and soon enough you will no longer be a leader.

The currency of leadership is not popularity: it is respect. Achieving respect requires the courage to do the right things, including:

- Having difficult but constructive conversations about performance of team members.
- Setting high expectations in terms of performance.
- Making difficult decisions about people and work.

Do these things well and in a supportive manner, and you will gain respect from your team. The skills required to manage performance, delegate well and make decisions are relatively easy to learn. The challenge is not the skill. The challenge is to develop the mindset to have the courage to put these skills to work.

Resilience

The nature of resilience changes when you take on your first leadership role. Previously, resilience was about dealing with long hours, high demands and often tedious work while learning your craft. As a front-line leader, the good news is that your work will rarely be boring. You may start to wish your work could be a little more boring and predictable.

As a front-line leader, you discover the truth that firms and teams are not always improving. They are constantly struggling to stay still. You are in the Red Queen's race:[2] 'Now, here, you see, it takes all the running you can do, to keep in the same place. If you want to get somewhere else, you must run at least twice as fast as that.' Firms are not constantly improving; they are constantly struggling with the forces of decay. Experienced team members leave and are replaced by inexperienced team members, competition makes things harder, customers want more for less, top management is always starting new initiatives which you have to implement and, simply, stuff happens. As a team member, you could ignore all of this and just do your job. As the team leader, you are in the front line of dealing with all of this. You are the firm's first line of defence against chaos. Success is not a matter of having the right skills: it is a matter of having the right mindset. You need deep resilience to deal with the day-to-day challenges that come your way.

For a team leader, resilience is the product of four other mindsets (see Table 9.3). As you look at the list in Table 9.3, you will probably recognize some front-line leaders who have the resilient mindset, and some who fall into the traps. It should be clear which the better leader is and which you would prefer to work for.

Table 9.3 The making of the resilient mindset for front-line leaders

	Resilient mindset	Traps
Positive	Finding solutions, future focused, celebrating success	Complaining, blaming, 'why me?'
Accountable	Control what you can, influence what you cannot control	Hiding from problems, passing the buck
Collaborative	Enlist support from your team, peers and bosses	Being the lone hero to look good; not trusting others
Growth	Use every challenge as a chance to learn and adapt	'My way or no way', rigid thinking

Positive

Being positive is at the heart of the resilient mindset and the success mindset. Put simply, you only excel at what you enjoy. If you do not enjoy something, then it becomes ever harder to put in the discretionary effort and the extra hours that are required year after year. Enjoyment in this context does not mean the enjoyment that comes from wining and dining. It is what psychologists refer to as 'flow'. Flow is those occasions when you have been so absorbed in doing something that you have not noticed the time; you have probably forgotten about eating and it is getting late without you realizing it. If you find each hour drags out, then you are probably (like Macbeth) in the wrong role:

Tomorrow, and tomorrow, and tomorrow,

Creeps in this petty pace from day to day,

To the last syllable of recorded time.[3]

The positive mindset becomes essential for the front-line leader because a core part of your job is to motivate your team. Most team leaders (61 per cent) think they are pretty good at motivation; most team members (65 per cent) think that their team leader is not good at motivation. This is not the place to explore how to motivate teams, but you can only create a positive team if you are positive about yourself and your team. A cynical and negative team leader does not motivate, inspire or create a positive atmosphere. If you want to see what your mindset is really like, look at your team. The way your team behaves will often mirror the way you behave and think. People take their lead from their leader.

Accountable

As a team member, accountability meant holding yourself to account. As a team leader, it means you have to hold other team members to account as well. Many people struggle with this, especially if they are managing people who were their peers or friends, or they are managing older people and experts. Most humans are conflict averse: we do not enjoy giving people bad news or confronting people. But as a team leader, you have to manage performance. Your firm will have a performance management system with annual reviews, management by objectives, development systems and such like. Having a system is easy, putting it into practice is tough.

There is a trick to developing the accountability mindset: don't look back. Accountability normally means looking back at performance and seeing how well people performed. It is a demeaning process which treats adults like school children who are being marked on their homework. No wonder new leaders struggle with performance management.

Instead of looking back, look forward to what needs to happen by when. And then be ruthless about holding the team member to account for the agreed deliverables. If they are not delivered, have another conversation about what it will take to make it happen, what needs to be done differently to avoid a similar setback. Make sure they are confident that they can deliver and have the support they ask for. If they consistently fail to deliver, then you can have a conversation with them about what sort of work will best play to their strengths, inside or outside your team. The essence is to move from a judging mindset to a supporting and developing mindset focused on clear goals: you achieve the accountability without the conflict.

Collaborative

As a first-time leader your mindset makes a radical shift from 'how do I do this?' to 'who can do this?' Your job is no longer to make things happen, it is to make things happen through other people. Many first-time leaders struggle with this. They often find it difficult to delegate, for two reasons: lack of trust and fear of losing control.

To delegate well, you have to learn to trust your team. You need to adopt the mindset of positive regard: assume that your team is competent and wants to do well. The alternative is that you only really trust yourself to do things well. This is natural, but is also the route to hubris and arrogance. If you do not trust your team, they will become demoralized and you create a vicious circle of declining performance and lowering trust. If you trust them, most teams rise to the challenge and you create a virtuous spiral of rising trust and performance.

The second element of learning to collaborate with your team is to recognize that control does not mean doing it all yourself. You exert more control, not less, if you enlist the full support of your team. If you try to do it all yourself you will become overwhelmed and you will burn out and crash out. You can only achieve all you need to achieve through your team. Do not become the leader in the locker room: the player that cannot make the transition to becoming the coach.

Growth

For the first-time leader, everything changes as you move from managing yourself to managing others. You have to do something very unnatural: you have to discard the success formula which got you promoted and you have to learn new rules of survival and success. Some of these changes are listed in Table 9.4.

You can only succeed if you have the courage to learn new ways of working and leading. Building this growth mindset is fundamental to your career because the rules of engagement keep on changing. Policy manuals tell you all the boring rules about expense policies; nowhere is there a manual which tells you what the rules of survival

Table 9.4 Managing yourself and managing others

Managing self	Managing others
How do I do this?	Who can do this?
Deliver performance	Manage performance of others
Receive and act on feedback	Give feedback
Seek direction and support	Give direction and support
Take on challenges	Delegate challenges
Be positive	Be a role model for others
Work to clear goals	Manage ambiguity and change

and success are. You have to work these out each time you start a new role. There is no point in learning to be a great swimmer if your next task is to climb a mountain. You have to keep on learning and keep on changing.

Ruthless

Most leaders dislike being called ruthless, because that makes them seem like unpleasant human beings. But if you are going to lead well, you have to do some difficult things in terms of managing performance and managing people. At minimum, you need to find your hard edge. You need a hard edge to drive performance. There are always reasons why a deadline cannot be met, or why a deliverable needs to be watered down. Once you accept excuses, you accept failure. There are times you have to learn to be unreasonable about the goals, while being reasonable and flexible over the means of achieving the goals. The performance culture also means being hard edged about your team. You should support your team, but you also need to make sure you deliver. Recognize that some team members may be better off elsewhere. Ultimately, the survival of the team takes precedence over survival of the individual: you have to ensure the survival of the team as a whole.

The ruthless mindset is not about being nasty to people. It is about being very focused on achieving set goals. Once you have goal focus, then you can hold people to account and you can manage performance. If you compromise on your goals, then you have a recipe for underperformance. As a leader, you have to be tough and tender: tough in sticking to your goals, tender in how you deal with people. This means you will have to have difficult conversations with team members about performance: difficult can be positive, supportive and future focused or unpleasant, blaming and personal. Effective leaders learn to be ruthless and positive at the same time.

Managing a function

Leading from the middle is often the hardest role in management. At the bottom of the firm, you have little autonomy, but at least you normally have high clarity about what to do: meet your sales target, teach your class, prepare that report. In the middle, you still have low autonomy as you have to deal with competing and often conflicting demands from across the organization. You will find that demands routinely exceed resources and responsibilities exceed authority. At the top of the firm, things become easier: you have authority to match your responsibilities, you can shape your own role and you can direct resources where you want them. Whisper it quietly, but the job of CEO is easier and less stressful than the job of the middle manager.

Table 9.5 summarizes the challenge of leading from the middle. Leading from the middle is a big step up from front-line leadership. You move from managing a team to managing a group of teams. You no longer manage individuals: you manage managers. Once again, you find that the rules of survival and success change. You have to grow and change as your situation changes. As you move up, you still need all the skills and mindset you acquired as a front-line leader. But you need to layer in more skills and develop your mindset even further, as Table 9.6 shows.

This changing context means that the mindset of success has to evolve once again. High degrees of resilience are required to survive

Table 9.5 The challenge of leading from the middle

	Entry level	Leading from the middle	Top-level leadership
Autonomy	Low: do as you are told	Low: caught in the matrix	High: you can decide what to do
Role clarity	High: clear goals	Low: many conflicting demands from across firm	Low: high flexibility and ambiguity. Create the role as you see fit
Resources	Clear, given; long hours	Demands routinely exceed resources	High; with high control
Authority	Low responsibility matches low authority	Responsibility routinely exceeds authority	High responsibility matches high authority

Table 9.6 Developing skills and mindset as a leader in the middle

Managing others (front-line leadership)	Managing a function (several teams)
Managing front-line workers	Managing managers
Focus on making individuals work well	Focus on making the organization work well
Dealing with people	Dealing with politics
Reacting to events	Planning the future
Maintaining performance today	Changing, optimizing how things can work in future
Focus on today and this week	Focus on the future
Manage activities	Manage budgets and resources

the ambiguity and pressure to perform in the middle. And collaboration takes on a whole new meaning: it becomes a deeply political skill and mindset which you have to master.

The following are how the mindsets of success evolve for a middle leader.

High aspirations

As a front-line leader, you will have learned to read the agenda of top management, and show how that can be applied in your team. As a middle manager, you still need to do that. But now you need to show that you can raise the game. You have to be prepared to stretch and challenge your teams. That is not a matter of making them work harder, but work smarter. In other words, you need to stretch the teams to achieve business not as usual. You have to find new ways of working which deliver the agenda of top management. This is a sea change in how you think about your role. You no longer react to events, you shape events; you move from dealing with today's crisis to planning for the future; you move from maintaining the current way of working to changing the current way of working.

Having clear, high aspirations are vital to your success. High aspirations mean that you have a clear goal and a clear sense of priorities. In the middle of the firm, goal clarity makes all the difference. Once you have a clear agenda, you are in control of your destiny. If you are not clear about what you want to achieve, then you are at the mercy of events and you will find yourself struggling with endless conflicting priorities being pushed at you from the rest of the firm. Goal clarity is also essential to building your claim to fame. If you are to progress, you need to be known for something. Beating budget by 5.6 per cent is worthy but unexceptional. You have to do something different, relevant and ambitious.

Courage

As a middle leader, you require courage for three reasons.

First, courage flows from high aspirations. If you are going to make a difference, to stretch your teams and encourage business not as usual, you are going to have to change things. That takes courage, because change normally involves the risk that it may not work, and it normally involves opposition from people who do not like change.

Second, you need to be prepared to fight battles within the firm. These battles will be for securing budget and resources for your group, agreeing the goals and priorities which you think your group needs and fighting unwanted interference from peers and bosses. If you cannot fight these battles, you quickly lose control over your agenda and your destiny.

Third, you need to have difficult conversations. These are harder than the difficult conversations you had as a middle leader with your team. There, you had the benefit of authority on your side. As a middle leader, many of your difficult conversations will be with peers and bosses whom you do not control. These are the conversations about budgets, resources, goals and priorities.

The challenge is how to develop the courage you need. The reality is, you probably already have it. That means you do not have to develop courage, you simply have to discover the courage you already have. High aspirations are, again, the key to the courage mindset. If you genuinely believe in, and you are committed to, the goals you have then you will do what is necessary to achieve those goals. You will have the difficult conversations, you will fight the right battles. If you are unclear or uncommitted, you will simply compromise.

Resilience

The nature of resilience changes as you progress through the firm. As you started out on your leadership journey, resilience was about dealing with long hours and mundane work. In the middle, you may still have long hours and much of your work will seem mundane to you. But in the middle, you face a different set of pressures which come from two sources: ambiguity and lack of control. You face conflicting pressures and demands from your team, your bosses and your peers. This can cause real stress. You have to find a way of managing the stress in the middle before the stress burns you out.

The clue to managing stress is taking control. The difference between pressure and stress is control. Most of us respond well to pressure. Put the other way around, lack of pressure does not bring out the best in us. Pressure is about rising to meet challenging demands. Most leaders like to rise to a challenge, if we are in control of our fate. Now try keeping the pressure and taking away the control: you still have the deadline, but now you depend on peers and third parties to help you deliver. Your needs are not their most urgent needs. Suddenly, the pressure starts to turn to stress: your fate depends on other people. That is the reality of leading from the middle.

Leading from the middle you cannot control everything and everyone. You have to learn a new way of leading, which is about leading through influence: persuading, aligning agendas, building trust and commitment. The more you learn how to control your agenda and control your destiny, the less you will feel the stress of middle leadership. You will be adding another layer of resilience to your armoury.

Positive

In the middle, you need all of the positive mindsets you learned in the first two stages of your leadership journey. Now you need to add one more layer. The trick is in how you think about the endless challenges you face as a middle leader. If every challenge is a burden, then you will be crushed. The best leaders in the middle see challenges not as a problem, but as an opportunity. They are opportunities to shine, to learn, to make a difference and to be noticed. Suddenly, this means that challenges are not to be shunned; they are to be embraced.

This utopian vision of middle management leads the cynics to talk about having opportunities which have to be solved. And not every challenge is life enhancing. Some are mundane but vital; get it right and no one notices, get it wrong and the sky falls down. In practice, you have to choose which challenges you are going to take on personally, and which you can delegate. A mundane challenge for you can be a major learning opportunity for one of your team. Frame challenges the right way and they can be enjoyed, not endured.

Accountable

It is easy to get lost in the middle of a large organization, where responsibilities may be shared across functions and groups. It is easy to hide but hard to shine in the middle of a matrix. Many leaders in the middle choose to keep their heads down and avoid trouble. You can survive that way, for a while, but you cannot succeed.

The success mindset actively seeks out accountability, for a simple reason: success requires that you have a claim to fame. A claim to fame is something which gets noticed by management at least two levels above you. So it has to be relevant and meaningful to the agenda of top management. You have to make a difference. This way of thinking becomes increasingly important as you move towards more senior roles. The more senior you become, the greater the ambiguity of your role and the greater your freedom in deciding your agenda. Less successful leaders muddle along and follow the agenda they inherited. The best leaders pick one or two things where they really want to make a difference, and they focus their efforts accordingly. You still have to worry about business as usual; that is what you have your team for. But you also have to be clear about where you personally will make a difference and be held to account. You have to learn to get out of the weeds of detail, and start working on what matters most.

Collaborative

The collaborative mindset takes on two new meanings for leaders in the middle.

First, you have to think differently about how you manage your team. You are now managing managers. Experienced managers want autonomy and do not like being micro-managed. Many of your managers may also be first-time managers who are inexperienced and are making the vital, and painful, transition from being a team player to a team manager. For both types of manager, there is an effective way of managing them: coach them. The coaching mindset is fundamentally different from the traditional managing mindset. In the managing mindset, the boss has the brains and the team has the hands: the job of the boss is to tell the team what to do and then tell them if they have done it well. The coaching mindset works the other way around. It does not assume that the boss has all the answers. It assumes that the team has the answers. So the job of the leader is not to tell the team the answers, but to help the team discover the answers. This works if you are managing experienced managers, because you let them flaunt their expertise. It works for new managers, because your coaching helps them learn what works best. It works for both groups of managers because the solution they come up with will be their solution. That means they own the solution and they will be committed to making it happen. You never want to hear your team doing something because 'that is what the boss wants'. Coach your team to success.

Second, the collaborative mindset is also the political mindset. Politics is often seen as grubby, but politics is the art of making the organization work for you, when you do not have power over it. It is a vital skill set to master. If your mindset is that your power is limited by your formal authority, then you struggle to achieve what you need to achieve. Instead of focusing on power and authority, focus on your ability to influence. With influence, your power stretches as far as you want it to stretch. The core skills of influence include building trust, aligning agendas, fighting the right battles, holding persuasive conversations and creating alliances based on common interests.[4] Effective leaders do not wait to be given power, they create their own networks of influence and power which help them achieve exceptional results.

Growth

We have already seen how the mindset of success grows and changes when you move from being a front-line leader to a leader in the middle. The words remain the same but their meaning changes: high aspirations, courage, resilience, positive, accountable and collaborative mindsets all have to be re-learned and grown.

But there is a growth trap for leaders in the middle. You not only have to learn the rules of surviving and succeeding, you also have to prepare to step up to leading the whole organization. That means you need to see beyond your function, beyond today's agenda and beyond your own skill set. You need to act not just as a middle leader today, but as a top leader in waiting. You will find very little help in knowing what this looks like. At junior levels it is very clear what you have to do to succeed: you meet and beat targets which have been set for you. But what is required for you to become a top leader? What do you have to do and show? Nothing is written down for you. There is a Japanese expression for this: *kuuki o yomu*, which means 'read the air'. This involves knowing what to do, how to behave, who to work with, what agenda to follow and how to position yourself. Put simply, you have to be able to see the world through the eyes of the CEO and the board: understand their needs and concerns and where you fit in their agenda. You have to rise above your current role.

Not everyone is comfortable with growing into the top role. And there is a gender bias here: men are typically happy to go for the top job when they are 30–40 per cent ready. They think they can learn on the job where they need to. So they apply early and often for top roles. If they get rejected, they assume that the appointments panel has made a mistake. Men have the self-belief to blag their way to the top. Typically, women (not all) are more cautious: they want to know they are 100 per cent ready for the top job. But the reality is that you can never be 100 per cent ready: there is always more you have to learn on the job. And then when they get rejected they assume that rejection shows that they were not ready for the top job, as they feared. Clearly, these are stereotypes. But they have their basis in reality.[5]

If you want to become a top leader you need to start seeing the world through the eyes of a top leader. And you need the self-belief to then put yourself forward for a top role. The good news is that looking at most top leaders should convince you that if they can do it, you can do it. As one highly entrepreneurial top leader expressed it: 'I use to be in awe of these older people with big titles in big roles. Then I realized they were all idiots. Just like the rest of us. It was then I realized that I could make it. You don't have to be super human to succeed, you just have to be human.'

Ruthless

For better or for worse, increasing seniority brings with it increasing ruthlessness. As a front-line leader, you are concerned about individual jobs and roles. As a middle leader you may change or eliminate entire teams. As a top leader, you may be changing or eliminating entire functions and businesses. You may not like making these decisions, and few leaders do like them, but these are the decisions that ensure the health of the firm overall.

But for a middle leader, ruthlessness not only increases in scale, it also changes in form. As a middle leader, you are struggling with competing agendas. You discover that the greatest competition is not in the market place, but is sitting at a desk near you. Your peers are competing with you for a limited amount of budget, management time and support and promotions. You have to collaborate closely with your competitors in the office. This is a difficult balancing act, and it is easy to fall over. If you are too collaborative then you become weak and you never get to enforce your agenda. If you are too competitive you become the office psychopath that everyone wants to fail.

The way to balance collaboration and competitiveness is through the accountable mindset, where you make sure you hold yourself to account for one or two big agenda items where you can make your mark. Once you know what your vital interests are, you can be ruthless in pursuing those interests while being highly collaborative with your peers on their non-conflicting agendas. Ruthlessness comes from complete goal clarity; if you don't know what you want to achieve, then you will always compromise and always come up short. Know what you want and make sure you get it.

Managing a business: top leadership

Once you reach the top, you may think you have finished your journey. You have not finished your journey: you have embarked on a new journey which will define the success or otherwise of your career.

Top leaders face many traps to trip them up. The biggest traps are not about markets, competition, the economy and regulation. They are all avoidable mindset traps. The four biggest traps for leaders at the top are:

- Failing to lead.
- Hubris.
- Failing to learn.
- Not knowing your role.

Each of these traps is deadly. We will explore each one in turn.

Failing to lead

Just because you have a leadership title, that does not mean you are leading. Do not confuse title with performance. The definition of a leader is someone who takes people where they would not have got by themselves. Against this benchmark, you should have been leading for many years before you become a top leader. But as you become more senior, the performance bar rises. You have to do much more to show that you really are taking people where they would not have got by themselves. Many leaders, even prime ministers and presidents, make minor changes which make them think they are leading. History then shows that they were just tinkering with a legacy which they inherited. Your first challenge is to think and act like a leader: what are you doing to take people where they would not have got by themselves?

Hubris

Once you get to the top, life changes. Suddenly all your jokes become funny and all your ideas become brilliant. You find yourself surrounded by sycophants who all want your time, your support, your budget, your approval. There is no such thing as an honest conversation. Everyone wants to use you, and everyone wants to flatter you. It is very easy to be seduced by this flattery and to believe it. From there it is a short step to believing that you are indispensable, like dictators around the world who believe no one can or should replace them. To avoid this trap, Romans got a slave to whisper memento homo ('remember, you are mortal') to generals on their triumphal marches.[6] This is not a choice you have, but you can remember to be human and remember that leadership is a team sport. Graveyards are full of irreplaceable people. Be humble and recognize that you are part of a team. Your job is not to be the super hero that knows and does everything. Your job is to be the super hero that builds the team which knows and does everything.

Failing to learn

By the time you reach the top you will have a lifetime of experience which tells you what works and what does not work. You will, naturally, want to apply your success formula. That way, disaster lies. Typically, marketers see marketing and revenue generation as the solution, accountants see costs as the solution, engineers see operational excellence as the solution. These solutions may have worked for you in the past. If you are lucky, they will work for you as a CEO. But hope is not a strategy and luck is not a method. You have to learn new ways of succeeding. As we have seen, at every stage of the leadership journey the rules of survival and success change. The transition to top leadership is no different.

Not knowing your role

Your title is clear – it will be something like CEO. But that tells you nothing about what you do. And the answer is very different if you are leading a start-up with three people or leading a business with 3,000 people. The larger your firm, the less you should do. In the start-up, you are likely to be your own IT help desk, receptionist and accounts receivables department. If you are doing these things when you are in charge of 3,000 people you are doing the wrong thing. As the CEO you have to shape your own role; no one is going to tell you what it should be. As the firm grows, you focus on fewer things. Ultimately, just three things matter in what can be called the IPM agenda. You need the right Idea (I) about how you are going to make a difference. Then you need to build the right team with the right people

(P) to make the idea happen. And finally, you have to sweat the money (M). Even as CEO, you have to learn to grow and adapt your role as your firm grows and adapts. Growth never stops.

High aspirations

At the top, you have to discover vision. Fortunately, this does not mean you have to be a visionary. It means you need a very clear idea about what you and your firm will do. Your idea is simply a story in three parts:

1 This is where we are.

2 This is where we are going.

3 This is how we will get there.

If you want to motivate your team, add one more element: 'This is your very important role in helping us get there.' Give your team a sense of purpose, relevance and ambition. Let them rise to your challenge and to their potential. The limit of the firm's ambition is the limit of your ambition. The firm will not be more ambitious than you are, so dare to stretch your team.

Thinking of your vision as a story shows the nature of high aspirations for a top leader. As a top leader, your vision has to:

- be very simple, so everyone can understand it;
- stretch the team, so that they achieve what they would not have achieved without you;
- focus the efforts of the firm, so they know what their priorities should be;
- be unique, relevant and meaningful to each part of your team; everyone should know how they can contribute to achieving the vision.

The idea may be simple, but making it happen is always hard and complicated. As a top leader, you have to create clarity out of ambiguity and simplicity out of complexity. Be clear about your choices and stick to them.

Courage

Having a vision requires courage. At its simplest, it means you chose to do *a*, *b* and *c*, and not do *x*, *y* and *z*. There will always be people who are happy to drip feed the cancer of doubt into your firm (behind your back), suggesting that *a*, *b* and *c* are all wrong and you should pay more attention to *x*, *y* and *z*. Remember the advice of Rudyard Kipling in the poem *If—*:

> ... trust yourself when all men doubt you,
>
> But make allowance for their doubting too.

Making clear and bold choices takes courage. As a leader, you will have been growing your courage at every step of your leadership journey. This is not the time for turning back.

Resilience

You may hear people say 'It's lonely at the top' or 'It's tough at the top'. This is hogwash. It is neither lonely nor tough at the top. Once you break out of middle leadership and reach top leadership, the need for resilience reduces. As a middle leader, you were not in control of your destiny, your responsibilities exceeded your authority, you faced conflicting demands and your obligations were greater than your resources. You need real resilience to deal with that. But at the top, the challenges of middle leadership vanish: you are in control of your destiny, your authority matches your responsibility and your resources match your obligations. You are the one that decides what the goals should be. If you face conflicting goals, look in the mirror and sort it out.

Among all the mindsets, resilience is unique because it becomes less demanding at the top. But that does not mean it disappears completely. Top leaders need a special sort of resilience which comes from pursuing a clear and focused agenda.

First, you need resilience to avoid distractions and stay focused on your agenda. There will be endless demands from your team which will distract you. Many of these will be urgent matters. But you have to stay focused on what is important; if you get trapped by dealing with what is urgent, you become a firefighter, not a leader. You have a team which should be capable of dealing with urgent stuff; trust them and empower them to deal with what is urgent.

Second, you need resilience to push your agenda. One CEO remarked after three years in the job that he had not understood what it would really take: 'I probably only spent 5 per cent of my time figuring out the solution. I have spent 50 per cent of my time communicating the solution, and the rest of the time dealing with noise.' You have to be relentless in communicating your vision. Your vision is obvious to you, because you thought of it and you live with it. You need to make it real and relevant for everyone in the firm; make sure that it flows through the agendas of everyone from top to bottom of the firm. Never grow tired of communicating and pushing your vision.

Positive

In your leadership journey, you will have learned how to be positive about what you do, who you are and how you think. As a top leader, that is not enough. As noted earlier, leaders are dealers in hope. You have to show everyone that there is a better and brighter future ahead, even if today is tough. That is part of what you have to communicate in your vision.

When times are good, it is easy to be positive and to project confidence. When times are good, everything is easy. But that is not the real test of leadership. Your test starts when things go wrong and the future looks bleak. This is not the time to express doubt; your little cloud of doubt will expand into a major depression across your firm. People take their cues from their leaders. Even if you feel doubt and uncertainty, your followers want hope and certainty. Give them what they need. That does not mean you have to stay on the wrong path; if you need to change direction, then change direction with vigour and certainty.

As a top leader, you will find you live life in a goldfish bowl: everyone is always looking at you and observing you, whether you like it or not. So being positive is not just about what you say and do. It is also about how you say and do things. There are different ways of being positive: you can be energetic and enthusiastic; you can be quiet and supportive. Be true to yourself, but dial up your more positive qualities to the maximum. Your team will respond to how you are as much as to what you do.

Accountable

By the time you reach the top, you should have acquired the account-ability mindset. But a short review of firms' annual reports show that accountability is often treated as a one-way street by people at the top. If things go well, then clearly management take the credit and take the bonus. If things go wrong, the excuses start pouring out: the economy, regulators, competition, weather, political uncertainty. The problem with making excuses is that it sets precisely the wrong culture for the rest of the firm. Everyone else becomes cynical about the talent and honesty of top management; everyone assumes that making excuses or pointing the finger of blame is the way to deal with setbacks.

As a top leader, you need to create not just an accountability framework, but an accountability culture. This starts with how you behave. Care is needed. If you create a culture of 'no excuses' then you create a highly political environment where everyone plays the blame game. If you create a culture of 'bring me solutions, not problems', then every problem will be hidden until it blows up as a fully-fledged crisis. If you can create a culture which is genuinely open and honest, you have a chance of driving accountability. This means hearing about problems early, and dealing with them positively and constructively so that no one fears surfacing problems in the future.

Culture eats strategy and organization for breakfast. As the top leader, you set the culture of the firm not through speeches, motivational posters, rallies and values statements on brass plaques. You set the culture by how you behave, especially when things go wrong. That is your moment to show what sort of behaviour you value most.

Collaborative

For top leaders the collaborative mindset means two things. First, leadership is a team sport. This leads to the second collaborative mindset, which is valuing diversity.

You have to build the right team for your strategy. That often means making real and painful changes, but the future of the firm takes precedence over the future of the individual in a harsh, Darwinian fashion. Even if you do not have to make big changes to the team, you have to change the way you think about people around you. For the first time in your career, you have to value staff and support groups. In the past HR, IT, finance, legal and compliance were the functions you loved to hate because they always stopped you doing what you wanted to do. Now you have to love them, because these functions will stop disaster happening and will help you keep control and make good things happen.

Because leadership is a team sport, you have to learn to value diversity of thought, talent and expertise. You cannot be an expert at everything and you do not need to be. You need to pull together the right talent for the firm to succeed. The huge trap here is building a team of people who you like and are like you. You need a diversity of talents and ways of working, you need to challenge group think and you need people who can see different problems and opportunities for you. Your mindset has to shift from distrusting and disliking some groups and types of people, to valuing and including them in your leadership team.

Growth

Nothing can prepare you fully for the top job. It is always a shock. Everyone treats you differently. They start being nice to you and flattering you, and they at least pretend to take your ideas seriously. In practice, you do not stop growing and learning when you reach the top. We have already seen how dealing with people changes in the collaborative mindset. But you also have to learn new skills and to think on a different time horizon.

Skills

As the top leader, you have responsibility for the fate of the firm, and for many people and livelihoods which depend on the firm. At a crude level, you need to hone your financial skills and strategic skills as these are core to a general manager's role. You cannot master every leadership skill yourself, so the core skill focuses on building the team which can help you achieve the goals you set. If you are to make a difference, you have to think big. Ask yourself the easy questions which are hard to answer: 'What will be really different in five years' time?' 'What is the one thing I want to be remembered for achieving?'

Time horizon

The good leader knows that an old-fashioned watch has three hands: the second hand, the minute hand and the hour hand. You have to keep track of all three hands. The second hand is about the here and now: even at the top, you will have to deal with urgent issues as well as important issues. The hour hand is about seeing the long-term future: are you building the foundations of future success or are you just pumping up performance for this year's bonus? The hour hand finds expression in your big idea: how are you going to make a difference and take people where they would not have got by themselves? The minute hand is those critical change projects which form the bridge between today and tomorrow; there will be two or three which are important enough for you to take direct ownership. As the top leader, you have to deal with today, but you also have to think further into the future than ever before.

Ruthless

By the time people reach the top, they often find it easy to be ruthless. They do not even realize that they are being ruthless. They are simply being goal focused.

Early on in a career being ruthless is tough because you have never had to be it before, and because being ruthless is often highly personal. You have to move people on or out. At the top, you will still have to make some hard personal decisions about your top team. But these will be relatively easy; you have made such decisions before and if you are really committed to your goals you will know you have to make these decisions.

At the top, the most ruthless decisions are often the easiest to make. These are the decisions you make to sell or close a business, to outsource work, to start a takeover. These decisions seriously mess with people's lives, but they do so in a highly impersonal way from your perspective. You are focused on the big strategic question. The grubby, messy reality of changing or eliminating jobs and roles is borne by your middle leaders. As the top leader, your concern is for the future, not the past. That means you focus on the morale of the survivors, not the leavers.

As ever, your ruthlessness will come from your commitment to clear goals. If you want to make a difference, you have to make hard decisions.

Managing a group: beyond top leadership

The purpose of this section is to give some insight into how leaders of very large organizations think and act. Once you see the world through their eyes, you have a chance of influencing them positively. Because they are in a different place, they will see the world differently. Because they have more power than you do, it is worth understanding their view of the world.

First, it pays to know who these leaders are and where to find them. This raises a basic question: how can there be anything beyond top leadership? If top leadership is defined as running a business, then running a group of businesses is clearly a step up. And chairing a business is also a step up. Running a group of businesses is proactive: you make the decisions. Chairing a business is reactive: you react to events and to proposals from top management. In other ways, they are similar. In both cases you become sufficiently removed from the front line that it becomes impossible to know what is happening everywhere all the time. You cannot be personally in control of the business. So you need a different way of thinking about how you control and lead the firm. At the extreme, how do you lead the United States or any other country? You have no way of knowing what is going on everywhere, even within your government departments. This remoteness raises four questions which you have to deal with at this level:

- What's my idea?
- How do I stay in control?
- Who do I need on my team?
- What is my role?

What's my idea?

We have already explored the importance of having a simple idea: how you will make a difference and take your firm or your country where they would not have got by themselves. By definition, you should have big and simple ideas. As a test, think of the great leaders of history or of your country. Doubtless they achieved many things, but there will be one or two things that you will remember most clearly. What will your legacy be?

How do I stay in control?

You cannot control everything that happens in a huge firm or a country; other people do that for you. You make a difference by pushing for one or two big ideas. In terms of mindset, this is a significant evolution from your CEO role. You do not try to control everything. Instead you rely on a combination of building a team you trust and building robust systems and processes which provides assurance that things happen the way they are meant to happen. Political leaders routinely fail to pay enough attention to the systems and processes of government, with the result that they are constantly surprised that policies do not work out the way they were intended.

Aside from formal control systems, it is commonplace to see leaders at this level apparently wasting time by visiting work sites, clients and stakeholders where in practice they can make little difference because they do not know the detail of what is happening and how things work. But they have two reasons for wasting time by wandering around:

- They are desperate to find out what is really going on. They only partly trust all the formal reports and presentations they receive. They put disproportionate value on what they discover for themselves. This is a huge opportunity for leaders lower in the organization to influence and shape events. Make sure they discover what you want them to discover when they come wandering in your part of the business.

- They want to sell their agenda, and see if their agenda is being understood and acted on. Again, this is a wonderful chance for leaders lower down in the firm to shine; make sure you understand the big agenda and show that you are making it happen. You will find that you suddenly have a very powerful friend and ally.

Who do I need on my team?

By now, you will know that as a leader you have to have the right team. But you have reached a level where each of your team members will be very powerful in their own right. It is easy to lose control over the agenda to these power barons. The most powerful power barons follow the corporate adage: 'It is easier to ask forgiveness than to ask for permission.' They act first and then seek permission later. There are two antidotes to this. The first is to set a very clear agenda, which is easy if you know what your big idea is. The second is to be ruthless about enforcing your agenda.

Corporate reorganizations never find the perfect solution, because the perfect solution does not exist. But they help in two other ways. First, they send a signal to everyone about what is important. It forces people to take notice of your agenda. If you decide customers are the key to the future, reorganize from product groups to customer groups, for instance. The second purpose of any reorganization is political: move out dangerous power barons and move in loyalists. An exemplary redundancy or two at the top level concentrates the minds of the other power barons very well.

If you have picked the right team, you may need to adapt your management style. You still need to hold your team to account, but you are managing seasoned and effective leaders. They do not need micro-managing. Instead, you have to create a partnership mentality, where you are working together on a common agenda. This makes your role as a leader closer to that of a partner, coach or consultant than a traditional line manager. As ever, you have to learn to grow and adapt on your leadership journey.

What is my role?

Again, your title may be clear but your role is what you make it. In practice, you will have two roles. The first role is compulsory. You become a role model, for better or for worse. Think back to all the leaders you have worked for: you may be vaguely aware of one or two things they achieved, but you will recall vividly how they behaved and what they were like to work for. People will not remember you achieve. They will remember you for how you are. You can decide what sort of a role model you want to be. Choose well.

The second part of your role is optional: you can shape your role as you want it to be. The critical question you have to answer is: 'What is it I can do that no one else can do?' Shaping the agenda and picking your team are essentials. For politicians, being great communicators is a vital skill. Beyond that, there is not much; at the top, you can afford to be lazy. But you also have to be ruthless in pursuing your agenda. Throughout the ages, the most powerful leaders have shown no hesitation in fighting the battles that need to be fought; more precisely, they have sent young men to get killed in pursuit of their agenda. Your decisions may not be life threatening, but they will be livelihood threatening. You still have to make them.

Mindset at the very top

This brief review of leadership at the very top shows that the nature of leadership changes all the time. It changes with seniority, role, context and the scale of the firm. When conditions change, you have to change as well: you have to change your role, your focus, your skills and your mindset. The leadership journey is also a learning journey.

Below is a very short summary of how mindset develops at the very top, when you are leading a group of businesses, a government or a large and complex firm:

High aspirations
Focus on one or two must-win battles where you will secure your legacy and create a better future for the firm.

Courage
Be brave enough to trust your team to deliver. Learn to step back and stop interfering; this is remarkably hard to do for leaders who have spent their entire careers believing that success comes from delivery. At this level, success comes from getting others to deliver.

Resilience
You need to be persistent and focused, but you are past the need for deep resilience. Complaining about your intense travel schedule does not count if you travel first class around the world: you are showing off.

Positive
You are now a role model, and you are under constant observation. Act the way you would want to be remembered, because people will remember you more for how you are and less for what you achieve.

Accountable
Define your role, knowing that less is more. What is it that you, and only you, can do? Everything else has to be delegated. As with courage, learn to let go.

Collaborative

Very experienced leaders now report to you. They will resent being micro-managed. Instead, you have to forge a relationship which is about partnership, coaching and consulting.

Growth

Your role has changed again, but there is no one to tell you what your role is or how to perform it. The rules of survival and success have not changed, because there are no rules; you have to make the rules yourself. Your challenge is to make the right rules.

Ruthless

Stay focused on your goal and do what it takes to get there. In practice, leaders below you will have to do most of the dirty work.

Summary

Your leadership career is a journey. The rules of survival and success change at every stage of your journey. This helps explain why many people stall or drop out at each level: they fail to adapt. Do not let yourself become a prisoner of your own success where you apply your previous success model to your new context. Keep on learning, keep on changing.

Here is what you have to do to manage your leadership journey:

Look and learn from leaders one or two levels above you

- Learn what they do well and copy it.
- Learn from their mistakes and avoid them.
- Understand their agenda and show how your work helps them.
- See the world through their eyes, so that you can influence them better.

Do not become a prisoner of success

- Realize that what worked in the past will not work in the future in a different context.

- See every new role as a chance to learn and grow.

Manage your learning journey

- You need to learn both hard skills ('know what') and soft skills ('know how').

- Build technical skills at the start of your career; build people and political skills to progress your career further.

- Do not succumb to the random walk of experience; make sure you get the right roles where you can develop the leadership skills for the future.

- Get help from mentors, coaches, books and courses so that you can structure your learning and make sense of the nonsense you encounter.

Finally, remember that you are accountable for your leadership journey. You are the only person that makes your journey a success, so make the most of it.

Conclusion

Return to the bright side – enjoy your journey

Mindset means becoming the best of who you are.

Remember that even leaders are human. To quote Shakespeare:

> If you prick us do we not bleed?
>
> If you tickle us do we not laugh?
>
> If you poison us do we not die?
>
> And if you wrong us shall we not revenge?[1]

Where there is humanity, there is glorious diversity: good and bad, smart and slow, strong and weak, funny and serious. There is no such thing as a perfect human, and there is no such thing as a perfect leader: 'No leader gets ticks in all the boxes.'[2] This is hugely reassuring to all of us who suspect that we may be less than 100 per cent perfect. We do not need to be perfect.

Nor do we need to be like someone else. The ideal of leadership is occasionally held up to be some implausible combination of Genghis Khan and Mother Theresa. Just for a moment, try swapping the two of them around. Watch Mother Theresa lead the Mongol hordes as they rampage across Asia and into Europe. Then watch Genghis Khan sort out the slums of Calcutta: he might succeed, but not to the advantage of the locals. So leadership is about context. We have to find the context where we can play to our strengths, and then we have to build a team around us to compensate for any (very minor) weaknesses we may have.

But if we cannot succeed by trying to be someone else, nor can we succeed simply by being ourselves. If we hang around like a teenager in full hormonal angst waiting for the world to recognize our innate genius and humanity, we could be in for a very long wait. This paradox appears to leave no way forward: we cannot succeed by being ourselves nor by being someone else.

The solution to the paradox is that we have to be the very best of who we are. That means the growth mindset is vital. We have to keep on learning, growing and building on our strengths. That makes leadership a journey, not a destination.

If leadership is the art of taking people where they would not have gone by themselves, then our leadership journey starts as soon as we want it to, even at school. Leadership is about what you do, not about your title. Whatever your position is, you can make change happen by building support with the right people. To lead change is to lead.

Our leadership journey often starts by building technical skills. We have to learn our craft, our profession. Accountants need to know how to do a stock check. But if you are still doing stock checks at the age of 50, you probably have not gone far on your leadership journey. To sustain your journey you need much more than technical skills. And technical skills are a commodity: plenty of people have them. The people with the freshest technical skills tend to be young, cheap and hungry; if you rely on technical skills you have to compete against those people, and cheaper resources from low-income countries. You have to have much more than technical skills.

The next layer of talent you have to acquire on your leadership journey are people and political skills. People skills are essential to making things happen through people you may not control and you may not like. These are the skills of motivation, delegation, performance management, coaching and support. Less obvious is the need to build political skills. Politics can be benign: it is the art of making things happen with and through other departments. That calls for skills in negotiating, collaborating, aligning agendas and dealing with conflict productively.

All of these skills are normally learned through experience: either personal experience or watching how others do these well or less well.

It is an apprenticeship in leadership. What it lacks in theoretical elegance, it makes up for in practicality and relevance.

With all these technical, people and political skills you can become a very good leader. But there is an invisible barrier that separates the very good leader from the great leader. The very good leader can move things forward in steady steps; the great leader will take people far beyond where they thought was possible. These best leaders often do not have the outward skills of normal leaders. They have something else: they have the right mindset.

With the right mindset you have an invisible advantage over everyone else. Skills you can observe and copy. It is much harder to observe and copy mindset. The right mindset means that you react differently to others in the same situation: perhaps because you have more courage, more resilience or you see things more positively. Because you think differently, you get a different result.

Mindset not only means you react differently. It means you take a different journey from your peers. You put yourself in positions where you learn and grow faster; you take on the more challenging opportunities; you see opportunity where others see risk; you see the world differently. The result is likely to be a life led with the record button on: it will be vivid and memorable, even if it is at times more exciting than comfortable. And with the right mindset, the roller coaster of life is enjoyable: the occasional dips are not valleys of death, but the springboard to the next summit.

Mindset is your secret weapon that will let you go further than you imagine today. It is not a commodity that can be offshored to the cheapest labour. It is not something others can copy. And it does not ask you to become a different person. It simply helps you to become the best of who you are. The secret of success is in your head. Unleash it.

No one can predict the future. All of our journeys diverge and go on different paths. If the destination is uncertain, then we should make the most of our journey. And we only excel at what we enjoy. So whatever your journey is, enjoy it.

ENDNOTES

Introduction

1 Department of Education quoted in *Wall Street Journal*, 6 January 2013.

2 Throughout the text, I respect leaders' requests for anonymity where appropriate. This refers to the CEO of a large financial services and travel group.

3 Fry and Osborne, Oxford Martin School, 18 September 2013 [Online] www.futuretech.ox.ac.uk/news-release-oxford-martin-school-study-shows-nearly-half-us-jobs-could-be-risk-computerisation.

4 Jim Lewis, Robots of Arabia, *Wired* [Online] http://archive.wired.com/wired/archive/13.11/camel.html?pg=1&topic=camel&topic_set=.

5 [Online] www.bbc.co.uk/news/technology-28484536, 25 July 2014; Starwood Hotels are also Testing a Robot Butler (www.bloomberg.com/news/2014-08-19/robot-butler-debuts-at-cupertino-ca-hotel.html). Google are testing driverless cars; IBM created Watson, which won US gameshow Jeopardy; IPSoft have created Amelia, which can have natural language conversations, learns and solves problems (http://online.wsj.com/articles/amelia-a-machine-thinks-like-you-do-1411948078). Human skills are being tested by technology as never before.

6 Miller and Atkinson argue that robots will increase productivity, prosperity and jobs, but accept that up to 30 per cent of current jobs are at risk just with current technology [Online] www2.itif.org/2013-are-robots-taking-jobs.pdf.

7 Matlda is a robot that has no gender, race or faith bias and unerringly detects your facial expressions and emotions. She, or he or it, may be a better interviewer than humans [Online] https://www.ft.com/content/b71f0afa-9c36-11e6-8324-be63473ce146.

8 FRBSF Economic Newsletter, 5 May 2014 [Online] www.frbsf.org/economic-research/publications/economic-letter/2014/may/is-college-worth-it-education-tuition-wages/.

9 From *Forbes*, 16 June 2014 [Online] www.forbes.com/billionaires/list/#tab:overall. Inherited wealth excluded (eg Walton family).

10 I am co-founder of Teach First, which gets great graduates to teach in the most challenging schools. It is now the largest graduate recruiter in the UK.

11 Jim Collins (2001) *Good to Great*, Random House Business.

12 Robert H Waterman Jr and Tom Peters (2004) *In Search of Excellence: Lessons from America's best-run companies* (2nd edn) Profile Books.

13 [Online] www.businessweek.com/articles/2012-07-19/how-to-write-a-bestselling-business-book. Other estimates rise as far as 50,000 business books per year.

14 Some overconfidence can help. Overconfident people tend to be rated more highly by their peers than underconfident people, irrespective of their actual performance. So appearing confident matters, but we need to avoid believing our own propaganda too much. See S Lamba and V Nityananda (2014) Self-deceived individuals are better at deceiving others, *PLoS ONE*, 9 (8): e104562; doi:10.1371/journal.pone.0104562, 27 August.

15 Ola Svenson (February 1981) Are we all less risky and more skilful than our fellow drivers? *Acta Psychologica*, 47 (2), pp 143–48. Similar results were obtained from Swedish drivers, although they were slightly less self-confident than their American counterparts.

16 Mark D Alicke and Olesya Govorun (2005) The better-than-average effect, in *The Self in Social Judgment: Studies in self and identity*, ed Mark D Alicke, David A Dunning and Joachim I Krueger, pp 85–106, Psychology Press.

17 *Social Psychology Quarterly* (American Sociological Association), 64 (3), pp 207–23.

18 The 'cowardly' lion does not realize he is brave until given a magic liquid by the wizard (in the book) or a medal (in the film).

19 Over 90 per cent of Fortune 500 American CEOs are above average height, *Economist* (23 December 1995). According to the same article, tall people are also paid more, and are preferred by the opposite sex, parents and voters.

20 See www.leadershippartnership.com; also contact Jo Owen at jo@ilead.guru.

Chapter 1

1 You may be able to find the speech on YouTube. Copyright restrictions make it difficult to quote or use the speech without payment: is pursuit of the dream giving way to pursuit of the cash?

2 Wendy Kopp is the CEO and founder of Teach for America. I first spoke with her in autumn 2001.

3 Independent verification from High Fliers [Online] www.highfliers.co.uk/download/GMReport14.pdf.

4 Real case; name changed.

5 Brett Wigdortz, CEO, Teach First.

6 James Toop, CEO, Teaching Leaders.

7 Consider, for example, Alexander the Great, also known as Alexander the Barbarian in Persia as a result of his destruction of that ancient empire. Thus a hero in one part of the world can be a villain in another.

8 Full name withheld.

9 The warlord was acting in accordance with a long and living tradition. Cattle have been capital since ancient times. Capital, chattels and cattle have the same etymological origin; the Latin for money is pecunia, which comes from pecus meaning cattle. See Jeremy Rifkin on cattle and capitalism [Online] www.columbia.edu/~lnp3/mydocs/ecology/cattle.htm. I found cattle being used as capital while conducting research with tribes in Mali: the Fulani are nomadic herders and informal bankers to other tribes in the region. See Jo Owen (2008) *Tribal Business School: Lessons in business survival and success from the ultimate survivors*, Wiley.

10 The SAS is the Special Air Service: the elite British special forces.

11 Rice University, 12 September 1962. You can see the speech at [Online] http://er.jsc.nasa.gov/seh/ricetalk.htm.

12 From the same Rice University speech, as above.

13 Taylor was copying a term popularized by Louis Brandeis in 1910; Taylor was one of many practitioners and theorists, such as Max Weber, who were all pushing in the same direction.

14 This follows Karl Popper's falsification principle set out in *Conjectures and Refutations: The growth of scientific knowledge*

(1963). Obviously, there is more to scientific method: observation, hypothesis, testing, prediction, replicability, etc.

15 Mike Tobin, recent CEO, Telecity.

16 See Carol Dwyer, American Psychological Association [Online] www.apa.org/education/k12/using-praise.aspx.

17 See Elizabeth Gunderson *et al* (2013) Parent praise to 1- to 3-year-olds predicts children's motivational frameworks 5 years later, *Child Development*, 84 (5), pp 1526–41, September/October.

18 Named after Canadian psychologist Laurence J Peter; see Peter J Laurence and R Hull (1969) *The Peter Principle: Why things always go wrong*, William Morrow and Company, p 8.

19 Alessandro Pluchino *et al* (2010) Statistical mechanics and its applications, *Physica A*, 389 (3), 1 February, pp 467–72.

20 [Online] http://www.etoncollege.com/FamousOEs.aspx.

21 WAGs: 'wives and girlfriends', normally of top footballers. Marrying into money, power and fame is not a new idea.

22 RV Levine and A Norenzayan (1999) The pace of life in 31 countries, *Journal of Cross-Cultural Psychology*, 30 (2), March, pp 178–205. They also found: 'Faster places also tended to have higher rates of death from coronary heart disease, higher smoking rates, and greater subjective well-being.' Lilongwe in Malawi had the slowest pace of life recorded. Make your choice.

23 There are many variations of this law, which effectively states that the entropy (disorder) of the universe always increases, which helps to explain why time flows only in one direction. A teenager's bedroom is a good example of the law in action: it is always finding its way to maximum disorder.

24 *The Collected Essays, Journalism and Letters of George Orwell: In front of your nose, 1945–1950* (1968) ed Sonia Orwell and Ian Angus, Harcourt Brace Jovanovich, p 125.

25 [Online] www.youtube.com/watch?v=y6qgoM89ekM.

26 [Online] www.startupnow.org.uk.

27 Also known as Prince Turki bin Faisal Al Saud.

28 See [Online] www.outwardboundoman.com/ and http://www.universityofthedesert.com/about-us/#.U4hpvijHn9Y.

29 [Online] http://businessjournal.gallup.com/content/106912/turning-around-your-turnover-problem.aspx. The survey indicates that over 75 per cent of departures are based on factors that managers could control, but also confirms that most organizations have similar problems.

Chapter 2

1 Also known as Boudica, Boudicca or even Buddug in Welsh. In any event, she led a revolt of 100,000 Iceni against Roman rule around AD 60. A force to be reckoned with.

2 This paraphrases, and strengthens, Henry Kissinger's definition of leadership: 'The task of the leader is to get his [*sic*] people from where they are to where they have not been.'

3 Jo Owen (2008) *Tribal Business School: Lessons in business survival and success from the ultimate survivors*, Wiley. I use tribes loosely to describe all traditional societies, not all of which are organized on tribal lines.

4 Economist Frank Knight defined risk as the unknown outcome of a known probability distribution such as tossing a coin; businesses can deal with this. In contrast, uncertainty is where the probabilities are unknown; this is the 'uncertainty' that businesses always bleat about. Frank H Knight (1921) *Risk, Uncertainty, and Profit*, Hart, Schaffner & Marx; Houghton Mifflin Company.

5 See W Edwards Deming (1986) *Out of the Crisis*, MIT Press; and W Edwards Deming (1993) *The New Economics for Industry, Government, and Education*, MIT Press.

6 Sir David is Vice Chancellor of Reading University and was Permanent Secretary at the Department for Education.

7 This is an annual event, then called Teach First Week, which encourages opinion formers to experience the reality of urban education by teaching one lesson. It challenges perceptions of teaching, teachers and urban schools.

8 All his fire fighters are male.

9 This is disputable. Different surveys give different results against different benchmarks. See examples at [Online] http://answers.google.com/answers/threadview/id/47686.html.

10 The programme was *World in Action* (1984). See [Online] www.speaking.co.uk/AtkinsonCommunications/claptrap.html.

11 The charity is STIR Education [Online]: http://stireducation.org/. Disclosure: the author is the founding chairman of STIR Education.

12 Name changed at the request of the interviewee.

13 Jo Owen (2008) *Tribal Business School: Lessons in business survival and success from the ultimate survivers*, Wiley.

14 James Surowiecki (2005) *The Wisdom of Crowds*, Anchor Books, p xv. Even Surowiecki recognizes that the wisdom of crowds is highly conditional and breaks down where there is centralization, homogeneity or an information cascade: the normal condition of most firms.

15 For a full discussion on how to manage your fear and an interesting mind management model, try Steve Peters (2012) *The Chimp Paradox*, Ebury Publishing.

16 See Andrew Caruso (2005) *Sports Psychology Basics: For serious players and coaches*, Reedswain Inc; also Tony Morris, Michael Spittle and Anthony P Watt (2005) *Imagery in Sport: The mental approach to sport*, Human Kinetics.

Chapter 3

1 David Herbert Donald (1996) *Lincoln*, Simon and Schuster.

2 *Winston Churchill: The wilderness years* is an eight-part 1981 drama serial based on the politician's life, and particularly his years in enforced exile from political power during the 1920s and 1930s.

3 This speech is in dispute: some place it at an Oxford graduation ceremony after his second term as prime minister, when he was over 80. Other sources claim that his Harrow speech included the phrase above but was much longer. The legend has taken over from history.

4 Brett Wigdortz, CEO of Teach First, also subsequent quotation.

5 Dame Sue John, head of Lampton School, also subsequent quotation.

6 This may be a paraphrase of Nietzsche, who wrote: 'Out of life's school of war: What does not destroy me, makes me stronger.' Section 8, *Götzen-Dämmerung, oder, Wie man mit dem Hammer philosophirt* (Twilight of the Idols, or How to Philosophize with a Hammer), written in 1888 and published in 1889.

7 Jim Stockdale (1984) *In Love and War: The story of a family's ordeal and sacrifice during the Vietnam years*, Harper & Row. Senator McCain's record was widely discussed, and attacked, when he unsuccessfully stood as the Republican candidate for the president in 2008.

8 Jim Collins, The Stockdale Paradox [Online] www.venchar.com/ 2005/01/the_stockdale_p.htmland;.http://www.jimcollins.com/ media_topics/brutal-facts.html.

9 Viktor Emil Frankl (2000) *Viktor Frankl Recollections: An autobiography*, Basic Books.

10 Viktor Emil Frankl (2006) *Man's Search for Meaning*, Beacon Press.

11 [Online] www.ppc.sas.upenn.edu/prpsum.htm.

12 Charles Dickens (1859) *A Tale of Two Cities*, starts with: 'It was the best of times, it was the worst of times.'

13 [Online] www.standard.co.uk/sport/cricket/angus-fraser-when-i-asked-the-middlesex-players-about-visiting-auschwitz-they-all-wanted-to-go-9189302.html.

14 [Online] www.bbc.co.uk/news/entertainment-arts-27587898.

15 Different versions of this exist. According to a *Sun-Sentinel* interview (2012) Mike Tyson said: 'Everybody has a plan until they get hit. Then, like a rat, they stop in fear and freeze' [Online] http://articles.sun-sentinel.com/2012-11-09/sports/sfl-mike-tyson-explains-one-of-his-most-famous-quotes-20121109_1_mike-tyson-undisputed-truth-famous-quotes.

16 [Online] http://socialcarecurryclub.wordpress.com.

17 [Online] www.bbc.co.uk/news/blogs-ouch-26371243.

18 Anthony Willoughby is an adventurer with whom I have done fieldwork in Kenya and Papua New Guinea.

19 [Online] www.washingtonpost.com/business/capitalbusiness/ career-coach-dealing-with-rejection-and-setbacks/2012/05/04/ gIQAfS3J6T_story.html.

20 *Independent*, 12 December 2013.

21 Malcolm Gladwell (2008) *Outliers*, pp vii–ix, Little, Brown.

22 The Danger of Delegating Education to Journalists [Online] www.psy.fsu.edu/faculty/ericsson/2012%20Ericssons%20reply.

23 David Epstein (2013) *The Sports Gene*, Yellow Jersey.

24 Abraham H Maslow (1943) A theory of human motivation, *Psychological Review*, 50 (4), pp 370–96.

25 This follows poet William Blake: 'You never know what is enough unless you know what is more than enough', from 'Proverbs of Hell', 1790–93.

26 Frederick Herzberg (1959) *The Motivation to Work*, John Wiley.

27 Economic History Association [Online] https://eh.net/encyclopedia/hours-of-work-in-u-s-history/.

28 [Online] www.teachfirst.org.uk/home. Disclosure: the author is a co-founder of Teach First.

29 [Online] http://stireducation.org/. Disclosure: the author is the founding chairman of STIR Education.

30 Education for All Global Monitoring Report 2012 (UNESCO) [Online] http://unesdoc.unesco.org/images/0021/002193/219349E.pdf.

31 This was before he received his knighthood.

32 David J Becker *et al* (2007) Mortality and the Baseball Hall of Fame: an investigation into the role of status in life expectancy, paper at iHEA 6th World Congress: Explorations in Health Economics.

33 Redelmeier and Singh [Online] http://fisher.utstat.toronto.edu/reid/sta442f/2009/aawards.pdf.

34 Rablen and Oswald (2008) Mortality and Immortality: The Nobel Prize as an experiment into the effect of status upon longevity [Online] www.warwick.ac.uk/fac/soc/economics/staff/academic/oswald/nobel16may2008.pdf.

35 Klaus Fliessbach *et al* (2007) Social comparison affects reward-related brain activity in the human ventral striatum, *Science*, 23 November.

36 Christopher J Boyce, Gordon D A Brown and Simon C Moore (2010) Money and happiness: rank of income, not income, affects life satisfaction, *Psychological Science*, 9 March.

37 Sonia Blandford, CEO of Achievement for All.

38 Susan Michie (2002) Causes and management of stress at work, *Occupational & Environmental Medicine*, **59** (1). Also looks at broader causes of stress.

39 One infamous survey for deodorants found housewives reporting higher levels of stress than CEOs [Online] www.stress.org/workplace-stress/.

40 [Online] www.manchester.ac.uk/discover/news/article/?id=9783. The study required 600 hours of observing monkeys and then collecting their faecal samples. Anyone want to do the same for their colleagues?

41 Health and Safety Executive [Online] www.hse.gov.uk/stress/ furtheradvice/signsandsymptoms.htm#individuals.

42 Melitta Weiss Adamson (2004) *Food in Medieval Times*, Greenwood Press.

43 Dental care was hopeless [Online] see www.nature.com/bdj/journal/ v197/n7/full/4811723a.html.

44 A M Williamson and Anne-Marie Feyer (2000) Moderate sleep deprivation produces impairments in cognitive and motor perfor- mance equivalent to legally prescribed levels of alcohol intoxication, *Occupational & Environmental Medicine*, **57** (10). See [Online] http://oem.bmj.com/content/57/10/649.short.

45 Federal Highway Commission (1999) publication number: FHWA-RD-94-046, February. See [Online] www.fhwa.dot.gov/ publications/research/safety/humanfac/94046/index.cfm.

46 Research is showing that sleep deprivation affects gene expression in blood cells: it changes the body. Believe the research, not the anecdotes. See Carla S Möller-Levet *et al* (2012) Effects of insufficient sleep on circadian rhythmicity and expression amplitude of the human blood transcriptome, *PNAS*, **110** (12), E1132–E1141, doi: 10.1073/pnas.1217154110.

47 I am grateful to Sarah Furlan and Giunti O S for sharing their work on anti-fragility.

48 William Blake (1790–93) Proverbs of Hell, line 46, in *The Marriage of Heaven and Hell*.

49 A study by Professor Richard Dunbar of the University of Oxford (2011) to show that laughter really does reduce pain through release of endorphins. See [Online] www.ox.ac.uk/media/news_stories/ 2011/111409_1.html.

Chapter 4

1 Timothy W Smith *et al* (1988) Cynical hostility at home and work: psychosocial vulnerability across domains, *Journal of Research in Personality*, **22** (4), December, pp 525–48.

2 Elisa Neuvonen *et al* (2014) Late-life cynical distrust, risk of incident dementia, and mortality in a population-based cohort, *Neurology*, **10**, March [Online] www.neurology.org/content/early/2014/05/28/WNL.0000000000000528.

3 University of Pittsburgh, Women's Health Initiative, reported in *Oregonian* [Online] http://blog.oregonlive.com/pulse/2009/03/cynically_hostile_women_get_wh.html.

4 Harvard Medical School (2008) Why optimists enjoy better health, *Harvard Health*, May [Online] www.health.harvard.edu/press_releases/why-optimists-enjoy-better-health.

5 Ciro Conversano *et al* (2010) Optimism and its impact on mental and physical well-being, *Clinical Practice* & *Epidemiology in Mental Health*, **6**, pp 25–29, 14 May. Has a comprehensive overview of studies on the effects of optimism.

6 David Snowdon (2011) *Aging with Grace*, Fourth Estate.

7 Steve Munby is the CEO of Education Development Trust and previously of the NCSL (National College of School Leadership) and was kindly part of the leadership panel for this book.

8 Optimism (2009) a report from the Social Issues Research Centre, February [Online] www.sirc.org/publik/optimism.pdf.

9 Martin Seligman (1998) *Learned Optimism*, chapter 6, Pocket Books.

10 Richard Wiseman (2004) *The Luck Factor*, Arrow.

11 He told his troops before Bannockburn: 'If at first you don't succeed, try, try and try again.' W C Fields created his own version: 'If at first you don't succeed, try, try again. Then quit. There's no point in being a damn fool about it.' Take your pick. Read more at [Online] www.brainyquote.com/quotes/quotes/w/wcfields108002.html#wyefkPlkzIwTH4IG.99.

12 This comes from an original and trustworthy source (not on the leadership panel), but is unverified. There are obvious challenges involved in attribution and verification of this story.

13 Many resources are available to help your self-talk; for instance [Online] http://stress.about.com/od/optimismspirituality/a/positiveselftak.htm; www.college.ucla.edu/ucadvconf/powerpoint/cog-restr-talk.doc.

14 See for instance C D Batson (1998) Altruism and prosocial behavior, in *The Handbook of Social Psychology, Vol 2* (4th edn) ed Daniel Todd Gilbert, Susan T Fiske and Gardner Lindzey, McGraw Hill, pp 282–316. Also: E Gil Clary and Mark Snyder (1999) The motivations to volunteer: theoretical and practical considerations, *Current Directions in Psychological Science*, 8, 156–59.

15 Robert Cialdini (2007) *Influence: The psychology of persuasion*, Harper Business.

16 Attributed to the Chinese philosopher Laozi (*c*.604 BC–*c*.531 BC) in the *Tao Te Ching*, chapter 64.

17 [Online] www.betterhealth.vic.gov.au/bhcv2/bhcarticles.nsf/pages/ Breathing_to_reduce_stress.

18 Sarah Novotny and Len Kravitz, The Science of Breathing [Online] www.unm.edu/~lkravitz/Article%20folder/Breathing.html.

19 Thomas Graham, Jr (2002) *Disarmament Sketches: Three decades of arms control and international law*, University of Washington Press.

Chapter 5

1 Noel Tichy and Stratford Sherman (2005) *Control Your Destiny or Someone Else Will*, reprint edn, Harper Business. Tells of GE's transformation under Jack Welch, CEO 1981–2001.

2 Scientific management is the movement started by Frederick Wilmslow Taylor at the end of the 19th century, pushed hard by Louis Brandeis who coined the term 'scientific management'. Taylor's monograph in 1911, *Scientific Management*, enshrined the world of time and motion, close observation and maximizing efficiency: hence the ever-increasing speed of assembly lines. Much disliked by workers and unions.

3 RACI: common tool used, especially by consultants, to define who in an organization is Responsible (R) for an activity, who is Accountable (A) for it, who needs to be Consulted or Cooperate (C) and who needs only to be kept Informed (I). A useful tool for clarifying who does what.

4 There is an argument that these self-beliefs, plus the other two core self-beliefs of self-esteem and neuroticism are all linked closely. See Timothy A Judge *et al* (2002) Are measures of self-esteem, neuroticism, locus of control, and generalized self-efficacy indicators of a common core construct?, *Journal of Personality and Social Psychology*, 83 (3), pp 693–710.

5 See Paul E Spector (1982) Behavior in organizations as a functioning of employees' locus of control, *Psychological Bulletin*, 91 (3), pp 482–97.

6 This follows Alfred Bandura's definition of self-efficacy. A Bandura (1982) Self-efficacy mechanism in human agency, *American Psychologist*, 37 (2), pp 122–47.

7 Extensive research is available [Online] www.ppc.sas.upenn.edu/lh.htm.

8 Ellen J Langer and Judith Rodin (1976) The effects of choice and enhanced personal responsibility for the aged: a field experiment in an institutional setting, *Journal of Personality and Social Psychology*, 34 (2), 191–98. Test largely replicated by Lois M Brandriet, unpublished PhD thesis (1993) University of Utah.

9 Aleksandra Luszczynska and Ralf Schwarzer (2005) Social cognitive theory, in *Predicting Health Behaviour* (2nd edn) ed Mark Conner and Paul Norman, pp 127–69.

10 Shakespeare, *Hamlet*, Act 5, Scene 2.

11 Alfred Adler (2013) *The Science of Living*, Routledge, pp 96–97. Adler (1870–1937) was a colleague of Sigmund Freud, a qualified medical doctor and one of the founders of the psychoanalysis movement.

12 Brett Wigdortz is CEO and co-founder of Teach First. Disclosure: the author is a co-founder and board member of Teach First.

13 Christopher Peterson and Martin Seligman (2004) *Character Strengths and Virtues: A handbook and classification*, APA Press.

14 [Online] www.authentichappiness.sas.upenn.edu.

15 These tools are largely based on practical experience with groups and on the work by Bandura and others on social cognitive theory. Albert Bandura (2001) Social cognitive theory: an agentic perspective, *Annual Review of Psychology*, 52 (1), pp 1–2, and on the principle of locus of control by Julian Rutter; see Julian B Rotter (1966) Generalized expectancies for internal versus external control of reinforcement, *Psychological Monographs: General and Applied*, **80** (1), pp 1–28, and many others on self-efficacy; for instance Jeanne E Ormrod (2006) *Educational Psychology: Developing learners* (5th edn) Pearson/ Merrill Prentice Hall. They are, broadly, better at diagnosis than prescription. There is no magic formula for improving your accountability mindset.

16 Shakespeare, *Hamlet*, Act 3, Scene 1. Hamlet's famous 'to be or not to be' speech. He then goes on to contemplate taking his own life – which is not your next step.

17 David Begg, principal of Tanaka Business School at Imperial College, 2003–11.

18 Future Leaders 2009–12 investigated why male participants were putting themselves forward and gaining headship positions earlier than female participants. Significant issues around role models, parental expectations and school governor bias emerged; but there was also a noticeable attitude and belief difference between the genders.

19 NLP (neurolinguistic programming) takes this idea to an extreme. As a leader, you do not need to become an NLP expert: you need simple tools to check your language and thoughts. You can find out more here: Richard Bandler and John Grinder (1975) *The Structure of Magic I: A book about language and therapy*, Science and Behavior Books Inc, pp 5–6.

Chapter 6

1 This was extensive research that I conducted from 2001 to 2003 for *How To Lead* (Pearson). The research asked over 1,000 staff at all levels what they wanted from their boss, which gave a new perspective on what makes a good leader.

2 James Toop, CEO, Teaching Leaders.

3 The Myers and Briggs foundation has useful resources [Online] http://www.myersbriggs.org/.

4 See Jo Owen (2010) *How to Influence and Persuade*, Pearson.

5 Radio 4 *Today* programme, interview with John Humphrys, 5 May 2005.

6 Boswell quotes Johnson as saying, 'Hell is paved with good intentions', 16 April 1775, but no 'road to...'. Other attributions go back to St Bernard of Clairvaux (1091–1153), as 'Hell is full of good intentions or desires.' Again, no road. The true source of this is lost in the mists of time.

7 This is by reputation, and different agencies will have different methods. Some go for honey traps and blackmail, but these are unstable relationships built on fear. The lasting and productive relationships are built on commitment and trust.

8 Proceedings of the National Academy of Sciences (PNAS) (2014) Cortisol shifts financial risk preferences, ed Burton H Singer, University of Florida. This piece of research came to light from listening to a conversation among strangers in a coffee shop. An erudite conversation, which shows that opportunity is always around us if we look and listen for it.

9 Daniel Kahneman and Amos Tversky (1984) Choices, values, and frames, *American Psychologist*, **39** (4), pp 341–50; doi:10.1037/0003-066x.39.4.341.

10 Roland G Fryer *et al* (2012) Enhancing the efficacy of teacher incentives through loss aversion, Harvard University. Disclaimer: I am not advocating this approach in schools.

11 Dennis T Regan (1971) Effects of a favor and liking on compliance, *Journal of Experimental Social Psychology*, 7, pp 627–39; doi:10.1016/0022-1031(71)90025-4.

12 See for instance Robert Axelrod (1984) *The Evolution of Cooperation*, Basic Books; Richard Dawkins (1989) *The Selfish Gene*, Oxford University Press.

13 Elain Chan and Jaideep Sengupta (2010) Insincere flattery actually works: a dual attitudes perspective, *Journal of Marketing Research*, 47 (1), February.

14 [Online] www.economist.com/node/16990691, 9 September 2010.

15 Baroness Morgan, senior adviser to Tony Blair and chair of OFSTED.

16 Kim Jong-un is the leader of North Korea, the 'Great Successor' to 'Dear Leader', his father Kim Jong-il; they neatly marry communism and the principle of hereditary power and wealth.

17 Functions at a school might be heads of behaviour, literacy, parental engagement, special educational needs and disabilities (SEND), coordination, etc, not to mention key administrative roles such as finance and HR.

18 Deductive logic is top down: it starts with the principles and works down to the detail. Inductive logic is bottom up: it starts with concrete detail and works out the principles from that.

19 Mr Men have been a long-standing cartoon series created by Roger Hargreaves; they are wonderful. See [Online] www.mrmen.com/. He does a series of Little Miss to sit alongside Mr Men.

20 Dame Sue John, head of Lampton School.

21 At risk of shameless self promotion, my preferred source is Jo Owen (2014) *The Leadership Skills Handbook* (3rd edn) Kogan Page, pp 73–77. The second edition was CMI Book of the Year for new managers 2013. The fourth edition is even better.

22 See *The Leadership Skills Handbook*, pp 97–102, for a manager's practical approach to coaching.

23 This is a fundamental construct identified by Eric Berne in his therapeutic approach Transactional Analysis: see Eric Berne (1964) *Games People Play: The psychology of human relations*, Grove Press.

24 Eric Berne (2010) *Games People Play*, Penguin Books.

Chapter 7

1 Agriculture is widely seen to have driven the rise of civilization: food surpluses allowed for organized society beyond that of hunter gatherer tribes. See V Gordon Childe (1942) *What Happened in History*, Penguin; and V Gordon Childe (1951) *Man Makes Himself*, Harmondsworth. Civilization is derived from the Latin *Civitas* or city state: no agriculture, no city state.

2 *Financial Times*, 5 June 2014.

3 *Farmers Weekly*, 6 June 2014 [Online] www.fwi.co.uk/articles/06/06/ 2014/144916/gps-steering-tops-readers39-poll-of-best-farm-technology.htm.

4 OECD statistics [Online] http://stats.oecd.org/Index.aspx? DataSetCode=TENURE_AVE.

5 Bureau of Labour Statistics, 18 September 2012 [Online] www.bls.gov/news.release/tenure.nr0.htm. The United States uses a median average, OECD uses a mean average, so the two numbers are not directly comparable.

6 Office for National Statistics [Online] www.ons.gov.uk/ons/rel/census/ 2011-census-analysis/170-years-of-industry/170-years-of-industrial-changeponent.html.

7 [Online] http://news.fool.co.uk/news/investing/investing-strategy/ 2009/05/27/25-years-of-the-ftse-100.aspx.

8 Comparison of 1955 list at [Online] http://archive.fortune.com/ magazines/fortune/fortune500_archive/full/1955/index.html and the 2014 list at http://fortune.com/fortune500/wal-mart-stores-inc-1/. Some have gone private or survive under other ownership.

9 The tables that follow were based on research I conducted 2001–03, which was first published in Jo Owen (2011) *How to Lead*, Pearson.

10 Disclosure: the author is one of the founders and a board member of Future Leaders.

11 This is normally attributed to Charles Darwin. The Wikipedia entry on Darwin insists it is a misattribution. This is what the entry says (on 6 June 2014): 'The earliest known appearance of this basic statement is a paraphrase of Darwin in the writings of Leon C Megginson, a management sociologist at Louisiana State University.' (Leon C Megginson (1963) Lessons from Europe for American business, *Southwestern Social Science Quarterly*, **44** (1), pp 3–13.)

12 Elizabeth A Kensinger (2004) Remembering emotional experiences: the contribution of valence and arousal, *Reviews in the Neurosciences*, **15** (4), pp 241–51.

13 Elizabeth F Loftus, Geoffrey R Loftus and Jane Messo (1987) Some facts about 'weapon focus', *Law and Human Behavior*, **11**, pp 55–62; doi:10.1007/BF01044839.

14 For a sharp distinction between fixed and growth mindsets see Carol Dweck (2007) *Mindset: The new psychology of success*, Ballantine Books.

15 Excellent examples of this sort of disruptive competition are given in Gary Hamel and C K Prahalad (1996) *Competing for the Future*, Harvard Business School Press.

16 Homo sapiens have lasted about 200,000 years; dinosaurs lasted about 200 million years until the impact event in Yucatan about 66 million years ago and/or the Deccan traps of the same era: both changed the climate dramatically. See Luis W Alvarez *et al* (1980) Extraterrestrial cause for the Cretaceous–Tertiary extinction, *Science*, **208** (4448), pp 1095–1118. See Michael Hopkin (2005), Ethiopia is top choice for cradle of Homo sapiens, *Nature News*, doi:10.1038/news050214-10.

17 Andrew S Grove (1998) *Only the Paranoid Survive*, Profile Books.

18 From the ancient Greek words: *phobos* (fear) and *atyches* (unfortunate).

19 Carol Dwyer, American Psychological Association [Online] www.apa.org/education/k12/using-praise.aspx.

20 Michelangelo took four years, 1508–12, on this commission; painting a ceiling is very uncomfortable, and it is a fresco – which increases the challenge; plus Michelangelo was primarily a sculptor, not a painter. But you do not refuse a pope, especially not Julius II, the Warrior Pope.

21 Don E Hamachek (1978) Psychodynamics of normal and neurotic perfectionism, *Psychology*, **15**, pp 27–33.

22 Kaizen simply means 'good change'. It has become associated with continuous improvement in process industries, as championed by Toyota.

23 See Jo Owen (2008) *Tribal Business School: Lessons in business survival and success from the ultimate survivors*, Wiley.

Chapter 8

1 'You could be great, you know, and Slytherin will help you on the way to greatness, no doubt about that' – the Sorting Hat to Harry Potter. J K Rowling (1997) *Harry Potter and the Philosopher's Stone*, Bloomsbury.

2 Sonia Blandford, CEO, Achievement for All.

3 Sally (Baroness) Morgan, adviser to Tony Blair when he was prime minister.

4 James Darley, director of recruiting, Teach First.

5 Steve Munby, CEO, Education Development Trust.

6 Reuben Moore, Teach First, Leadership Development.

7 From a senior corporate partner who, like most leaders, did not want to be seen as ruthless although they act that way.

8 Kevan Collins, CEO, Education Endowment Foundation.

9 Sir Alexander Fleming discovered penicillin in September 1928 (although antibacterial moulds have been used since ancient times). But isolating it and producing it in stable, large quantities proved elusive: the war created the urgency to find a solution. See History of Antibiotics, Princeton University [Online] http://web.archive.org/web/20020514111940/; www.molbio.princeton.edu/courses/mb427/2001/projects/02/antibiotics.htm.

10 I have heard this story anecdotally. It appears to be confirmed by a University of Oxford history of penicillin [Online] www.ox.ac.uk/media/science_blog/100716.html.

11 Level four is the expected level of achievement for primary-school children in the UK.

12 Free school meals (FSM) are a commonly used proxy for social deprivation: school lunches are free to children from low-income households. It is also used as a proxy for educational challenge: FSM pupils underperform the national average; 100 per cent FSM is very rare, anything above 30 per cent is commonly regarded as a challenge.

13 Related by Steve Munby, CEO, Education Development Trust.

14 *Lives of the Caesars*, 'Divus Julius', section 32.

15 Richard A Gabriel (2002) *The Great Armies of Antiquity*, Greenwood Publishing Group.

16 Attributed to Margaret Mead, in Frank G Sommers and Tana Dineen (1984) *Curing Nuclear Madness*, Methuen, p 158.

17 *Harvard Business Review* has a good piece on the mistakes that people make in such conversations [Online] http://hbr.org/web/slideshows/difficult-conversations-nine-common-mistakes/4-slide.

18 Acas, the arbitration service, provides a quick guide [Online] www.acas.org.uk/media/pdf/3/t/Table-Challenging_conversations_and_how_to_manage_them_APRIL-2012.pdf.

19 Adapted from Hervey Cleckley (1982) *The Mask of Sanity*, revised edn, Mosby Medical Library. First published in 1941, he originally identified 16 traits, which I have cut in order to save space.

20 Work by Robert Hare suggests that about 1 per cent of the population has psychopathic tendencies, and men outnumber women by about seven to one in this trait. Noah C Venables, J R Hall and Christopher J Patrick (2013) Differentiating psychopathy from antisocial personality disorder: a triarchic model perspective, *Psychological Medicine*, **9** (July), pp 1–9. Hare has a 20-point test for psychopaths.

21 From Jo Owen (2014) *The Leadership Skills Handbook* (3rd edn) Kogan Page, p 140.

22 Gary Hamel and C K Prahalad (1989) Strategic intent, *Harvard Business Review*, July; C K Prahalad and Gary Hamel (1990) Core competence of the corporation, *Harvard Business Review*, May. I worked for two years with C K Prahalad on implementing strategic intent/core competence: from the outset, the myths about them were divorced from their reality.

23 This has been attributed to Gore Vidal and to American theatre producer David Merrick, among others.

24 After a military victory, the Roman general was allowed to enter Rome in triumph with his booty and captives. He would wear a gold-embroidered purple tunic to show he was nearly divine or royal, but was expected to act humbly: hence the slave saying, 'Remember, you are mortal.' Caesar liked to wear his purple tunic at all times, a sign of his kingly aspirations. Brutus eventually proved to Caesar that he was mortal by murdering him.

25 Miguel de Cervantes, *Don Quixote*, Part 1, Chapter VIII, Of the valorous Don Quixote's success in the dreadful and never before imagined 'Adventure of the Windmills', with other events worthy of happy record.

26 Sun Tzu (2009) *The Art of War*, Pax Librorum. Sun Tzu was a Chinese general, active in the 6th century BC.

27 Cult 1980 British science-fiction film based on a cartoon strip of the same name, created by Alex Raymond.

Chapter 9

1   See Jo Owen (2015) *How to Lead*, Pearson. Original research shows that ambition is one of the five key markers for a future leader.

2   From Lewis Carroll's *Through the Looking-Glass* (1871).

3   Shakespeare, *Macbeth*, Act 5, Scene 5.

4   See Jo Owen (2012) *How to Influence and Persuade*, Pearson.

5   Proprietary research on promotion of senior teachers to head teacher roles at Future Leaders showed that there was a marked gender bias in the early years of the programme, for the reasons outlined in the text.

6   This was the role of the Auriga, a slave gladiator. Caesar, famously, was supposed to have used the services of the Auriga. It did not do him any good; he still got murdered.

Conclusion

1   Shakespeare, *The Merchant of Venice*, Act 3, Scene 1. Shylock showing that Jews and Christians are humans alike.

2   Interview with Dominic Casserley, then director at McKinsey, now CEO of Willis.

INDEX

Note: bold page numbers indicate figures; italic numbers indicate tables.

CPSIA information can be obtained
at www.ICGtesting.com
Printed in the USA
JSHW041359280621
16381JS00008B/201